# Changiya Rukh

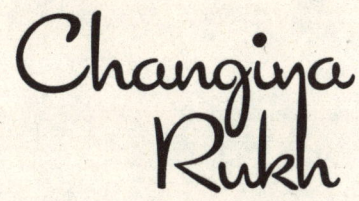

# Changiya Rukh

## Against the Night

An Autobiography

Balbir Madhopuri

Translated from Punjabi by Tripti Jain

With an introduction by Harish Puri

OXFORD
UNIVERSITY PRESS

# OXFORD
## UNIVERSITY PRESS

Oxford University Press is a department of the University of Oxford.
It furthers the University's objective of excellence in research, scholarship,
and education by publishing worldwide in. Oxford is a registered trademark of
Oxford University Press in the UK and in certain other countries

Published in India by
Oxford University Press

22 Workspace, 2nd Floor, 1/22 Asaf Ali Road, New Delhi 110002

© Oxford University Press 2010

The moral rights of the author have been asserted
Database right Oxford University Press (maker)

First published 2010

12th impression 2025

MR. Omayal Achi MR. Arunachalam Trust was set up in 1976 to further education
and health care particularly in rural areas. The MR. AR. Educational Society was
later established by the Trust. One of the Society's activities is to sponsor Indian
literature. This translation is entirely funded by MR. AR. Educational Society

ISBN-13: 978-0-19-806550-0
ISBN-10: 0-19-806550-7

Typeset in Arno Pro 11/13
by Sai Graphic, New Delhi 110 055
Printed by Saurabh Printers Pvt. Ltd., Noida, UP

*To the memory of my beloved husband*
*Surendra*

# Contents

# Author's Note

The writing of my autobiography was not something of an epiphany. The idea did not even occur to me. Its origin lay in something direct, natural, and simple. On reading an excerpt of Sheoraj Singh's autobiography in a Hindi magazine, I remarked to my friend, the dalit-thinker, S.S. Gautam, 'There is neither any remarkable content in this nor ideology. My family has faced far more difficult situations.' 'If you can write better than this, then do it,' he answered tersely. I felt somewhat abashed. Off and on, he reminded me, 'What? When are you going to write?' Then one day I wrote 'My Daadi—a History' for Bhapa Pritam Singh's publication. He cleared his table to publish my piece in the December 1997 issue. 'Write your autobiography. I will publish it,' he said. Within the next few days, I was flooded with complimentary phone calls and messages, and Ajit Kaur commended my point of view in an interview on Doordarshan.

As I unravelled myself and held conversations with myself, I found I was writing the autobiography of my community. It was no longer just my story.

There were many discouraging questions and remarks as well; not the least of which was that an autobiography is somehow considered less than top-class literature.

It took me four years to complete my autobiography. My language and our lifestyles, characters and incidents described are all true, as are the names. The essence of this work is to explain the dalit heritage and culture to contemporary India and to the future, and to both depict the poverty amongst the dalits and expose the cruel reality of the oppression they suffer at every step. I steadfastly held in my mind's eye the events and problems of grave socio-economic significance, in order to portray them without bias or sentimentality. I think of the times when only *chattala*, a low-quality fodder was available. Then came *berseem*. Red rice has since been replaced by many varieties of white rice. There have also been great changes in the quality of cotton, wheat, and other crops; even deserts have blossomed. But has the life of peasant India or the urban poor changed?

I sometimes feel that the most a writer like myself can do is to place a stone on the foundation of the edifice of a new society which is yet to come into existence. Dr B.R. Ambedkar's writings inspired me in the preparation of this work, the object of which is to spread the message of socio-economic equality and human rights in line with the vision of 'Begampura' by Guru Ravidas.

It is my moral responsibility to thank every person who ever supported my enterprise whole-heartedly: its language, dialect, and point of view. I have no words to express my gratitude to, and regard for, Tripti Jain for her excellent translation, her humility, and cooperation. For selecting my autobiography to be translated into English and for her skilful editing and dedication, I thank Mini Krishnan. I am grateful to Dr Harish Puri for his comprehensive introduction and to Dr Ronki Ram for his valuable suggestions.

New Delhi                                                    BALBIR MADHOPURI
2009

# Translator's Note

It was with some trepidation that I took up the task of translating *Changiya Rukh* (*Against the Night*). I had heard of Balbir Madhopuri's book, and had been told that it might be difficult to translate as the author had freely used his native dialect. I was also informed that it could be a little uncomfortable for a woman to translate, as there were many abusive words. This did not bother me; and the complete work is now in the hands of its readers …

It has been a labour of love for me. The milieu that the book describes is familiar; it is my own—though I have not lived in Punjab for many decades now. The setting itself took me back to a time when I spent my happy, college-going years—in Punjab, where my father was posted. The language was a little strange, yet fully comprehensible. I knew and understood the socio-political history and was fully aware of the burden of caste issues in our society.

Balbir has described the life that he, his family and kin have lived. The pain that underlay the true-life narrative gripped me. The humiliation that was a daily affair, the indignity that was life, depicted by the author in a simple yet heartrending manner inspired me to take up the task—for it needed to be given a wider audience.

Balbir writes both honestly and objectively. He tells us of the tribulations faced from both man and nature, the battles fought every day. Yet he dared to dream, and his father showed him the way by impressing upon him that education alone would help him break out of the suffocating hold of the caste system. All this is narrated in a stark manner, using the dialect that is his mother tongue. There is no rancour, no bitterness. He does not once despair, though fully aware that the road ahead was filled with difficulties.

The literal translation of the words 'Changiya Rukh' is 'lopped' or 'hacked tree' the resonance of which appears at the end of Chapter 13, 'The Banyan Tree of the Chamars'. However, I felt that in English it lacked the force it has in the original Punjabi and therefore thought of *Against the Night* because it conveys the helplssness and pain the author endured, and the resistance he in turn put up against the many forces of the 'night' that tried to suppress him.

Balbir and I worked together right from the beginning. We agreed on most things, but differed on some. It has been a happy and very satisfying collaboration.

The translation took me longer than I had planned. During this period I suffered a personal bereavement, but the work gave me great solace and peace when I needed it the most.

I am very grateful to my editor Mini Krishnan, for all her patience, tact, and support. I am extremely thankful to Balbir Madhopuri and his sweet wife, for all their help and support. They were there for me, willing to clarify and explain things that sometimes baffled me. The love, advice, and support that I have received from my sister Dr Jasbir Jain, all my life, is something I will always cherish and be grateful for.

Ajmer                                                                TRIPTI JAIN

# Introduction

*As I put my nice-looking belt around my waist,*
*I feel that someone is trying to tie a broom behind me*
*To get me to sweep away my own history*
                              —Satish Chandar, translated from Telugu
                                          by Velcheru Narayana Rao

*Changiya Rukh* means a tree lopped from the top, slashed and dwarfed. As the title of his autobiography, Balbir Madhopuri has used it as a metaphor for the dalit or an 'untouchable' Indian whose potential for growth has been 'robbed by the Hindu social order'.

Leafless trees look like my kin, my brothers and sisters ... When they start growing, their heads are cut mercilessly; the arms and feet are chopped, like branches hacked down. As such thoughts came to mind, the third or fourth part of the slashed tree would take the shape of my father, uncles, and their sons.

Significantly, the lopped tree also denotes its inherent and defiant resilience that brings forth fresh shoots of branches and leaves. Written originally in Punjabi, Madhopuri's autobiography is the story of a dalit's angst of deprivation, social exclusion, and humiliation, as well as of resistance, achievement, and hope. The subjective narrative of a dalit writer tends to universalize the caste-based experience of his community. Indeed, it goes further and resonates with numerous Black American autobiographies. No wonder that when Martin Luther King was reminded of his social status, during his visit to India in 1958, while in Kerala, he hastened to declare, 'Yes, I am an untouchable, every Negro in the United States is an untouchable.'[1] Though the burden of being a dalit in India may be different from that of a Black in America, there is much in common in their real-life experience of pain and humiliation, as also in the purpose and process of autobiography writing. As far as deprivation of land rights and ostracization go, there are echoes between the Aborigines in Australia and dalits in India.

Born in 1955 in the Ad Dharmi caste, a category of the Chamar caste of ex-untouchables, Madhopuri is a Punjabi poet, with two collections of poems, *Maroothal da Birkh* (*Tree of the Desert*, 1998) and *Bhakhda Pataal* (*The Smouldering Netherworld*, 1992). Presently working as a civil servant with the Government of India and serving as the editor of the Punjabi edition of the monthly magazine, *Yojana*, he has also translated a number of novels from English into Punjabi, in addition to a pictorial book on the monuments of Delhi. It was his autobiography, *Changiya Rukh*, however, having gone through five reprints in the last six years, and subsequently translated into Hindi, which brought him recognition in the literary world. Through this translation, *Changiya Rukh* will be the first Punjabi dalit autobiography to appear in English.

Madhopuri's education and his association with progressive writers and the Communist Party of India (CPI) enabled him to view things in a broader ideological perspective. But he was troubled by questions such as, why these same progressive intellectuals had silently watched the brutality against dalits in our society for so long; why they had failed to overcome their upper caste arrogance in their dealings with low caste comrades; and why were mainstream Punjabi writers so blatantly indifferent to dalit history? As an educated dalit, he realized that dalits should start telling their own stories. Any recollection of the past by

---

1. Martin Luther King, from his sermon at Ebenezer Baptist Church, 4 July 1965. Cited in his autobiography, *I Have a Dream*, Ch. 13, 'Pilgrimage to Non-Violence'; cf., *readerswords.wordpress.com 2007/2/19/Martin-Luther-King-racism and Dalits*. See also, Sanjukta Dasgupta, 'A New Dawn', *The Statesman*, 11 January 2009.

a dalit who had progressed in life and moved out of his village was bound to be a painful exercise. 'Believe me,' he writes, 'as I read again what I had myself written about many of the actual events of my life, my eyes blurred and I felt choked.' Much of what the reader finds in the misery and suffering in Madhopuri's recollections of his childhood was probably the fate of poorest families of small farmers, artisans, and landless labourers in India's villages—whether dalit or non-dalit. But the social exclusion and insult of being treated as unclean and polluted, on grounds of birth, was a kind of emotional violence reserved for dalits. This autobiography, therefore, is also a strong critique of caste and 'untouchability'. What strikes the reader, however, is the author's poise and ability to narrate his story without sentimentality or hatred towards his tormentors.

## The Context of India

There are nearly 170 million dalits in India. This means that one in every six Indians is a dalit. The term dalit, first used by B.R. Ambedkar, is a Marathi word derived from the Sanskrit, and means ground-down, downtrodden, broken, or oppressed. It is an emotive term used to denote the former 'untouchables'. Eleanor Zelliot has pointed out that, 'The term is one of pride—untouchables have been oppressed by others'(Anand and Zelliot 1992: 1). In the traditional caste hierarchy, the ritual status of those at the bottom of the pyramid was that of physical 'impurity', as against the 'purity' of the upper castes. In theory, 'untouchability' was abolished at India's Independence, and its practice in any form became a criminal offence. All such caste communities, numbering more than 750 at present, according to the Anthropological Survey of India (ASI), came to be termed as 'Scheduled Castes' for the purpose of a variety of constitutional and legal protections and affirmative action by the state. B R Ambedkar used a number of alternative terms—untouchables, depressed classed, exterior castes, and dalit—according to the context. Mahatma Gandhi's description of these people as *Harijans* (children of god), also remained in currency until the late 1970s. For Gandhi, removal of untouchability from the minds of Hindu upper castes was a question of social morality. Since the rise of a militant dalit Panther movement in Maharashtra in the early 1970s, the term dalit has come to replace the term Harijan, as an ideological alternative to the legal term, 'Scheduled Castes'. At the local level, however, most dalits tend to identify themselves as belonging to their particular *jati* such as Chamar, Jatav, Mahar, Mang, Mala, Madiga, Pallar, Parayar, Namsudra, Valmiki, etc. In their own communities, they maintain their own hierarchy which prohibits the acceptance and exchange of water and food (Singh 1995: 11).

Four out of every five dalits who live in the villages of India are landless. They are the real face of India's notorious and endemic poverty. A glance into an office, a college, or a railway compartment will afford no signals about who belongs to what caste, but within minutes of one's arrival in an Indian village, the caste divisions and labels will be quite stark. All the unclean and degrading, exhausting tasks are usually assigned to the dalits. Despite the abolition of untouchability six decades ago, the imposition of a variety of social disabilities on persons, for reasons of their birth into particular castes, remains a part of social reality in rural India. This social exclusion affects not only their outward lives but also their inner worlds. The practice of caste-based exclusion and discrimination was a plan to block access not only to economic but also to civil, cultural, and political rights, and has been rightly described as a 'living mode exclusion'. While varying from region to region in India, the prejudice against the castes stigmatized as untouchable continues to remain deeply embedded.

The highest concentration of dalits is in Uttar Pradesh (UP), India's largest state, known for electing a dalit as its chief minister for the fourth time. Yet the dalits have been the target of obnoxious human rights violations, caste atrocities, social boycotts, and police abuse. Amazingly, even the judiciary was not immune to caste prejudice. In 1998, a Judge of Allahabad High Court ordered his chambers to be 'purified with *Ganga Jal*' ('water from the "holy" river Ganges') because its former occupant was a dalit Judge. There is a huge gap between the moral values inscribed in laws and institutions of governance and social practice. Under the impact of liberalization when there has been a retreat of the state from its constitutional moral commitments, and when civil society, yielding to consumerism and self-gratification, appears to make a mockery of public good, dalits continue to feel deprived and apprehensive about the future.

## The Context of Punjab

Not many people outside Punjab may be able to appreciate that, owing to a variety of historical and cultural reasons, the ideological basis of untouchability was markedly weaker in this region than in other parts of India. According to the 2001 Census, it is this state which has the highest proportion of Scheduled Castes in India, comprising 28.9 per cent of its total population—almost twice their share of 16.5 per cent in India's population. Another important difference lies in the historically non-Hindu character of the region. Before the Partition of the subcontinent in 1947, Punjab had a Muslim majority (53 per cent in 1941). After Partition and following the reorganization of the Indian part of Punjab (through demarcation of predominantly Hindu and Hindi-speaking areas of Haryana and Himachal Pradesh) in 1966, it became a Sikh-majority state. So the history of the oppression of dalits in Punjab was related more to the structure of economy, ownership of land, and the politics of power relations, rather than the Brahmanical worldview.

To make sense of the dalit experience in this autobiography, it is important that the narrative is placed in the context of the historical and contemporary realities of social life in Punjab. It is vital to understand that the dalits of India do not share a monolithic identity. The diversity of their particular historical/cultural experience in different regions may help us in making sense of the multiplicity of interests and conflicts in perspectives among dalit activists regarding their common struggle for dignity and justice.

As the frontier region of the subcontinent, Punjab has faced hordes of invaders over thousands of years—the Greeks, the Shakas, the Parthians, the Kushans, and still later, the Turks, the Persians, and others from central Asia, such as the Indo-Scythians, have all invaded it. Many of them were absorbed into this frontier population. Historian Buddha Prakash, described the phenomenon as 'The Socio-Cultural *Panmixia* of Punjab'. According to him, Brahminical orthodoxy had 'practically abandoned' the Punjab region and shifted to the Indo-Gangetic region, quite early in history (Prakash 1976: 8). Again, Denzil Ibbetson of the Indian Civil Service (ICS), who conducted the first serious study of the castes of Punjab in 1881, discovered that the region was 'a notable exception' to the caste system in India. He found it to be 'more Mohammedan than Hindu' and also commented that Islam in Punjab was 'as a rule free from fanaticism'. As the report in *The People of India* series, published by the ASI, observes, 'Punjab probably represents the finest example of syncretism that emerged in the medieval period' (Singh 2003: xv).

## Influence of Sikhism

B R Ambedkar pointed out to Mahatama Gandhi that the most serious evil in Hinduism was not the practice of caste hierarchy and exclusion, as such, but the upholding of the caste order as a 'religious ideal'. Rejection of the Hindu religious texts on which the Hindu social order was built was, according to him, basic to the struggle against caste. Ambedkar campaigned, saying, 'to leave inequality between class and class ... which is the soul of Hindu society untouched and to go on passing legislation relating to economic issues is to make a farce of our Constitution and to build a palace on a dung heap' (1995, vol 14, 1: 1325).

Sikhism, on the other hand, was distinguished from Hinduism by its rejection of caste and the authority of religious texts such as the *Dharamsastras*, *Smritis*, and *Puranas*. Guru Nanak (1469–1539), the first Guru of the Sikh faith, declared that:

Nanak seeks the company of those who are of low caste among the lowly, nay rather the lowest of the low. Why should he (he has no desire to) rival the lofty. Where the poor are looked after, there does rain the look of Thy grace, O' Lord!

(*Adi Granth*, *Sri Rag* 15.9; translation by Manmohan Singh)

The Sikh holy book *Adi Granth* includes the compositions of not only the Sikh Gurus but also of Muslim Sufi saints such as Sheikh Farid, and of Bhakti saint–poets like Kabir and Ravidas who belonged to the low castes. Great importance was given to *kirtan* (congregational singing of sacred poetry) and *langar* (community eating without distinction of high and low). By cultivating his land, Guru Nanak personally demonstrated the dignity of physical labour. Sikh temples were expected to welcome all without caste distinction. It made a considerable difference at the level of ideas and beliefs. The peasants, artisans, and menials were, therefore, attracted to the new religion of

Punjab. In fact, large-scale group conversion of low castes to Islam, Sikhism, and later Christianity—religions which did not believe in ritual pollution and 'karmic retribution'—appeared to be the first step towards an upward mobilization. However, the social reality of cultural dynamics and relations of power was quite different. The outcastes of Hinduism did not cease to be outcastes after joining the Sikh *Panth*. The social roots of caste ran deep, and there was a wide gap between theological position and social practice. In fact, the Sikh community evolved a new caste hierarchy parallel to that of the Hindu community (Marenco 1976; cf. Puri 2004: 207–8). Exclusion and discrimination in that community, as we will see, are only a shade less prevalent than in the Hindu community. The Census 1931 records more than 25 Sikh castes (cf. Ram 2007: 4068). There was a time when after his famous rejection of Hinduism and his declaration in 1935 that even though he was born a Hindu he would not die a Hindu, Ambedkar considered converting '60 million untouchables' to Sikhism in 1936. But when he became aware of the empirical social reality, the idea was quietly dropped. When the Constitution of India was being drafted, it was the only non-Hindu community whose leadership fought to claim Scheduled Caste status for the 'Sikh untouchable castes'. Ironically, the Rai Sikh, a backward Sikh caste, is the most recent one to stake its claim to and win Scheduled Caste status in Punjab (2005).

## *Ad Dharm*: Religious Route to Dalit Identity and Politics

Madhopuri refers to his heritage of the Ad Dharm movement as a source of pride. This was a powerful movement of dalits, launched in 1926, for transformation through a religious dissociation from Hinduism. Its leaders came from the educated, forward looking and affluent Chamar (leather-workers) caste. 'We are not Hindus,' it was declared and also that their religion was Ad Dharm (from *aadi*, that is, original or ancient, and *dharm* or religion), one that existed before the Hindus prevailed. Saint Ravidas (fifteenth century) who was a Chamar, was a bhakti radical and was the first to ideate an Indian utopia in his song, 'Begumpura Shahar' ('The city without sorrow'). He was hailed as their Guru, and they adopted distinct rituals of worship, prayers, and salutations. Requesting the British government of India to grant recognition to Ad Dharm as a distinct religion, or community (*qaum*)[2] similar to Hindu, Muslim, and Sikh *qaums*, was a political act. It was meant to assert that the 'untouchables' were a people, not castes. Interestingly, the government conceded their demand and notified Ad Dharm as a separate religion. At the time of the 1931 Census, over 400,000 dalits registered themselves as Ad Dharmi in the face of militant opposition by sections of Hindus and Sikhs. Composed almost totally of the Chamar caste, Ad Dharmis became the most progressive and politically active community among the dalits. It supported Ambedkar's struggle against Gandhi on the issue of the Communal Award in 1932. However, by upholding its distance from Ambedkar's movement in the region, it restricted the influence of Ambedkar's ideas in Punjab. The examples of Ad Dharm and Ravidasi religion of Chamar caste encouraged other lower castes to construct their separate caste-based religious sects such as the Kabirpanth of the Julaha (weaver) caste and Valmiki Dharm of the sweeper caste. The religious *bhakti* route that the dalits prominently took to separate jati identity, tended to block the secular political solidarity of dalits and marginalize the Ambedkarites.

## Post-Independence Culture

The culture and history of oppression of dalits in Punjab has been prominently related to the structure of the agricultural economy and the ruling interests of the land-owning 'agricultural castes'. Contrary to the Hindu religious texts' view of Brahmins being on top of the caste hierarchy, it is the concept of 'dominant caste' given by India's well-known sociologist M N Srinivas that is appropriate for understanding the vast diversity and changing character of hierarchy and caste behaviour. The dominant caste in the villages of Punjab is that of the Jats.

Socio-cultural life in Punjab underwent a marked change after India's Independence. After the rehabilitation of refugees and consolidation of holdings, a far-reaching impact was made by the Green Revolution. One manifest consequence of the new form of capitalist agriculture that privileged the big landowning entrepreneur was the rise of *Jattvaad*,

---

2. *Qaum* (originally Urdu) is a commonly used term to denote a distinct nationality or nation and also for a community. An inherent fuzziness in its meaning in English translation can lead to controversies.

signifying a Jat swagger based on power and arrogance. For the rural dalits, this became the keyword for their oppression and humiliation (Ajmer Singh 2003: 292–300). The Jats' ownership of most of the agricultural land in post-Independence Punjab, their preponderant numerical strength in the Sikh community (about 65 per cent), and their concentration in rural areas (over 70 per cent of rural population) determined their high status and their influence on the culture of the region. On the basis of his study, anthropologist Indera Pal Singh noted that 'most of the Sikh values are jat values, and the jats assert that they occupy the highest position among the Sikh castes' (1977: 70). In fact, the growing emphasis on religious identity and communalization of politics around 'Sikh grievances' and 'Sikh demands'(for example, the Anandpur Sahib Resolution) became a promising route to promotion of the Jats' economic and political power interests, leading to greater coercion of the lower castes in rural areas. Another consequence of capitalist agriculture was the end of the hereditary feudal patron-client (landlord-attached labour/servant) or *Jajmani*[3] relations of the dalits, bondage. Historically, the outcastes such as Valmiki, Mazhabi (Chuhra Sikhs), Chamar, Ramdasi (Chamar Sikhs), etc., were not allowed ownership of land. Under British rule, the Land Alienation Act of 1901 had debarred them from buying land. The village commons on which these outcastes were allowed to reside—in temporary structures on the western margin of the village—were the property of the landowning caste (belonging to the village in legal terms). The 'outcastes' were not allowed to build any brick structures and could be expelled from the land. On the other hand, as a 1914 notification reproduced in the text shows, legal provision had been made for obligatory services (including unpaid services known as *begaar*), by families of different menial castes. All such laws/orders were repealed after Independence because of a spirited initiative taken by Ambedkar, as India's first law minister. But the political clout of the Jat landlord did not allow the implementation

3. *Jajmani* is a Punjabi term for the traditional feudal customary relationship between the zamindar (landlord) and the attached servant. The dalit servant received, from the Zamindar, a custom-fixed amount of grains at harvest time, and on festive and other specified occasions for different kind of services. It was a kind of social bondage in which there was a possibility of patronizing human touch, and of help for the servant, in times of emergency.

of the legislated land reforms. The dalits practically remained landless and were forced to work as agricultural labourers. Their share in the total cultivable land, at present, comes to only about 2.4 per cent.

Different kinds of other consequences, however, followed from new Constitutional and other affirmative measures. Untouchability was abolished and its practice in any form was made a crime punishable under law, and the Constitution guaranteed equality under law. Political representation according to the proportion of Scheduled Castes in the total population was guaranteed at different levels through reservation of seats in all elected institutions. Special welfare measures, free education, and reservation in jobs for the upliftment of dalits contributed to far-reaching changes in social and political spheres. Though the pace of change was slow, a new sense of self-respect and hope was in the air. By the end of twentieth century, over 200,000 Punjabi dalits were employed in government jobs—many in India's higher civil, police, health, and engineering services—through reservation. Many of the Chamars, today, are big and small industrialists and traders. Jalandhar city alone boasts many dalit millionaires. Emigration of large numbers of dalits to foreign countries led to dalit prosperity altering the rural landscape, particularly the Doaba region to which Madhopuri belongs. A big difference was also made by the series of elections to representative bodies from the village council to the Parliament of India. Prominent participation of dalits in these elections tended to alter their perception of their political worth, as also the sense of their stake in the democratic system.

## Punjabi Dalit Literature

The beginning and early growth of Punjabi language and literature is traced back to the writings of Sufi saints like Sheikh Farid and the Sikh Gurus. The principal theme in their writings was human suffering and its alleviation. Compassion for the oppressed and helpless, as well as resisting tyranny, constituted a significant element in Punjabi literature. Another powerful influence on Punjabi writers during the twentieth century was that of Marxist ideology with its thrust on revolutionary change. However, the tragedy of caste-rooted indignities was out of focus in Punjabi literature until the publication of Gurdial Singh's novel, *Marhi da Deeva* (*The Flickering Lamp*, 1964).

Dalit literature in Punjabi is only about three decades old. A powerful voice calling attention to caste-based victimization of dalits appeared in the poetry of three prominent dalit poets, Sant Ram Udasi, Gurdas Ram Alam, and Lal Singh Dil.

*These prostitutes, women and girls,*
*are my mothers, sisters and daughters*
*and yours too.*
*These are mothers, sisters and daughters*
*of the cow-worshipping India*

(Lal Singh Dil)

He speaks of the numbness and fatigue he feels when he hears that his brother has gone mad, or that the police have undressed his mother in public. He has so little strength to respond. Another verse of his says

*You love me, do you?/Even though you belong/ to another caste*
*But do you know/our elders do not/even cremate their dead/at the same*
*place*

(translated by Nirupama Dutt)

Dalit fiction, as in Gurucharan Singh Rao's *Mashalchi*, (The Torch Bearer, 1986), the first Punjabi novel by a dalit writer portrayed the woeful living conditions of the outcastes in the *Vehra* (locality of the outcaste) and cruelty of the landlord to his bonded dalit labourer. The present generation's resistance and rage against the 'slavish mentality' of the older generation is a popular method to signify change and a new assertiveness among dalits. Going beyond the jati identity, the writers recognized the cumulative impact of the Dalit Panther Movement in Maharashtra, the ideology of Ambedkar, and Kanshi Ram's political struggle on their writings. Dalit narratives, the prominent form of expression, reflect dalit anxiety and tension between the modern and the traditional sensibilities. Literature as a form of political activism gained ground after the Punjabi translation of Shravan Kumar Limbale's autobiography, *Akkarmashi* (originally written in Marathi), and Om Prakash Valmiki's *Joothan* (originally in Hindi) became available. The last decade has witnessed a tremendous proliferation of writing about dalits and creative literature by dalit writers, including the increasing circulation of a number of magazines brought out by dalit publishers and editors.

## Madhopuri's Self-Narrative

Madhopuri's narrative of his struggle is not merely a record of the subjective perceptions of a dalit. It opens a window to the objective conditions that existed in the past, as well as to the social relations that have been changing after India's Independence. The new generation of dalits have learnt to confront injustice with reason and with a sense of confidence. Repeated reminders of the change, by Madhopuri's elders, made a big difference to his struggle. When he was in school, they would tell him, 'Between now and then there's a world of difference (as between the Earth and the Sky)'. Hopelessness and despair of Bakha in Mulk Raj Anand's *Untouchable* was in the past: 'Those days are gone when we would be standing like beggars at your (landlord's) door.' An important characteristic of this change was a marked determination in the author's community to overcome obstacles and raise their status. (I would, nevertheless, hasten to emphasize that this is not the case in all the regions of India.) The key to that change was education: '*Parhai kar ke zaat badalni*' (altering caste status by acquiring education). This was the mantra that Babasaheb Ambedkar had given his people. '*Putt dab ke parh lai, daliddar chukk ho joo; Jattan di gulami na karni paoo*' (Son, work hard for an education, the wretchedness would be removed, there would be no slaving for the Jats). But the humiliation of caste prejudice persisted even after joining the elite club of the educated. Though the author does not expect an early end to the deeply embedded 'caste mindedness' in Indian society, his writings exude confidence and hope. No less marked is the writer's ability to avoid exaggeration and sentimentality, and to appreciate the positive and encouraging aspects of an otherwise ugly social reality

Madhopuri's recollections of his past, show his sensitive eye for detail in day-to-day village life. The two segments of the living space were clearly marked: *Pind* (the village) on one hand, and *Vehra* or *Chamarli*, the segregated row of dalit houses located on the lower western periphery of the village, on the other. Separate wells, temples, and cremation grounds divided the worlds of the two segments of the village. He captures the smells, colours, and sounds of the Vehra of his childhood which enable the reader to empathize with the misery of poverty—smelly, filth-laden streets, lice-infested clothes, foods like the meat of dead cattle; hard agricultural labour on the lands of zamindars, caste abuse, insults, swearing; the body language of fear, tension, outrage, and clashes; their strategies of coping and the typical local language and accents. The last wish of the dying grandmother to have a taste of 'meat curry' seems as typical of dalit eating as the savouring of leftovers from zamindar homes. No less illustrative in such a personal account is the dalits' resort to what James Scott described as 'weapons of the weak' and the 'subterranean forms of resistance', which reveal 'the hidden transcripts of what is said behind the back of power' (Menon 2008). Angry expressions are frequently heard among the rural dalits: 'Just because they own four acres ... they behave like our God ... Give us just about two or three acres for each family, and you'll see how we thrash the Jat's upper caste arrogance.' Talking to a migrant dalit labourer from UP, Madhopuri's elders lament about not owning any land. But the poor migrant's comment, 'You people talk of a piece of land ... it seems to me that our poor people's wives and daughters are *their* common property ... You are better off than us ... What if you don't have land! You at least have some honour', leaves them speechless. His thoughts stray from a broken cot to illiteracy, to poverty, to women: 'Sometimes poverty appeared to be changing into woman and sometime woman into poverty ... like our (fate) existence: what is there in poor woman's existence!'

Earlier, the resistance of lower caste people against insult or unwelcome commands by the Jats meant inviting trouble: 'Jats were a terror for dalits,' says Madhopuri. Therefore, the dalit's preferred course of action used to be concealment of anger, telling of lies, and an affected show of submission or deference. Now the younger generation of Scheduled Castes make it known that caste insult would meet with instant retaliation. The Jats routinely lamented that 'The Mazhabis wanted to behave like the Jats', or that 'one day they will start beating the Jats' (Judge 2003: 82, 86; Puri 2008: 329). The literary genre of autobiographical writing, like Madhopuri's, appears most apt for description of everyday forms of resistance and their 'symbolic and ideological underpinnings'.

Difference and distance from the upper castes is not, however, the only aspect of a rural dalit's experience. There is another dimension to the context of social dynamics, that is, an 'intimate other-ness'. The physical proximity between the dalit landless worker and the Jat landowner, while working in the field, made laxity in ritual distance more pragmatic and practical. The landlords and their women could not ignore the value of skills and services which only dalits would provide to them, as per their needs. Therefore, overt expressions of deference and kinship towards the dalits did not appear oddly generous to the Jats even when distance and discrimination were common. Madhopuri's narrative, in the meaningfully titled chapter 'Daadi's Saga', draws our attention to the layered dynamics of the relationship between the proverbial oppressor and the oppressed. Mutual cooperation and empathy was not an insignificant part of that relationship. The normal usage of affectionate kinship terms of addressing elders—*Bebe, Tai, Taaya, Chaacha, Bua, Massi*, etc.; cordial as well as hot exchanges between the two sections; the not uncommon practice of seeking the advice of a seasoned old dalit, the grandmother of the author, by upper-caste ladies on a host of matters; the not so ungrudging submission by the latter to her rebukes and commands; as well as the spectacle of the massive outpouring of village kinship in the mourning at her funeral, are a part of that reality. Alongside cruelty, uncommon cases of human care and generosity are a part of the complex empirical reality. The story, meaningfully titled 'An Oasis in a Desert', underlines an aspect of Jat-Dalit family-level relationship, which, as he reflects, 'appeared sometime to fill up the breach' of the caste divide. The author seems to suggest the need for understanding the local dynamics of caste.

The author's references to a fellow Ad Dharmi who, upon conversion to Sikhism, identifies himself as Ramdasia—apparently a notch higher in status—and refuses to accept water from the well used by his former kinsmen, or, to a retort by an Ad Dharmi, 'now do not equate us with the Churahs (sweeper caste)', are some meaningful pointers to the paradox of internal caste hierarchy and prejudice among the victims of the caste system. Another dimension of that mental attitude is reflected in the author's revulsion against those of his kinsmen who, after rising to a class higher than their original one, tend to hide or mask their real caste identity. If the sense of caste hierarchy and discrimination is so deeply embedded in the minds of those whose liberation is believed to be bound up with the end of caste-mindedness, the challenge to social change is indeed formidable.

Madhopuri is sensitive about the portrayal of a certain uneasy co-existence of the 'big tradition' and 'little tradition' around religious and cultural practices in the village. Besides the more visible presence of separate Gurdwaras and Deras, such as the Sachkhand at village Ballan of the Ravidasis, there is a more or less shared subaltern tradition of gods, faiths, and rituals. The worship of local Muslim saints like Khwaja Khizar, the Hindu Siddh Devta, serpent shrines, listening to the *Katha* of 'Guga Pir' and the religious preaching by the Chamar saints such as Gharib Das, the belief in the 'ghost of the Pir', witchcraft, local healing practices (traditions largely linked with dalits) are not confined to the dalits' world alone. A good proportion of upper caste Jats participate in these rituals, even if some of them politely avoid eating of ritual prasad offered by the low castes.

Madhopuri regards himself an atheist, and views the obsession with religion and spiritualism among dalits as an escapist distraction from the larger project of social democracy. However, contrary to the emphasis on political solidarity of dalits that Ambedkar struggled to instil among his caste divided people, the surge in dalit self-awareness and assertion in Punjab is oriented towards distinct caste-based religious identity. In Punjab's 12,000 villages, the number of different denominational dalit temples and Deras is estimated to be around 10,000. Most major dalit clashes with Jats, for example, the prolonged confrontation in Talhan village of Jalandhar district in 2003, are cantered on the village dalits' claim to their share in that part of the public domain of power (Judge 2004: 11; Ram 2007: 4072). But the most telling instance was the recent (May 2009) violent riots carried out by hordes of outraged Ravidasi Dalits in a number of cities and towns, lasting for nearly one week. This violent reaction of Ravidasi Dalits in protest of the murder of a Ravidasi Sant in Austria seemed like the eruption of a long simmering angst against the caste indignities routinely suffered by dalits and their present day urge to assert their identity and autonomy.

The present generation believes that the practice of 'untouchability' or the purity-pollution question is not an issue anymore, except when it comes to arranging marriages, which is still the practice in India.

Nearly 90 per cent of dalits (barring a section of the Valmikis) have
moved out of their hereditary occupations; no more than 15 per cent
work as agricultural labourers any longer. Education, urbanization,
modernization, and jobs in higher civil services have given them a
consciousness of self-respect and hope. Yet, a dalit, even after a high
level of achievement in secular and material terms, apprehends a subtle
form of caste prejudice. The emotional experience of insults in public
spaces—the village, the school, the rented house—or in the company of
colleagues in the higher civil service, represents a kind of apprehension
that non-dalits are generally unable to understand. The school is, in
fact, often the first major site of assault on a dalit child's psyche where,
like Madhopuri, he is reminded of his vulnerability. 'What is the point
in going to school?' asked Lal Singh Dil, 'if the only thing you were
taught was about your low origin' (1998: 26) Madhopuri poignantly
describes his sorrow in his verse.

> *Many a time*
> *I'm dwarfed*
> *Like a tree cut at the top*
> *Over whom passes the power line*
> *I get pruned out of season*
> *When in passing*
> *Someone is curious to know what my caste is.*
> —Bhakhda Pataal (*The Inferno*, 1998), p. 41

Kanshi Ram, the founder of the Bahujan Samaj, emphasized that, 'Our
problem is humiliation, not deprivation.' What could dalits, individually
or collectively, do to deal with such insular 'caste mindedness' which
robs a person of his dignity? This is an issue Madhopuri takes up in a
chapter titled 'Humanist Slap'. He understands that the slaps that one
of his friends metes out to an upper caste tormentor in his presence is
a natural and perhaps a heart-warming reaction, but that still leaves the
author distressed; 'The past is not dead', and the plausibility of the end
of that caste-mindedness in the near future appeared remote.

Madhopuri wants dalits to raise their status by their individual effort
but at the same time suspects that an individualistic 'mobility syndrome'
negatively impacts their desired collective struggle for justice and

dignity. The mounting salience of an insular kind of jati (caste or sub-caste) identity and the politics of feuding political groups have come to hound the protagonists of dalit solidarity. Given the persistence of caste prejudice in the non-Hindu religious communities, it is difficult to sustain the 'myth' that the root cause lies only in the Hindu 'religious sanctions'. Madhopuri's dilemma is that while he seeks his identity in his dalithood, his Ad Dharm caste, he yet looks forward to a kind of social change whereby an individual would not be identified by his caste. He believes that howsoever slow and difficult it may be, the only rational course of struggle for dalits is both modernization and their solidarity with the non-dalit poor and oppressed, in order to create a new social order to match Ambedkar's dream.

I have benefited a lot from the observations and suggestion made by Harsharan Singh, Ronki Ram, Paramjit Judge, Atamjit and Amarjit Chandan on earlier drafts. To Mini Krishanan, in particular, I owe special thanks for help in the final editing of the text. The responsibility for the present text is, of course, entirely mine.

HARISH K. PURI

## References

Anand, Mulk Raj and Eleanor Zelliot. 1992. *An Anthology of Dalit Literature ( Poems)*. New Delhi: Gyan Publishing House.

Dil, Lal Singh. 1998. *Dastaan: Swaijivani*. Ludhiana: Chetna Parkashan.

Government of India. 1908. *Imperial Gazetteer of India: Provincial Series, Punjab Part 1*. Calcutta.

Ibbetson, Denzil. 1993 [1916]. *Punjab Castes* (a reprint of the chapter, 'Races, Castes and Tribes of the People in the Census of 1881'). New Delhi: D.K. Publishers.

Judge, Paramjit Singh. 2003. *Peetu*. Jalandhar: Kuknoos Prakashan.

———. 2004. 'Recent Caste Clash in Talhan in Punjab', *Dalit International Newsletter*, vol. 9, no. 1(February).

Juergensmeyer, Mark. 1982. *Religion as Social Vision: The Movement Against Untouchability in 20th Century Punjab*. Berkeley: University of California Press.

Marenco, Ethne K. 1976. *The Transformation of Sikh Society*. New Delhi: Heritage Publishers.

Mendelsohn, Oliver and Marika Vicziany. 2000. *The Untouchables: Subordination, Poverty and the State in Modern India*. New Delhi: Foundation Books.

Menon, Dilip. 2008. 'Peasants, States and Civilizations: An Interview with James C. Scott', *The Hindu*, 3 December (Op-Ed), p. 9.

Prakash, Buddha. 1976. 'Ancient Punjab: A Panoramic View', in Harbans Singh and N. G. Barrier (eds), *Punjab Past and Present: Essays in Honour of Dr. Ganda Singh*. Patiala: Punjabi University.

Puri, Harish K. 2003. 'Scheduled Castes in the Sikh Community: A Historical Perspective', *Economic and Political Weekly* (28 June).

———. 2008. 'Understanding Change in the Lives of Dalits of Punjab After 1947', in K.L. Tuteja and Sunita Pathania (eds), *Historical Diversities: Society, Politics and Culture*. New Delhi: Manohar Books, pp. 315–38.

Ram, Ronki. 2004. 'Limits of Untouchability: Dalit Assertion and Caste Violence in Punjab', in Harish K. Puri (ed.) *Dalits in Regional Context*. Jaipur: Rawat Publications, pp.132–189.

———. 2007. 'Social Exclusion, Resistance and Deras: Exploring the Myth of Casteless Sikh Society in Punjab', *Economic and Political Weekly*, vol. 52, no. 40 (6 October).

Singh, Ajmer. 2003. *Veehvin Sadi dee Sikh Rajneeti*. Chandigarh: Self-published.

Singh, Indera Pal. 1977. 'Caste in a Sikh Village', in Harjinder Singh (ed.), *Caste Among Non-Hindus in India*. New Delhi: National Publishing House.

Singh, K.S. 1995. *The People of India: The Scheduled Castes, vol. II*. New Delhi: Oxford University Press.

———. 2003. *People of India*, PUNJAB, vol. XXXII. New Delhi: ASI-Manohar Publishers.

# 1

# My Birthplace
## *Madhopur*

*Sim sim paniya*
*Qugi tihai aa …*
(Ooze o water, ooze/the dove is thirsty … )

My friends and I would dig shallow holes in the earth with our small fingers and recite these lines again and again. In no time, these pits would be full of water. And when we dug a pit with our heels, making shallow round holes, they would immediately fill and brim over.

Actually, Madhopur in district Jalandhar is one of the villages located in the *mand*—the land where the river Beas once flowed.

Beas, which is one of the five rivers of the Punjab, has its source in Rohtang (Kulu district) and flows through the districts of Kangra (Himachal Pradesh) and Hoshiarpur of Punjab, to complete its journey of 290 miles by merging with the river Sutlej on the edge of Kapurthala. The place where the two meet is called *Hari ka Pattan*, now in Taran Taran district.

When the river was diverted to the west, the land on the right was reclaimed, and groups of people settled on this land. These settlements grew and acquired the shape of villages. The river now flows at a distance of 21 kilometres from our village.

The land between the Sutlej and Beas—Jalandhar, Hoshiarapur, Nawan Shahar, and Kapurthala—is called the *Doaba*, land between two waters. Some of the villages of district Jalandhar are called *Sirowal*, because water trickles continuously. Numerous narrow jets of water join to form a channel. In summers, we bathed in the small seasonal streams of very clear water which flowed from hillocks in the western part of the village. This stream was the life support of many creatures— rabbits, animals, and birds. The groves of *tahli* trees along its bank were evergreen.

The land being low, our wells were very deep. The Persian wheel would work from dawn to the afternoon, and then the ropes and buckets would come up without water, carrying only white golden gleaming sand. We saw all this, as we ran about in the village, after school. But the process of digging a new well was very interesting ... Achchroo the acrobat, would start beating the dhol, days ahead of the event. Before the area where the digging was to begin was marked, prayers would be said, and coins scattered, the way they were on the palanquin of a bride, as she left home with her bridegroom. The happy atmosphere would become sad when women began singing in voices laden with melancholy,

*Pardesan lakdi ji*
*Darshan kar lo sareji*
(The circular wooden frame is now an
outsider/all must come to see her)

The expression of this emotional attachment to a circular wooden base, made of mulberry wood, was enough to wrench your heart; many eyes were moist because this 18 inches wide wooden circle would have to stay buried underground all its life. A thirteen-inch wall would then be built on it. The diameter of this circle was determined by the size of the well that was to be dug. Divers from the Jhiwar, the water-carrier caste, would enter the water to fill the large iron pot with mud. They had to stay submerged for a long period, and this was enough to frighten you ... the work of the construction of a well had to be completed within a few days, and when this was done, gruel was distributed as thanksgiving for the benevolence shown by Khwaja Khizir. I myself saw the well of the carpenter, Budda Ram, son of Kooda Ram, being built in this manner. On that occasion, I heard a group of young Jats recite this witticism in the hearing of girls

*Khuh de chakk wango*
*Tu murke nahin aana ...*
(Like the wooden frame of the well/
you are not going to come back)

When the level of underground water sank, the slogan of the Green Revolution was raised and tube wells were installed, and then the low caste children were summoned by the beat of drum by Jagar the chowkidar, for their share of the gruel, which was distributed on that occasion.

The first well with two Persian wheels in my village was built by Baba Sangatia in 1800. It stood in the eastern part of the village. And proof for this is an inscription on a brick, which I took out from the wall of the well in 1981. I had it photographed, and placed it back into the wall of the parapet again. The inscription reads as follows:

*This well was built by Sangatia in 1800, and 419811 bricks were used in its construction.*

And yes, the water of this well was taken to irrigate Qureshian, five or six kilometres away. The well supplied drinking water to the whole village.

Sangatia originally came from Mugowal (near Tooto Majara, district Hoshiarpur). The research of British scholars, Sir Denzil Ibbestson and E.D. MacLogan in *Tribes and Castes of the Punjab and North West Frontier Province* has established that the Sangha Jats migrated from Mugowal and relocated in Sakruli, Langeri, Narialan (and perhaps Madhopur).

Baba Sangatia's home was laced by seasonal hill streams. In his search for arable land, he came across this green patch and gave it the name of Madho's Puri—the region of God. When he settled permanently in this area, it came to be known as Madhopur. The postal department, to make its own work simple, called it Madhopur Sirowal, as there is another village of the same name in this district.

Within a few years of Baba Sangatia's settling here, pucca houses came up in the area. As a result, the future generations were called *pucca wale*—of pucca houses—and the place from where sand was quarried is still called *gora chappar*—the fair pond. According to the official records of the patwari, this is common land and the lower castes still have the right to take mud from this place for plastering their mud-huts. Along with my family, I too have dug mud from here. But the Jats are gradually taking over these lands.

Sangatia arranged to have a Chamar family of the Virdi subcaste from Pandori village, which was near his paternal village, to settle on his lands in our village. This Chamar, Punjab Singh Ramdasia, had come from Sainpur in district Hoshiarpur, and settled here, about 150 years ago. The place where he sat making shoes, is still called *gandian da chappar*—the pond of the cobblers. A family of Jhiwars had been despatched to this place by the Sardars of the village Laroya, which is about five kilometres from here, in district Jalandhar, at the request of Sangatia. Then, families of Brahmins, goldsmiths, carpenters, barbers, and also a dhobi family from the Purab—the east, (from UP)—arrived.

The village appeared to be one, but every group had its own drinking wells. Later some Muslims also settled in the village and bought land for themselves. They did not practise untouchability against the dalits, but this could be because many of them had once belonged to the untouchable and artisan castes.

If a low-caste boy were to come out on the lanes of the village, all bathed and dressed in new clothes, his hair combed, one or the other of the Jats sitting under the trees would get up and throw mud on him. If he protested, he was sure to be beaten up. If an untouchable appeared in the village dressed in new clothes, he was certain to be given a beating on the pretext that the low castes were trying to become the equals of the higher castes; no one knew or could predict when such an incident would occur and where.

All the villagers were afraid of the *zaildar, jagirdar, safedposh,* and *nambardar.* A zaildar had many villages under him. He presided over a court and passed judgements. He enjoyed judicial powers. One had to comply with his decisions and pay fines, etc. Judgements were delivered after considering all the circumstances. It was said that a zaildar was forgiven five to seven murders by the government, and people did not have the courage to look him in the eye. The treatment meted out to the lower castes, specially untouchables, was oppressive and terrifying. The zaildar compelled them to do *begaar* in his field and on his construction sites. If there was no such work available, then he got them to dig up the fields and throw the mud excavated in this way outside the village. This meant that he did not the days fixed for forced labour. One can still see small mounds of earth outside the village.

A jagirdar maintained fifteen to thirty horses, and was rewarded with land by the British for his role in suppressing any attempt at rebellion by the people. He also compelled the untouchables to work free of charge for him, and often the only return they got were blows. He saw to it that they did not rise against him.

A safedposh kept a few horses, and supervised a few villages. The dalits were always to put in begaar. A safedposh was a government agent, and a spy. He was rewarded in cash by the government for his services.

A nambardar was a government employee. He was eager to serve his superiors. He had the power to force the dalits to do whatever he wanted, without any payment. People of all castes were afraid of him, because he could file complaints against anyone with the police or the zaildar. His voice was heard in all government circles. Judgements were delivered and decisions made the way he wanted; the law was his to use. He played a crucial role in mobilizing people in support of the government and its policies. All these office-holders were called toadies, or the camp followers of the government. The zamindars were encouraged by them to physically assault the untouchables. Innumerable such incidents are still related by scheduled caste persons who are about seventy years of age—the generation before mine.

This is what my birthplace is like ... My village is not very big. It has a population of about twelve hundred. Nor is it very old, only about 250 years old. According to records of 1914–15, its total area was 505 acres, and it had twelve wells. The revenue paid was Rs 885. At present, its area is more or less the same and the revenue is 1200 rupees. The common land is 17 acres and this includes the lanes and ponds of the village. There are thirty wells in the fields. But how much land do the untouchables have? Almost nothing! There are certain facts related to this. Under the British, land settlements were made three times. The first was in 1849–50, the second in 1880, and the third in 1914–15. I had the opportunity to read some extracts of the third settlement, which had become a part of our traditions and were known as 'Rules and Regulations'. Regulation number 10 lays down the various restrictions and responsibilities of the different *kameens*—dalit communities—in the following terms:

**Land Settlement (Rules) village, Madhopur, district Jalandhar (1914–15)**

| Names of low caste | Work of '*Kameens*' and their duties | Farmer will give in return |
|---|---|---|
| Carpenter | Will repair domestic and agricultural implements; wood will be supplied by the master. | One bundle at rabi/ kharif harvests per plough; rabi crop, 15 seers grains, 8 annas for daughter's wedding for making 'vedi'. |
| Potter | To make earthen ware according to needs of the house hold; walls of the well. | One bundle rabi/ kharif, per plough; 8 annas on son's/ daughter's wedding. |
| Blacksmith | Repair of domestic and agricultural imple ments of iron and repairs of iron cauldron. | A half share in the last picking of cotton crop; 8 annas at son and daughter's weddings. |
| Barber | To shave, to carry messages and run errands; to cook, perform various functions at weddings and sad occasions. | One sheaf per plough, 5 seers raw jaggery per plough; 5 annas for daughter's and 4 annas for son's wedding. |
| Scavenger/ Chamar or Cobblers | To sweep and clean as begar. | To clear away animals carcases. |
| Dhobi (Washerman) | To wash clothes and washing of '*koras*' - the cloths used to seat wedding parties. | One sheaf per plough on rabi/ kharif harvests; 5 seers raw jaggery. |
| Jhiwar (Water Carrier) | To render free labour, to fetch a pot of water morning/evening; to work at weddings and bereavements. | 1 maund grain every six months. 4 annas on son's/daughter's wedding. |

The above list makes it clear that the rights of the scavengers/ Chamars—that is, the untouchables'—encompassed only the right to provide free labour. In return for the begaar given by them, these downtrodden people, deprived of all human rights, were conferred the right to remove carcases of animals, and that also as a gesture of kindness on the part of the master who owned them. Government support to keep this social and economic inequality in place, and the support given by its advocates to see that it stayed intact, raised many painful questions in my heart.

The English may have conquered many countries, and there is a widely held opinion about them that they were just and scientific in their views. They played a crucial role in the development of their colonies and they also encouraged new attitudes and forward thinking in them. Many big projects were completed by them. They made a significant contribution to the spread of education, and it was through their efforts that people were made familiar with their own civilization, culture, and history. But there is a big question mark regarding British attitudes towards, and treatment of, the untouchables.

The British came to Punjab at the end of their conquest of India. Why did they not give the untouchables the rights of equality, education, property, and freedom of expression? It is evident that they were in league with the staunch adherents of the caste system and were influenced by them. During the hundred years of British rule in Punjab, the Punjab Land Revenue Act, 1887, remained in force, which prevented the untouchables from buying land even when they had the money. And the common land, the *marusi*, as it was called, which had been given to the low castes for their hutments, could not be owned by them. The untouchables depended on the mercy of the landlords and jagirdars and spent their lives in fear. The landlords were oppressive in their behaviour and extracted the free labour they were entitled to, and more. If the low castes tried to say 'no' to begaar, they were humiliated and beaten up. Those who were enslaved by the British demanded freedom, but they too did not bother about the freedom of those who were their own slaves. On the other hand, they asserted their right to keep them in bondage and justified it on the basis of the sacred books. It is this that underlies the decline of a society and a country.

There is no other example in the whole world of such an unjust, oppressive, and discriminatory social system that has survived for thousands of years. There is no other religion in the world that is the flag bearer of a system which upholds customs which incite hatred, and traditions that are discriminatory and inhuman. In no other country in the world is such oppressive and exploitative behaviour towards women and the working class tolerated; the process of slotting and dividing men has continued down the centuries, and some Indians take pride in it and proclaim that it is this system which has prevented social tension and violence from manifesting here! Even those people who are considered progressive uphold these ideas as they are from the higher castes and are able to enjoy life because of the services rendered by the untouchables.... Such an unjust system would not have survived for so many centuries, had not books like *Manusmriti* laid down strict regulations against shudras and *atishudras*. It is in this context that Dr Bhim Rao Ambedkar has written that these so-called sacred texts, which are full of conspiracies and are political in nature, are biased, their aim and intention being fraud and deceit. I also remember what the first prime minister of India, Jawaharlal Nehru said: 'The Hindu is certainly not tolerant and is actually more narrowminded than almost any person in any country ...' (Letter from Jawaharlal Nehru to Dr Rajendra Prasad, dated 17 November 1953). And I cannot forget Karl Marx's assertion that if a single hand was raised anywhere against injustice and in support of socio-economic equality, he would wholeheartedly support such an effort.

One such courageous and valiant Punjabi stepped forward to fights for social justice; and it was a unique coincidence that he was from Baba Sangatia's village, Mugowal. He was Ghaddari Baba, alias Babu Mangu Ram Mugowalia. He was imprisoned for opposing British rule in India and was sentenced to death, but he had absconded from prison to spend three years with the *adivasis* in the jungle. In the beginning of 1925, he left Manila and came back to southwestern India, where he worked with dedication. And then he returned to his own village. Here, he saw the grinding poverty and intolerable lives of the untouchables. He was shaken by the burden of the different levels of slavery. After a letter from Lala Hardayal, he threw himself wholeheartedly into the upliftment of untouchables, and also established contact with Dr Ambedkar. He convened a large assembly of over a lakh of people from different castes in his village Mugowal, to set up an *Adi Dharam Mandal*, on 11–12 June 1926. It was, in a way, the beginning of a cultural movement. He also started a newspaper under the name, *Adi Danka*, to protest against social oppression and inequality. Because of his participation in the social, political, and economic agitation, seven of his associates became members of the Legislative Assembly in 1937.

... An important fact is that Mangu Ram Mugowalia visited our village before 1947, and again after 1947. It is said that he was given a very warm welcome in which the whole village participated. He will always be remembered by the people of India for his role in the freedom struggle of the country and the liberation of the untouchables.

... The fourth land settlement under the East Punjab Land (And Prevention of Fragmentation) Holding Act, 1943, was done after the British had left India. It was initiated in 1948 and went on till 1960. Under this, every low-caste family in a village was given two *marla* of land for the dumping of household waste. Earlier, the waste of the landless was divided according to the share of the house owners. Those who did not own the land that they cultivated, used their waste in the fields they worked on. They did not have the right to sell their waste.

... Those enslaved by the British attained their freedom in August 1947. They were given many different rights, but *Rajatnama* (*Chaudary haq rajatnama*), the law under jagirdari settlement which maintained the system of sardars and chaudarys, remained as it was, even though the Constitution of India came into force on 26 January 1950. After a long drawn-out struggle to create awareness, the right of marusi was abrogated in 1957. The Kameens were granted the right to own their lands. The 'haq rajatnama' ultimately came to an end, thus terminating the ancient right to force dalits to work in return for this land. The Punjab Land Revenue Act (*Intiqale Arazi Act*), 1887, which prevented dalits from buying land had already lapsed, and the scheduled castes now had the right to buy and sell land.

... The settlements of the untouchables are always in the lower ends—the western part—of a village, in Punjab, as it is all over India. This is because this class of people, in accordance with the Hindu social system, are not a part of the caste system and do not belong within the four varnas; even their shadows are to be avoided. Though it is asserted that they are within the Hindu fold, actually this statement is meant to keep the dalits permanently enslaved. That is the why they have been kept out of the mainstream. The second factor was that the dirty water of the village flows towards the west, which is the lower part of the village; and it is believed that not only should they not pollute clean water but also that these people should live in dirt, mire, and slime. This hateful, inhuman system still prevails in the villages of India.

A family from our community had bought land before 1947 in the name of a Jat as they could not buy it in their name; the land was later transferred to this dalit family by the Jat. This event became a symbol of change and revolution in our society. An awareness for freedom was spreading. The Constitution gave equal rights to all citizens and the 'untouchables' traversed the road from Harijans to Scheduled Castes. But the attitude and social behaviour of the higher castes towards dalits have not changed as much as they should have in this scientific age. Many laws were not implemented properly and, thus, the purpose for which they were made was not achieved. In brief, all sections of society need to make a concerted effort, courageously and enthusiastically, to bring about social change. The need of the hour is a rational philosophy.

# 2

## Inscriptions on a Tender Mind

I should make it clear right at the beginning of my autobiography that the community into which I was born, did not arrange to have their horoscopes cast, nor believe that their lives would change for better by the giving of alms ... Therefore, my date of birth according to the school records is 24 July 1955, but this does not agree with my mother's account of my birth. She says that I was born on a Tuesday. And, I was the first in line of many generations, who had the opportunity to learn how to read and write.

—The Author

'Give these Chamar brats a shout and drive them off,' the Jat bhai of the gurudwara would say to whosoever stood near him on the occasion of *Sangrand*—the first day of the Indian solar month—or *Gurupurub*—the birthdays of the Gurus, when he saw us standing on our toes and clinging to the bars of the window, as he distributed the prasad to the congregation.

We would all run away, in the flicker of an eye, trampling the *jootis* that lay strewn outside the gurudwara. But as soon as he turned the other way, we would be back at the window, exactly like we had been earlier.

This ill-tempered bhai wore the traditional Sikh style *kachcha*, a shabby kurta of coarse cotton, and a turban tied anyhow. His clothes were so dirty that they seemed to merge with his greasy perspiring legs. The pock marks scattered on his face seemed as if someone had sprinkled water on the grey ashes of a dung cake. When he talked in his usual abrupt manner, his triangular white beard shook. We often made fun of his 'chinky' eyes.

'You can't control this litter. I myself will drive them away, the mother's—,' and he would jump up mouthing an obscenity, which we all completed in our minds.

When it was our turn to be given the prasad, he would scold us, 'Haven't I told you, "again and again" you low castes, to sit patiently in one place!' Yet, we contrived to stand stretching out our small hands cupped together, to receive the prasad. He would throw it into our palms without bending, but we were sharp enough to catch it before it hit the ground. At times, a child did fail to grab it in time, and it would fall on the ground, driving him to the verge of tears. And, before he could pick it up, Daboo the dog, lying in wait for a chance like this, would gobble it up. It also happened that the copper bowl I carried for the prasad fell from my hands a couple of times when the bhai was hurriedly throwing a small portion from above, lest his hand touch my bowl. And when this happened, it wiped the joy off my face, and it was a long time before it returned.

Once in a while, he would ask one of us, 'Haven't you taken your share earlier?'

'No, baba, I haven't,' would be the answer of whosoever had been questioned, after gulping down the prasad, and wiping his hands on the backside of his kachcha.

We would happily exchange notes on our way home, boasting of the records that we had created! We would brag about our exploits—'I also took it three times!'

'You don't know the crafty man, he gives a crooked deal! He gives a handful of prasad to the ones inside the hall, and only a pinch to us ...' When I heard Massa say this as he was passing by, something within me snapped, the same way the wall of our mud-house which was adjacent to the gurudwara had cracked during the earthquake.

Whenever I was alone, my thoughts would wend their way to the gurudwara and stand there, like a supplicant, whose silent voice was unheard by all but me. The only difference between the well-dressed girls and boys inside the gurudwara and me was that I had only one pair of shorts to cover my nakedness, and I was darker than them. Suddenly, the long sermon on karma delivered by the bhai would stretch before me, like the wide deep pond of the village which I never had the courage to swim across ... The crack in the wall of our mud-house would widen, and the roof would almost collapse. Amidst all this, the innocent face of a young girl of my own age, who had come from her mother's paternal village, and who had been close to tears when the dog had eaten my share of the prasad, would flash before my mind's eye. She was about to give me her share of the prasad, when a woman gripped her small plaits and dragged her away. She had trailed along, weeping and protesting, 'Maami, Maami.' Lost in my thoughts, I would resolve never to again step inside the courtyard of the gurudwara. What would I lose by not eating the prasad!

Many times, we caught sight of the roan mare of Bikkar of the Walis. Our whole group would run towards him, shouting. When Bikkar neared our homes, he would be leading the mare, holding its reins. The mare would continuously flick its tail up and sideways. We would walk behind it, crossing the havelis of the Hakanas, the Nangas, and also the Sheikhchillis, right up to the havelis of the Ghoras and the Mantris. I yearned to spring on to the back of the young colt which ran along its dam, nudging her and thrusting its head between its legs, sometimes from the front, and sometimes, from behind. But the thought of the game of karma would not leave me and compelled me to give up the idea. Often, we would retreat, screaming, when the mare stopped to drop dung. Once, when we had reached the pond of the Nangas, the boys started throwing shards of pottery into the pond. It was then that I saw the mango saplings. Their lower leaves were green and tender, and the buds were bursting forth. I tried to dig up the sapling along with a chunk of earth, but could not. Yet, with a great deal of patience and skill, I did manage to take out the sapling, root and all.

It was when I was digging in our courtyard to plant the sapling, that Bhaia snatched the hoe from my hand, and said, 'Maama, you are trying to ape the Jats! They have large lands and large havelis! We only have this much space where we can sit and relax.'

My heart wilted like the plant. A storm had blown away the flowers of my desire. Even so, I thought, we too should have a tree in our courtyard, so that the sparrows, doves, and parrots may come to perch and bicker on the branches.

I was still lost in my thoughts, when a little before sunset, my friend Pash came along, 'Gudd, there is a spirit on the path to our *shamshan*.'

He had come running and was out of breath. I was thunderstruck at the information, 'What's it like?'

'They say he is *ichchadhari*—one who can take the form of a man, or a goat, or a snake with cowries, or anything else that he may want to be!' His nervousness agitated me all the more.

'Many have seen him, and they say that he turns himself into a dwarf sadhu with long hair, and is dressed in black. Sometimes, the pupils of his eyes are dilated, and at other times, he squints and contracts his eyes. His face also changes colour.'

All these images flashed before my astonished eyes! I had earlier heard my grandmother, and also my friends, say that hyenas dig up the bodies of dead infants and children for it is the practice to either bury the bodies of infants in the shamshan or immerse them in a flowing river, and not cremate them. So I thought to myself that is why Mohan Lal, the postman, always carries a spear with a bunch of bells tied on it, and when he walks fast, he moves his staff, spear bells and all, so that they jingle loudly and frighten off the spirit from his path! The khaki cap he wears seemed to me like the cap of Suleiman, in my grandmother's stories. She had often said that all of one's adversities would vanish if one wore this cap!

I was slightly feverish that night. Thoughts of the ghost jostled about in my mind throughout the night. Frightened, I would close my eyes and then open them again. The small, blackened iron lamp, burning in an alcove in the inner wall of the courtyard tried to dispel the huge waves of fear that seemed to engulf me. When the flame trembled, my heart also sank, and I would think, 'If only I could get Suleiman's cap!'

... The next day I did not go to western side of the village to answer nature's call, but instead went to the land near the village itself, and afterwards, ran back home. I almost collided headlong with Mai Ishari in the lane. Though she was bent double and hunchbacked, thankfully she managed to save herself from falling by supporting herself against the wall. She did not recognize me and I escaped a severe reprimand.

'Just look the way you've dirtied your feet! They're filthy!' My mother scolded me as she cleaned me in the small brick-paved washing place near the outer wall and the door. Then, she went to the room at the back of the courtyard, and called out, 'My *puttar*, come here and take this sackful of grain to Ratta's and get some tea leaves.'

I would often go to Ratta Brahmin's shop which was in the central lane of the village, early in the morning, and see Khichi and Pashu, of the water-carrier caste, fetching water for the Jat and Brahmin families. Each carried a large earthen pot on his right shoulders with a smaller pot on top, very skilfully balanced on the neck. Though young, both were out of breath and had backs bent like old men. They walked rapidly with their heavy loads.

I often wanted to throw a pellet and break those pots so that Pashu, who was only five or six years older than me, could be rid of the burden he had to carry. His clothes were drenched from the overflowing pots. A little later, they would be running towards school. Their father, Diwan, also fetched water for many households, in a contraption devised with the help of a shoulder-pole that had two rope rings at each end. He would carry the pole across his shoulder front to back. He walked carefully steps, and the pots within the rings of the rope would bob and swing from side to side with each step.

A woman standing in a door would tell him, 'Diwan, fetch our water first, as we have to attend a condolence meeting.'

'Pancha,[1] you are sweating heavily so early in the morning!' a Jat asked, glancing at his clothes drenched with perspiration.

'I have to go somewhere and so thought it best to get an early start,' Diwan explained, speaking in his dialect of the Majha.[2]

I had also often seen Tai Sibo and her son Jeet, both of the Jhiwar caste, fetching water for various households. The wheel of destiny would seem to be on its perpetual journey, like the Persian wheel. It seemed that the new buckets strung on the wheel were full of water, like the symbol of the good deeds of the tales of holy men, and the old hole-ridden buckets were empty like the stories that could not be articulated. I often heard the bhai of the gurudwara reciting the Guru Granth, as I went up and down to the shops. But Bhaia would comment, 'The bhai seems to be muttering to himself! Yesterday he had started off with the first crow of the cock!'

1. Pancha is used as a form of respect for the Jhiwar water carrier caste.
2. Majha is the area between the rivers Ravi and Beas.

'Mind your tongue! What if someone were to overhear you?' Ma would softly admonish him.

My village, which disappeared every evening behind the dense black of night, would spring to life again as soon as the sun peeped out from the east. Bhaia would take a few hurried puffs at his hookah and then pick up a copper tumbler. By this time my uncle's sons would also arrive. They would also be carrying either a tumbler or a bowl tied in a corner of a thin *angocha*, a cloth, flung on their shoulders, or tucked into their pockets. They, too, would leave home for a day or half a day's work. My eyes would follow them. They would look back and wryly remark, 'Utensils are always scarce for us, in the homes we are going to! Now what!'

Speechless, I would wonder, 'These illiterates cannot read the written word, how can they read the question in my eyes?'

My mind was still caught up with thoughts of the ghost spinning out a web for itself … and a great part of the night would pass this way. Jackal howls scared me even more and often drove me to tears. I could hear the loud thumping of my heart! The long winter nights seemed unending. But when the sugarcane crop was harvested, then the jackals retreated from the village, and there was only an occasional howl.

The silence of the early hours of the winter morning would be shattered by the high tone of Gurudas Singh of the nambardars, who would go about reciting 'Jai Ali', 'Jai Ali'. Even in the cosy warmth of my bed, I would shiver and cling to my elder brother, Birju, sleeping by my side, and send up a prayer to the unseen god with fear in my heart. Many a time, sleep would descend only at the break of dawn.

Gurudas would pass our houses in the early hours of the morning, his hair loose and wet. His full white beard suited him; but he had the look of a giant or a ghost. He wore a dhoti, pulled up to his calves, and a kurta in the style of the *Nihangs*. He used to carry an iron bucket in his right hand, and a load of sugarcane on his left shoulder. He was a frightening sight, and I would hide behind our front door

'*Dharam naal*, he drinks a whole pot of cane juice! About five of seven days back, the boys at the cane crusher had given him a pot of cane juice and he drank it all up, and then started throwing up,' Swarana told my father one day as he saw Gurudas coming that way.

'God alone knows what the problem in their family is! He is a strapping man, but he goes to the well at midnight and yokes himself to the Persian wheel in place of animals and sets it rolling,' my father added to the talk.

'They have taken over all the lands, the pir is bound to trouble them—a Muslim pir does not let one off so easily,' Swarana glibly repeated what he had often heard the others say.

'He has had enough *akhand paths* held, but still ...' Bhaia remarked.

By this time Gurudas had come up and halted near them. I was watching through the door slats.

'Thakara, I tire myself out, turn my head round and round, speak in a loud voice, and at times even seem to lose my balance. The pir asks why did you demolish my grave. Now you must build a mausoleum for me, light candles every Thursday, and distribute alms. But I can do all this only when the family listens to me,' Das expressed the anguish in his heart, as he swung the bucket he held.

If the pir's grave does not exist anymore, then where does he live, and how does he speak? The one who frightens people at night, of whom is he frightened during the day? These thoughts assailed me.

After, a moment, Gurudas said, 'Swarana, come with me to the well. I hope your roller is working! Come soon.'

'Why are you so restless early in the morning, nambardar'? Bhaia asked.

'By god, my insides seem to be on fire.'

When Das and Swarana had passed beyond the house of the banyan tree, only then I and other children came out of our homes, and standing in the lane, began shouting in one voice, 'Jai Ali, Jai Ali'.

Swaran glanced at us; but Das could not look back properly ...

And Bhaia walked over to the cow and the buffalo tied under the banyan tree. Stroking the buffalo's back, he picked at the ticks and vermin sticking to its backside. Putting them on the ground, he would squash each one with the index finger of his right hand; but once in a while, one of the nits would start walking again. Stretching his arm, he picked up a shard of pottery from the ground and placing it near his right foot, he declared, 'Just look! The way they pretend to be dead! Now I shall set you right!' During this session of killing the ticks and vermin, I noticed that the buffalo had closed its eyes and had started chewing the cud. I don't know what came over Bhaia, but he told me, 'Gudd, go home and fetch my torn underpants lying in the manger.'

I immediately swung into action.

'Just see how thick the mud is,' he exclaimed, scrubbing the animal's back vigorously with the cloth I had brought. 'I will remove your ticks also,' he assured the brown cow, giving her a glance full of love. It was as if he communed perfectly with the animals.

... The winter was living out its last days. My friends and I would be busy making tops out of the dry leaves of the banyan tree. It stood, stark and bare, with all its leaves on the ground. The new reddish blossoms were already visible on the branches. When the autumn of 1962 ended, I started going to school.

I had often been to the school earlier, but that was only to play hide and seek. The three of us, Pash, Dhyan, and I, would start the Persian wheel of the well in the centre of the school courtyard. It was not very heavy and anyone of us would steer the whole round single-handed. The small iron buckets would rise to the top and empty themselves into the trough and fill it to the brim. On returning home, I happily related all this to Bhaia, who said, 'It was Jan Mohammad's haveli. He built the rooms, verandahs, and the mosque with great love and enthusiasm.' The whole family listened to him with interest. I noticed that Bhaia looked sad.

He went on as if trying to recall something, 'One evening I rushed up to Mohku, seated in the mausoleum and told him that his Jan was coming down the lane. All those who were sitting around, did not believe me, and I also was somewhat young at that time.' I could see the glow of happiness on Bhaia's face.

'I again told them to go and see for themselves. Then, Mohku got up and walked off rapidly to gather Jan to his chest.' Bhaia said all this with the air of one who had won a great battle.

'Had he run off after a fight at home?' I wanted to know and saw Bhaia's fine teeth gleaming.

'No, he was in the army during the Second World War, and there had been no information about him for a very long time, nor had he written to anyone. They had given up all hope,' Bhaia's story seemed to have no end.

By god! Jeewaan was overjoyed and celebrated his homecoming by distributing laddoos. She first came to me, and gave me rice as prasad, saying, 'you were the one who brought news of my son's return.' Bhaia had given the horses of his memory free rein—from Jan Mohammad's haveli to the school.

'Jan Mohammad's younger brother Aziz Mohammad, was my close friend,' Bhaia's voice had now become sweeter and deeper than it had been earlier. His dark cheeks had slackened. The silken thread he had woven at the loom of his memory now enveloped me.

The culmination of the story was that although sundry killings had already begun, their family was well when they had left here. When they boarded the truck, the whole village had come to see them off, Jeewaan and Mohku were weeping openly. Aziz embraced me and then cried ... It is not easy to abandon one's motherland!' Bhaia stopped, unable to go on.

After a short pause, 'As the truck started moving, Aziz stared at me. He looked ill and dazed. *Dharam naal*, he wept loudly. I also looked at him helplessly. Tears filled my eyes and everything was hazy ... As the evening fell, the whole village lay under a thick pall of silence, as if everyone had seen a ghost ... the wicked leaders had put stones in their boats.'

At bedtime, images of people being killed, of embraces, sounds of loud weeping, and the deep silence which had struck the village, flickered before my eyes. I saw the jamun tree standing in the school ground, shedding its leaves and the mosque shrouded in the darkened shadows of the night. I would think why had Bhaia not puffed at his hookah, as was his habit? And why had his voice dropped and grown deeper? And though I thought very hard, I got no answer to all the questions and gradually drifted into sleep. In the morning, no trace of those doubts remained, as if I had wiped clean the slate of my mind. By evening, however, they would all come rushing back, dark and ominous.

The thick cloud of fear enveloping my heart, however, did not seem to disperse. My apprehensions seemed to be focused on a single point. My night grew even longer.

It happened one evening, when the women of our area had gone out to get some grass and fodder, but had immediately returned saying, 'The police are in the nambardar's haveli.'

By this time, I too had seen three tall and well-built policemen. It was the first time I had seen a constable. They were all dressed in khaki shirts and shorts, with khaki turbans.

They held rods. Though it was summer, they wore stockings, doubled up and folded down to their ankles and sandals or boots. As they walked through, utter silence fell on our lane. Neither man nor beast was to be seen.

The women hiding behind our front door looked old and weary. The hoes and sickles they held were shaking, and they were whispering, 'That Mindho of the Panahgirs has not run away with same man. They say she was cut into three pieces, shoved into a sack, and thrown into the well under the silk-cotton tree.'

I stood near them, and out of sheer fright, collapsed under my own weight.

The door was opened after the policemen had departed. 'God alone knows which fool has recruited this Telang! The one at the back is running too fat, he already has a paunch, because he has been gobbling up things that don't belong to him!' Bhaia remarked loud enough for all assembled there to hear his opinion about the constables, thin and fat. Everyone laughed rather abruptly.

Bhaia went on, 'Saale! Arrogant ones! Why couldn't they have dispatched the *haraamzadi* elsewhere! How does it matter to the Barias (the Jats who had migrated from the Bar area, now in Pakistan)! It is not for nothing that it is said that the Jat is always at an advantage, and his hundred is made of seven twenties. Now, they will cool their heels all their lives in prison! And hasn't Gurmukh of the Barias kept their Karmi? But who bothers about Rakha Muji (Karmi's husband) at home.'

Right through the day my troubled thoughts ran wild like the multi-coloured rags of the balls with which we children often played.

I pictured the now dead Mindho bringing food and water, or tea, for her father, or carrying a head-load of fodder. At night, I would see her on the path now talking to this person and then to that! I would picture her body falling off in three pieces the head, torso, and limbs.

At night, before going to sleep, I would see a crowd gathered around the well, under the silk-cotton tree, and the police dragging the whole Panahgir family to the well. But when I talked about it to my brother, he would tell me, 'Take the name of god, you will be able to sleep.'

Events like this assailed my very being. I would add up many things and divide others, all in my mind, and many things would add up and other shatter.

All this was going on when someone come up to the hollow near the banyan tree and said, 'Durga Brahmin's radio gives the news that China has betrayed us and a war has broken out between China and India. The government has started recruiting for the army.'

Everyone was astonished and the positions of the hookahs changed. The taut pipes slackened and were then rolled up. The bullocks could be seen winding their way home, after a day's hard work in the fields.

This piece of news set off a big war in my heart and body. It seemed to me that apprehension and fear had erected a permanent camp in my mind. Whenever I recalled this, as we played under the banyan tree at dusk or on a moonlit night, a storm of fear raged within me.

… And one day Ma called out to me to bathe, but what happened was something else …

'Tell me, maama, will you eat mud again!' Suddenly Bhaia caught hold of my right wrist and dangled me over the edge of the well. From where had this cloud appeared to darken my clear skies? My breath hung somewhere in my chest, imprisoned within my ribs. I could hear my heart throb violently.

'Tell me,' he asked again, 'will you eat mud again?'

A current ran through my body, I could not even cry. I was breathing heavily with my heart in my mouth.

My mother was washing clothes seated on the brick-paved floor of the parapet of the well. She stopped and rushing up to the well, shouted, 'Will you take him out only when he stops breathing?' She stood there and again asked, 'What if your hold loosens …?'

'I have scolded him often enough, but he doesn't seem to care,' Bhaia retorted angrily.'

I looked at him with pleading eyes, and then looked down at the water, which was hardly a few spans beneath me.

'The boy is crying and you …'

Ma shouted and quickly lifted me out of the well. By now, I was almost lifeless. Even in the intense cold of winter. I was soaked in perspiration.

A little later, I thought of the last monsoon. At that time the water level in the well was as high the ground. Only when the rains weakened did it drop. Frogs of all sizes could be spotted swimming in the well. I had often worried about their not being able to come out of the well. Yet, many of them could be seen leaping about on the ground outside the well, and we could hear them croaking trr … trr … then, my own precarious situation came back to me. What if Bhaia's hold on my wrist had slackened? Could I have swum out of the well, like the frogs?

I was furious with Bhaia and thought of different ways of avenging myself, whenever an opportunity came my way. I'll fill his bottle of liquor with urine, or else, I'll throw a burning coal on his palm from his chillum …

Bhaia's action was frightening and my heart had sunk. It seemed as if a flying bird had been shot down in mid-flight with a slingshot.

'Shame on you! He is hysterical and you're slapping his temples! Look how they have swollen!' Ma's face was flushed with annoyance. I clung to her legs.

I had never seen her in such fury. She had never retaliated to Bhaia's daily abuse and beatings. But this new image of hers shook me. Sitting down and holding me against her breast, she wiped the tears streaming down my cheeks. After a brief pause, she turned on Bhaia, 'You are not aware of your own habits! Will you spare even a bit of pottery you stumble upon in the fields. You pick it up and chew it. Just see how your mouth stinks of tobacco! Go home, go!'

My mother's eyes were moist and red. Bhaia walked away and nearly slipped on the mossy floor of the trough of the Das family, but then saved himself. He muttered, 'Look at her blabbering!'

'It was he who took Gud along to work when the path to Laroya was being covered with mud and gravel. He learnt to eat mud at that time, as he played about in the pits along the path,' Ma told Mindo, the daughter-in-law of the Das family, who stood staring at me.

'This consolidation of land has only brought us trouble. We did not get any lands!' And then, after a pause, she went on, '*Hoon*! As if it will be our carts that will to pass on that mud road to the mills! That is why the cursed ones wanted our people to fill up the potholes with earth. They said, 'What do you do otherwise, idling the whole day long.' But our people fought back and worked on the basis of one man per household and told them that the days of *begaar* were over,' Ma said stretching her neck proudly. Perhaps, she wanted to prove that I had got into the habit of eating mud while throwing mud on the path for a fortnight.

By this time, Gelu of Rao caught hold of my arms and led me sobbing to the group playing under the banyan tree, and asked me, '*Phlatoo* (Aflatoon), tell where do your in-laws live?'

I was silent.

'You are my friend now tell me where is the house of your in-laws?'

'Kandhala village (Kandhala Sheiken, district Hoshiarpur, which was my mother's village), where else?' And as I said this they all laughed.

Gelu often asked me this in the presence of others, as if he were a *madari*, and I, his *jamoora*! But I could never understand why others laughed at my answers.

Early morning, Bhaia would fling aside the sheet of quilt covering me and my brother. Ma would call out, 'Sons, get up, the sun is over our heads.' Or, she would say, 'Gudd, go and fetch some embers from Bhagat's on a cow dung cake. I have to make tea.'

In our houses, the embers are buried under the ashes in the earthen *chulha* at night, to be rekindled the next morning. If one forgot to do this, then the next morning, some embers had to be collected from the neighbours. This way we saved on matches. During the cold and foggy winter mornings, we would gather around the chulha and stoke the fire by throwing dry leaves or scraps of dried sugar-cane on it.

There was neither a window nor a door in the kitchen, which had been constructed by raising four pillars in the courtyard and around the outer wall. The walls were made of woven rush and reed mats and plastered over to give the look of proper walls. The roof was not very wide, and was also made of rushes and bamboo cane. It had a thick layer of soot and smoke, and it was very difficult for anyone to make out what the material was. Occasionally strips of soot from the cane roof would come free and fall on the floor.

When I strained my tea into a glass, Bhaia would remark, 'It is not the rainy season for you to strain out any insects that may be in the jaggery. It doesn't go bad in winters.'

I would drink tea like drinking water, but couldn't blot out the image of the white insects in the tea which Ma strained through the end of her dupatta, during the monsoons.

A campfire would be lit outside our homes during winters. The old and the young would all gather around and keep the fire burning with the kindlings they brought from home. Anyone who did not bring kindling, would be elbowed out of the range of the heat of the fire. We would first stretch out our icy feet to the fire to warm them, and then run towards the school building. We were all barefoot. On the other hand, the children of landlords would each be wearing two jerseys. I would think if only someone were to give me even one sweater, it would keep me warm. Then, the chain of my thoughts would break and I would join the children in loud singing ...

*Suraja, suraja, patti sukha*
*Nahin sukahni, ghar nu ja*
(Sun, O sun, dry my wooden slate
If you can't do that then go home)

After a few moments, my thoughts would revert to my striped kachcha and kurta, which was more useful to wipe my runny nose than in keeping out the cold. My clothes were washed only on Sundays. I sat behind the wall of the trough and picked lice from the folds of my clothes. My mother would scrub my feet vigorously, as she bathed me at the well, saying, 'Just look at the layers of dirt!'

But I could not see much difference between my legs and feet. And then, as I would come out of my reverie, the sounds of 'Suraja, suraja, patti sukha' would still be heard, though very faintly.

Abandoning all attempts at pondering over the past, I would see Khushia, Bhima, or his younger brother Piari (whom the whole village called Aashiq, because of his dark complexion and the strange gait), carrying a dead calf in front of the school building. In those days, many cows, calves, and even bullocks died. The Jats sold their old buffaloes in the market.

They tied the hooves of the dead animal together and passed a pole through them, which they then carried across their shoulders, so that they could walk easily and comfortably. The animal hung upside down, and swung from side to side, its ears and neck shaking with every step.

The larger carcases were dragged away by four or five persons, who would call out instructions to each other, 'Piari, pull properly. You are putting the whole burden on me!'

They carried a carcass slung on a pole resting on their shoulders in such a manner that their heads and torsos would be bent forward. Their own weight was on their toes, and their knees would also be bent. At times, one of them came forward to pull the heavy weight. They would stop for a breather and wipe their foreheads with the *angochas* they carried on their shoulders, while we, who watched them, would all be shivering in the cold.

Sometimes, the other children of our community would join Bhima and his helpers during the recess. When the carcass was dragged along, its horns would leave a long trailing mark behind. Its eyes would protrude; its mouth would yawn open with its teeth bared and lower jaw sticking out. I would often hold the head of a carcass firmly so that it did not loll about. I didn't want its body to get scratched. Many a time, the dead animal would be carried away in an open cart with us children pushing the cart. On our way home, we would pluck the yellow mustard flowers from the fields around.

I had often noticed that whenever we used the tap, any Jat child who used it after us would wash the tap thoroughly before drinking from it. This often made me wonder what was wrong with my hands that others had to wash a tap after I had touched it. Was it because I had touched the animals? They, too, had often twisted the tail of the same live animal!

Massa often sat with a dying cow or a bullock and recited the *Geeta* in a loud voice. The animal would be writhing in pain and throw its legs about, and Massa would try to soothe it and say, 'The end is now near. You are going to get your *gati* now.'

'Massa, this bullock was so very useful,' Udham Singh, the father of Iqbal Singh, had once sadly remarked about an animal that had just died. But Massa just picked up the load of grain, flung it over his back, and walked off without responding.

Seated at his loom, Massa appeared to be more knowledgeable than even the bhai of the gurudwara, whenever he talked to people who were impressed with the references to Mahabharat and Ramayana, and the verses he quoted from the Gurubani, and the way he interpreted them. Often he would tell me—as I stood beside him—'Gudd, put some coals in the chillum.'

But whenever we talked of him at home, Bhaia would immediately retort, 'He is always talking about unattainable things. He behaves as if he has just come back from a meeting with god. Someone should ask him whether anyone has ever seen god.'

I thought Bhaia was right, then, at other times, Massa seemed to be right. I also wondered if an animal understood Punjabi or Hindi, in which the prayers are said? The word gati means both 'redemption' and 'speed'. I had taken the latter meaning. The whole issue still seemed very complicated, like the circles of a *jalebi*, which were difficult to know where they began and where they ended. My thoughts ran wild, seeking answers and yet none were forthcoming. Things seem dark and unfathomable, though the day was bright and sunny.

'Everyone …! Everyone … old or young, come out to the fields beating whatever you can get hold of—tins or thalis! The locusts are coming! We must save the maize crop!'

This loud proclamation by Jagar the chowkidar at daybreak woke me, and opening the door, I ran out. He had flattened the old, rusted, and discoloured tin with blows from his thick stick of mulberry wood. He covered the middle lane rapidly and disappeared, but his strident voice, calling out to save the maize crop, could still be heard. At that time—1963—I was in the second standard.

People ran in groups towards the field. Bhaia, my elder brother, and I picked up whatever we could and ran across the path into the nearby fields of Alballaeas and started beating tins, thalis, and metal trays. We had sown maize on half their fields after manuring it with the dung and refuse of our animals. The maize stalks were high, some as high as the span of my hand, and others even higher. They were lush green and tender. We had hoed and turned the soil only the day before.

As far as one could see, the locusts were flying in from the south of the village towards the mountains in the north. The rays of the sun filtered through the thick swarms of the locusts. Wherever they alighted, they gobbled up everything—maize, fodder, millet, and even the leaves of the sheesham trees. As soon as they descended upon whatever was at hand, they laid white eggs resembling grains of rice. The stink was unbearable, making one retch even on an empty stomach. The very sight of them was disgusting, and if one were to step on them inadvertently, one felt deep revulsion.

'I'll make you sing, maama!' Bhaia said trying to sweep away the hordes of locusts with his hands. I beat upon the thali with great force. It also occurred to me that if they were flying so fast, how did Jagar the chowkidar learn of their attack so quickly?

The sun was now fairly high in the sky. A few swarms were still lagging behind, and we quickly destroyed them. At once an army of ants materialized and busied itself upon the dead locusts, pulling them away out of sight, to feast on. These swarms of locusts seemed to me like the aeroplanes taking off from the Adampur airport. The long black stripes on the elongated bellies of their yellow bodies looked very attractive.

People were now going home. When we reached the crossroads near the haveli of the nambardars, my uncle Banta said, 'When you have four maunds of grain, Sardarji, only then will we able to get ten seers.'

'Thank god, not much damage has been done,' someone remarked. 'This is all due to Jagar! The moment the constable from the police station gave him the information, Jagar started beating the drum,' Taya Banta said.

'They said that wireless messages had come to the police station from Jalandhar.'

'When the locusts came in 1950, after the Partition, they even ate the leaves of all the trees at that time and stripped them bare. These swarms were nothing compared to those! At that time they even had to stop the trains,' Bhaia tried to set up a sequence of events. I stood near them, watching their dull faces. They were exchanging notes as they walked home.

'Come, my son, gather these dry twigs,' Taya Banta interrupted the conversation, and winked at me. I thought Taya must be wanting to smoke the *sulfa* in his pocket.

His son, Khushia, and I gathered small dry twigs. By this time he had collected hay and dry grass scattered around into a heap, and pulling some twigs over it, set it alight. A flame sprang up, and after it subsided, he opened the knot at the corner of his angocha in which there were dead locusts. Throwing them on to the fire, he stirred them with a twig and said, 'Chew them, they are now roasted.'

I stared at my uncle. He put a toasted locust into his mouth and giving me one, repeated, 'Eat, it doesn't have any bones!' Then laughing shortly, he remarked, 'I have eaten enough bones in my time!'

Hesitantly, I ate the roasted locust. It was salty and very tasty. Then, I scattered the embers and picking up the locusts, ate them. Khushia's hands and mouth were also busy.

This incident of my having eaten locusts spread through the school and the children teased me, calling me 'locust-eater' or 'locust-eater snake'.

This last word had perhaps been added because of my very dark complexion. I sank under the weight of this disgrace, and though I tried hard, I could not emerge from it. At times, I thought that my eating locusts had been a normal and ordinary thing; then, it would seem an abomination even to me. I would often argue with myself, 'mutton is cooked in all households on the occasion of Diwali and Dussehra and yet no one comments on it!' In a few days, even this thought had flown away like the locusts ... and my mind was rid of this subtle yet terrible burden. I was soon running after butterflies during the day and chasing gloworms at night again.

# 3

# The Tale of the Cracked Mirror

'If I don't pulp all these Chamars with my boots, I am not the son of a Jat!' shouted a zamindar as he rushed furiously through the central lane and stopped under the peepal and banyan trees to shout and rage.

'What has happened, sardara, why are you so angry?' old uncle Banta asked, emerging from his home, a small reed basket with pipes in one hand and a chillum in the other.

'They've cut the fodder from my field under the pretext of cutting weeds and grass! As if the field is their father's!'

Hearing this roar, both young and old in the neighbourhood came out of their homes. Their clothes were soiled and dirty, torn and patched all over. An odour of stale sweat, fouled the air. They were barefoot. The women's cracked heels, with crooked lines of deeply embedded mud in them, seemed like fissures of parched earth in the fields, as it sweltered under the impact of a long dry spell.

They stood in a half circle, perturbed and nonplussed, looking at each other's faces. I felt that a calamity was about to befall someone. Sheer fright made my heart beat rapidly and loudly.

'We nurture our crops by crushing the heads of snakes day and night, but these droves of cattle destroy everything, wherever they go! Sometimes they pluck corn cobs, or cut spinach, or sugarcane, or even green gram!'

As he spoke continuously and loudly, specks of foaming spittle collected at the corners of his lips, which he spat saying, 'thoo, thoo', every now and then.

'Sardara, you tell me who they were! And I will question them in your presence,' Uncle Banta told him patiently.

'This is the limit! Did they come from another village? They all looked the same! Now, no one wants to own up! I should have snatched their dupattas from their faces, in the fields! Thoo, thoo!' He was known in the village as 'thoo-thoo' because of this habit of his.

'Where else will we labourers and kameens go? It is from the fringes of your fields that we pluck grass. We also look after your buffaloes!' Taya Banta said in a manner of bringing the matter to an end.

'Don't try to be clever! You look after our buffaloes? As if you don't get your share! ... And then you puff your chest and claim three shares and say that we have only two!'

The issue had, by itself moved into the sphere of the rights of both the parties and, suddenly, temperatures rose. Uncle Banta was silent for a few moments, and then very humbly said, 'Sardar, this matter of *punj duwanji* that you are talking about, is not very simple. At times, the buffalo doesn't conceive, and then, again most of the time during its pregnancy, it is ill; at times, it is rendered barren—finally, we have to hand over the rope to the butcher. This Thakar, here, tended a buffalo for two and a half years. She was ill most of the time before calving, and then at the time of delivery, she died. We, too, bear these losses. It is not as if the women *cut* the crops from your field.'

'Don't you dare utter such nonsense! Either you yourself tell me who is responsible for destroying my crop, or I will call the panchayat.'

'May your sardari flourish! Forget you anger ...' Uncle said in an attempt to bring the matter to a close, and putting the reed basket on the ground, he stood scratching his bald pate.

'These Chamars will not see sense easily! 'Thoo-thoo' declared furiously, He abruptly folded his leg at the knee and tried to pull the leather boot off his foot.

'Do whatever you want. You are unnecessarily trying to frighten us, because no one protests! First go and ask Nangia's old man! I let him off the other day because he implored me with folded hands, or else I would have pulled out his intestines!' This was Phumman, my uncle's son, a high-school student, raising his right arm furiously.

A storm broke out all around us. Everybody was thunderstruck. My legs shook with fright and my whole body trembled. My mother, who stood beside me, looked at me from behind the dupatta covering her face, and placing my younger sister in my arms, went home. The women of the area, all my aunts, stood with their faces covered with their dupattas, which they kept adjusting to have a good look at things from time to time.

Uncle Banta and others caught hold of Phumman's arms and tried to take him away from there, but he refused to listen to anything anyone was saying, and shouted, 'Anybody and nobody rushes here to thunder at us. They snatch the hoes and sickles from the hands of our women, at times pull their dupattas off! This is the practice! The fodder may have been cut by their own men, but they will blame us for it—no one listens to us!'

'Fine! You will find out at the police station. I'll see you there. You are talking rubbish and so arrogantly!' 'Thoo-thoo' threatened us again.

'Threaten someone else; those days are gone when all of them scraped and bowed before you,' Phumman retaliated. After a moment's pause, he went on again, 'Now you lose your temper when you hear a few home truths! You are here every day, to threaten and frighten us!'

As I stood watching all this, it seemed to me that there was bound to be a struggle. Then it appeared to me that the matter had come to an end. The panic on the faces around me scared me. My throat was dry, and I had difficulty swallowing. My legs seemed numb, and my body felt chill. I felt I would collapse and drop my sister on her head.

'You will come to your senses—all of you who talk so aggressively now, when you are thrashed with boots! A widow's son (this was directed at my aunt) and a merchant's horse, never follow a straight path!' 'Thoo-thoo' vented his spleen yet again. After a short pause, and in a lower tone, he said, 'Saale! Sparrow, mice, and Chamars, all increase at a very fast rate!'

'Think before you speak, or else, I'll pluck you beard! The illegitimate son of your father should ask who struck my mother with a goad—he had to rub his nose on the ground at the police station. When they all tell you that you can take them to the gurudwara if they have harmed your interests ... even then you threaten them!' Phumman said passionately, as he freed himself from Taya Banta and other elders. His eyebrows were contracted and his brow wrinkled. As he spoke loudly, specks of saliva flew in the air.

When I heard Phumman, who was only some eight or ten years older than me speaking so courageously, my legs gained new strength. In a few moments, I was filled with the idea that I, too, should be brave and fearless like Phumman, and deal firmly with all those who frightened us. When I grew up, I should not submit to anyone but should deal clearly and effectively with everyone. I should own fields and go about twirling my moustache like the sons of landlords.

My other uncle, Rama (Ramlal), had also arrived and scolded Phumman. 'What's all this noise? Go home, or I'll hit you with my shoe!'

'No one says anything to those who harass us day and night! Do we not belong here that they have made life so difficult for us? They scold and terrorize us all the time. Merely because they have lands, they have become our gods! They are the ones who feed us! If we did not work so hard in your fields, you would starve! You will forget to drink and raise hell in the evening, the way you do!' He talked continuously and loudly, and spittle flecks of peppered the air. His eyes were red with anger, and his dark body tense.

It was the first time that I had seen Phumman speak like this. Everyone knew of his obstinate nature, but we also knew that he would not flinch if he was convinced that he was right. This event astonished me. I feared that the zamindars would come for us waving their lathis in the air.

Everyone's attention was suddenly diverted by the sound of jingling bells and all eyes turned in the direction it was coming from. A sanyasi had arrived, and he too joined the group standing around. But he kept raising and lowering his feet as if he was still walking, the way I used to while marking time with my friends at school. I forgot the tension of the moment and began imitating the sanyasi. I stopped only when he asked, 'What were you people saying about land? In the end, we will leave everything behind and take nothing with us.'

The sanyasi spoke in a mixture of Hindi and Punjabi and continued marking time as he spoke. Women, old and young, went home.

The others listened to what the sanyasi had to say. He talked about controlling emotions like lust, anger, avarice, arrogance, and pride, and finally raising his dhoti, he showed us his penis which was pierced with a copper ring. We youngsters were taken aback. He talked about freedom from worldly desires. In a few moments the atmosphere had changed. Uncle told 'Thoo-thoo', 'Now, no one will harm you. Don't worry, and drop the matter.'

'You are a member of the panchayat, how can I refuse you? Tell Phumman that he is young, and should be careful about what he says. If my sons were to hear it, who knows what they may do in a fit of anger. An angry Jat is capable of selling his land to kill a man.'

'Go, away from here …' Taya rebuked him.

My uncle's daughters-in-law had, by now, come up to our front door. I left the group and ran towards them. Jeeto bhabhi called out loudly, 'Chachi, send Gudd to collect rotis.'

Leaving my younger sister at home and picking up a small thali and a cloth, I set off with my sisters-in-law. This was a part of my daily routine. My father worked for different zamindars, and we would go to the houses of these zamindars, sit in their courtyards, and put out our bowls for rotis. Their women threw the rotis from the top and we would adroitly catch them. The dal and vegetables were also ladled out from above into our bowls, and sometimes blistering hot splashes fell on our feet.

On such occasions, I would often think of past events. … I had seen my father storing the grain in the granaries and bins at Iqbal Singh's house, and heard him mutter, 'Today, we walk barefoot on this mound of grain, but once it is stored, we would not be allowed to touch it, our touch contaminates it.' Who will let us come in here tomorrow!'

Defilement—I had confronted this word time and again, the way the rope in our well had frayed by constant rubbing against the wall. My thoughts would suddenly grow wings like the ones insects sprouted during the rains. I would think of the care the zamindars took of their animals—scrubbing and bathing, and tending them tenderly. Their dogs roamed freely in the courtyard and even entered the kitchen. Their children petted the cat all the time, feeding the kitten milk and … and … Bhaia and others like him have to carry their own tumblers and bowls from home, work hard for them the whole day, and still their animals are treated better than we human beings! And I wished that I didn't have to labour like this—somehow I should get some education and move to Delhi, like my aunt's son who was working in Delhi, and live there, wear new trousers and shirts, where no one would scold me, and there would be no one to fear.

At times, Bhaia was compelled to work on daily wages in homes where the food given was inedible. He often shared his feelings with us, 'I don't like to eat food cooked by that mean woman. I feel like throwing up. She gives rotis of bajra and masoor dal all badly cooked. The stupid woman does not have any children.'

At times my mother, instead of taking Bhaia's wages in cash, would get jaggery, onions, garlic, potatoes, wheat, maize, or other such commodities from the women of the Jat families he worked for. Bhaia would remark sarcastically, 'They increase the price of the commodities whenever they want, but our wages are not raised. We work like animals the whole day long!'

'Stop it, we are able to manage somehow or the other,' Ma tried to cut the conversation short.

'What do you know, sitting at home, of the way in which our skin burns under the blazing sun!'

'Who wants to argue with you! He says I sit at home!' With this, Ma went into the back room.

Bhaia would sit on the cot, tired and drained, or he would lie down and talk to himself, 'If only we had small piece of land, we would have been very comfortable. No one knows which bastard has deprived us of land. If I ever come to meet him, I shall tell that saala, that he should also work like a slave the way we do, and if his bum doesn't burst, then he may come and catch me!'

Red eyes. Wrinkled brow. Tense face. He would speak rapidly and bitterly. Watching all this, I would decide that when I grew up, I would buy land and have orchards of bananas, mangoes, and grow roses near the well, the way many of the Jats did.

I had seen the daily quarrels about money, the squabbles peaking at meal times. Bhaia would begin throwing the utensils around. The clatter in the kitchen could be heard by the people in the courtyard. At times it looked as if the very embers in the chulha would flare up. I was scared that Bhaia might hit Ma any moment now, vent his anger on her, and then sulk silently. He would then go to sleep without eating.

On such days, Ma would look at us two brothers, sadly. This would annoy Bhaia, 'Where should I go and hang myself! I have told you hundreds of times that I have not been able to get any money. But the same fight every day, complaints and abuses the whole day. Do the children belong to you alone?' The sadness in his voice expressed his deep helplessness.

'Don't look at me angrily, the month is over.'

'Should I steal from somewhere? I have asked, but no one is ready to give even a paisa.' Bhaia replied angrily. Then something came over him, and he said, 'I work very hard yet nothing seems to come of it! *Saali* our fate is like this. Who knows what sins we are being punished for! It would have been better had we not been born. It would not have been a loss to anyone, and then, on top of all this, *you*!'

'Be patient, listen to someone else once in a while. I say, tomorrow is Baisakhi, take them for a bath, before sunrise.'

It seemed as if raindrops had fallen on burning embers. Bhaia ran his fingers through the hair under the angocha on his head, and said, 'All right, whatever you say.'

Next morning, before sunrise, Bhaia took me and Birju towards the south of the village. As we walked silently, the moon seemed to be keeping pace with us. Clusters of plants bordered the path and the wind murmured through them. For a moment these soft whispers sent a wave of fear like a gust of wind through me. I rushed and clutched my brother's hand. When we reached the path on the periphery of the village of Jandit, a bitch rushed out of the deep pit used for boiling sugarcane juice to make jaggery, and started barking. Her litter followed her. Bhaia tried to drive them away and himself stood still and told us, 'Go quickly.'

'Oh God, I am dead!' I screamed and hobbled with pain, for I had stepped on a thorn bush. I sat down on the ground howling. Bhaia took out the thorns one by one, and then passing his hand over my sole asked, 'Does it hurt now?'

Looking around a little carefully, I discovered that it was the same place where I had come with Mangi, my uncle's son, for the Baisakhi mela last year. The village Diwan had set up a stall for golgappas. Khichchi and Pasha had served water to the customers and washing the dirty utensils. There were stalls of sweets and pakoras. Boys played kabbadi and a crowd of old and young stood in a semicircle watching them. And the sounds of pipe music, which I had heard at that time on our return home, echoed in my ears again.

'Take off your shirts and bathe quickly and then we can go back home. We have to go to Iqbal Singh's fields to cut the wheat,' Bhaia told us. Taking off his dirty old shirt, he advised, 'Sit here on the edge and bathe. There is a deep pit here.' The water flowing from the east, passed through clumps of reeds, and made a faint whispering sound as it rippled past us. The moonlight shone on the clear water, and we saw the trembling shadows of pine trees reflected in it.

When we had put on our clothes again, Bhaia took out a sickle from his bag and cut five swathes of rushes. He folded his hands and bowed to the earth and said, 'Hey Mata, be merciful, the children should never again suffer from such skin infection.'

Both of us had got a very bad skin infection and had scratched ourselves till we had deep oozing wounds. The children in the neighbourhood refused to play with us. Even members of our own family did not let us go out much, for they were afraid that we might infect others. We scratched practically the whole time. Though this was very annoying, sadly enough, we could not help ourselves.

Schools were still closed, as the new term was yet to begin. The results had just been declared and I had been promoted to the third class. Had this infection occurred during term time, I would have had to stay home, like my friend Sohan. I would not have been allowed to go out or play. These thoughts crowded my mind as I walked home.

There was a new confidence in Ma's face when we reached home. She consoled us saying, 'All these wounds will heal. Now don't scratch with your nails.' Then, after a brief pause, she continued, 'God will help us. We have not harmed Him.'

We were still talking when a voice was heard at the door,

*Gauraja is twelve years' old,*
*Parvati ji will bathe,*
*Shivji will have her darshan.*

Three sadhus with turbans decorated with peacock plumes—
normally worn by astrologers—had arrived to sing 'Gauraja' from home
to home. They would begin their round from our home, because it was
from here that the main lane of the village began. They would ring their
bells and one of them would recite the first line, and the other two the
next. They were dressed in white clothes, with the ends of their dhotis
tucked into their waists at the back. They had saffron-coloured cloths
on their shoulders.

I went into the inner room to get a bowl of flour from the earthenware
pot, to give them, when Bhaia angrily said, 'Couldn't you have fetched
less flour? You know grain is scarce! Then, this caste which begs for a
living, has nothing to do ... they don't even let the day begin, to come
begging.'

'Who knows when they started!' Ma said calmly.

'They've set up a camp under the tin shed of Bhogpur mill ... they
are not coming from Nawan Shahar right now!' Bhaia asserted. 'They
are our people, but these saalas—they pretend to be devotees of Shiva
and are ekeing out a living by singing paeans to his fair wife's beauty!'

'Is it easy to beg? Try it once ...!'

'I am not stupid that I should beg.'

Letting go of the argument, Ma went towards the courtyard, and I
followed the sadhus to the next house.

Listening to their songs very carefully, I was reminded again of
the colourful framed picture of Shiv-Parvati hanging in the courtyard
of Gurdas of the bargadwalas. Images of Parvati bathing in the pond
flickered before my mind's eye for a long time. For a while, I felt I was
Shiv. This thrilled me; but I dared not mention it to anyone.

Ma would stand at the threshold, with a small copper bucket and
summon me with a sign and say, 'Gudd, run and get some lassi from
Palo's.'

I would go running and jumping, with the bucket in my hand, into
the lane of the Jats. But when I reached the house of the Sheikhchillis
beyond the gurudwara, my legs and feet would grow limp and slow
down. I would think, 'Bhaia looks after their buffaloes, bathes and
cleans them, works in the sun and rain, and keeps them in a dry place
during the monsoons. He feeds them, yet when it is about to deliver, the
buffalo goes back to them. I want to tell Bhaia that just once we should

keep the buffalo. We also must drink its milk and lassi, and I want to play with its little one.'

At times, it seemed to me that Bhaia was aware of these feelings of mine. Milkha Singh Jat would boast about how strong his grandson was. 'Brother,' he would say, 'my Tochi (Tarlochan Singh) drinks milk and also urinates milk!' Then, I also wanted to be like him—tall and broad and strong like him.

I would put the bucket in the wide courtyard of the Barias, and stand with my head bowed. Various thoughts would crowd my mind like small clouds scattered over the skies, and fill my heart with dejection and sorrow. I would be filled with disgust and feel as if I was floating in the air, and that the different parts of my body no longer held together. The train of my thought would snap when Pallo called out from within, 'Gudd, come a little later. I am just about to churn the milk.'

We were buying milk from Pallo on a monthly basis. My first trip to her was to fetch milk every morning. Sometimes a quarter, and at other times half a litre.

But for lassi, I had to make more than one trip a day. ... And when I did not get any, Bhaia would scold me, 'Please go *now*, maama! I have told you hundreds of times that I cannot do without lassi.'

'If you need it so much, then this time keep both buffaloes— Meeni and Boori! Then the children would also have plenty to eat and drink ...'

'Look how she gabbles! Who is going to pay the loan we have taken from the zamindars, for the pillars that we got made? Your father?'

'Whenever you speak, you bring in my parents. You want to pick a quarrel with me and deliberately twist things.'

'I work like a donkey the whole day long, and *she* ...!' Bhaia started muttering to himself angrily, and emptied the ashes from his chillum and began refilling it.

At times I wanted to tell Bhaia that I couldn't go across half the village to fetch lassi, because I didn't like it. But the next morning, I would pick up the bucket and ask for lassi at one house or the other. The process went on. It was refreshing to drink lassi, morning and evening. If there was no dal or cooked vegetable, then we would make do with lassi. During the summer when milk was scarce, getting lassi was difficult, but we longed for it. We often drank tea without milk, but Bhaia made futile efforts to cool himself anyhow and cursed his fate continuously.

Sunk in these thoughts, I saw the Baba from Manikdheri with large bags slung on his shoulders, begging in the lane. He would fill flour in a sturdy khadi bag and store black gram in the other. He had a long tilak on his forehead and his saffron clothes gave him the appearance of a sadhu. He stood at every door, and called out in a loud voice, 'Bibiji, it is *puranmasi* tomorrow, and there will also be an eclipse.'

Innocently, I wondered how he knew that there would be an eclipse tomorrow? I understood this only when I saw him taking a long slim book from his bag and answering whatever the people wanted to know. Then, I would think, when he comes to our home to beg, then I will also ask him, 'When will the Meeni buffalo stay on with us at our home?' Or else, I'll ask him to arrange things so that this should happen—the way he arranges things for others, after taking grain from them. I will also ask him, will we ever have a big house like the one Ratta Brahmin has? I would say, as other villagers did, 'Do something and change the lines of our fate.' But my feelings remained unsaid, for he would go back after drinking tea at Taro aunty's house, which was a Jat's house, in the lane before ours. With this, the fragile mirror of my heart would shatter, and its silent anguish would circulate with my blood and soak my whole being. And this question would assail me all the time: they are sadhus, why don't they come to *our* mohalla to beg?

# 4

## Flowering of the Cactus

'Which bitch gave birth to you? Stop, or I'll cut you into pieces!' Suddenly, my grandmother, seated under the banyan tree in front of the house, could be heard shouting like the thunder before lightning. We all sat up at once.

'Who knows who she is scolding now!' My mother remarked, getting up from where she sat in the courtyard. I also followed her like a lamb. Going up to Daadi, she asked, 'What happened, mother?'

'The son of a pimp! Whenever he passes this way, he makes a lewd remark! Is there anyone older than me in this village? This bastard has no shame, he teases me!' Daadi protested as if she was trying to pass judgement on the right and wrong of the matter.

'But who was it?' Ma insisted.

'I couldn't recognize the pervert! Probably the one who eloped with his mother! I only recognize his bloody voice! I'll pull out his tongue, one of these days, let me just catch him!' Only the tongue could be seen moving in Daadi's toothless mouth, and her small eyes darted all over. Two tresses of thin, shining silvery hair hung on her temples. It seemed as if she would really annihilate that person, who seemed destined to die a violent death, when she found him.

Daadi got up, still talking loudly and walked along the path and crossed over to the middle lane of the village. I thought of asking her where was she going to lodge her complaint. But I was scared, and did not. Yet, I could see that despite her weak eyesight, Daadi was still erect and resolute. Whenever and wherever she saw an injustice being done to her or to another, she would be ready to protest ...; she was fearless, tenacious, and determined, and would not yield easily. She was out of breath in the race of life, but not yet defeated.

Daadi did not see the one she was looking for, and came back.

My group of aunts and children now surrounded Daadi in the courtyard. My younger sister came up and caught hold of my mother's hand. The bare-bodied toddlers stared at her. They all wore red or black threads tied up in a thick strand around their waists, and some were playing with the beads strung on to those strands, pulling them back and forth.

'But do tell what did he say?' One of my aunts asked her rather impatiently. My curiosity was further whetted. Not only the faces of those gathered around, but even their eyes had turned into questions. It seemed that my aunts were eager to discover the identity of the culprit and raise a storm, not hesitating from even going to his house.

Daadi's fair, wrinkled face was red with fury. Adjusting her dupatta to cover her head properly, she said, 'The remark was made by a person who should drown himself. As he passed by me, he said, "Satto has many lovers, some sweepers and other cobblers! I say, Satto may be your favourite mare"—bastard!' Daadi banged her stick on the ground, and the 'thak-thak' of the stick sounded like an assertion of her anger and pride. It seemed to me that she had an inexhaustible treasure of sharp and bitter words. Her victims might have escaped her, but Daadi, in full cry, was continually sending her barbs after him. No one could refute the logic of her arguments.

Hearing Daadi's din, Tai Taro and her elder sister Parkasho, who were married into the same Jat family, came up to us. As soon as they came up, Tai Taro asked, 'Haro, what happened for you to raise so much dust with your horns?'

My mind immediately started spinning a web. Tai Taro and her Jat women called my grandmother (who was nearing a hundred years), by her name. My classmates all addressed members of my community by their names, and in response they were called, 'Sardarji'. To us, every villager was uncle, aunt, or baba, and these people would call us by our first names, without any thought or hesitation. It also occurred to me that perhaps arrogance of caste and ownership of land lay behind this.

My reverie, however, halted when Daadi resumed her shouting, and it seemed to me that I had been jolted back from my journey in space and had fallen on hard, rough ground. My eyes had now begun to see and my ears finally hear. People were now listening to Daadi's complaints about what had just taken place.

'You are always ridiculing one and all, you sharp one. You start babbling about things, without learning the facts,' Daadi scolded Tai, shutting her up. It had to be accepted that Tai Taro also did not behave saucily with Daadi. This time too she kept quiet, letting the matter rest; but the other women were smiling, and we children stood watching silently.

Phumman reached the scene, like a gust of wind from nowhere, and as was his habit, began speaking loudly, 'Once I catch hold of him, I will smash him; the stupid fellow has a habit of making rude remarks.'

'Oh! But at least tell us who he is?' Tai Taro asked again.

'As if you do not know! You first start the fire and then try to play the mediator! Spread a little rumour here, cause a small fight there. Merely because they own a few acres of land, they cannot resist spitting at the moon!' Phumman said gritting his teeth. My lifeless body seemed to gain new energy, and I latched on to Daadi's stick. I shook all over. After a moment, I stood by her, like an obedient boy. But it seemed to me that my confrontation with the harsh realities of life had already begun.

'Have you forgotten what happened the other day? When we had to take Bhagta of the Babas' home? Everyone had started protesting at that time!' Daadi reminded the gathering of a past event.

'What happened at that time?' I asked her, though I was frightened that she would flare up again.

'Bhagta had come here to the weavers' pit and ordered Jagar the chowkidar to cut the fodder for him. Jagar replied that he had no time and Bhagta hit him with a stick!' Daadi took her hand away from mine with a jerk.

'Really? Then?' I was impatient to hear the end of the story.

'Then what! The whole Chamarli got after him. From that day, Bhagta has not dared to come to this mohalla or even to look this way. They are always trying to force people to do begaar for them!' Daadi exclaimed, as she met our astonished eyes! The pendulum of my thoughts at once began to swing to begaari, untouchability, the question of high and low, and jammed there, precisely in the manner the gramophone needle had on the record '*lak hille mijazan jaundi de*' (the beauty's hips sway, as she passed by) at the words '*lak hille*' (hips sway)! As I came out of my thoughts, I felt that if the needle could jam on a new record, then it was quite natural for me to think of these things time and again. Daadi, Bhaia, Taya, and the whole community talks about them every day. It dawned on me that I also had to work hard to get rid of this invisible, yet heavy burden. I realized that one has to push the needle forward to initiate new ideas and to inculcate a new ideology.

My mother urged again, 'Ma, let it be, you have created enough nuisance for them.'

'Ma, come and have your food. I will take care of that slippery fool who struts about!' Gripping Daadi's arm, Phumman steered her towards our home, and added, 'They taunt us about our caste! They hardly have any land, but pose like big landlords!'

'Phumman, why are you creating trouble? The snake has passed, what will you get by beating its track?' Tai Taro advised him.

'He says, "Lovers of your Satto are either sweepers or cobblers!" What's the difference between your girls and ours? Tell me, was the water not contaminated, or did your caste not matter, when my father once jumped fully clothed into the well to rescue the daughter of Dhanni the goldsmith?' Phumman said angrily.

Perspiration beaded his forehead and face heavily and streaked his kurta.

The hair on my body stood on end. I could visualize the scene—Dhanni's small daughter thrashing about, trying to save herself, and then my eldest uncle saving her. The very thought made me break out in sweat! My heart stopped for a few moments. Then, taking a deep breath, I came out of my thoughts.

A village girl had nearly drowned because as she was drawing up a loaded bucket from the well, its weight reversed the wheel and dragged her into the water. As all this happened so swiftly that she got no chance to let go of the rope that was pulling her to her death! My uncle, Pratap, had seen this as he was passing that way. Not pausing to think, he had jumped into the well and brought her out alive.

Daadi had just reached the threshold when the sound of the conch shell was heard. I looked around.

'It appears that the last ceremony of the old man of the "Ghoras" had ended,' Taro remarked so that all of us could hear. The sisters still stood at the entrance to our lane.

'It may be! But the sound of the conch shell is from the other side. Look, the Ram *gaiwalas* are coming this way from the Nangas, and it is they who are blowing the shell,' Tai Parkasho turned south and pointed out with both her hands to the group of men coming that way.

I, along with the other kids ran off towards the herd of cows. They had very thin, long horns, which shone brightly—being highly polished. Many were embellished with beautiful copper rings. The herd was advancing slowly towards our homes. Such strange cows appeared a couple of times every year, never more than thirty or thirty-five at a time. One or two were chestnut coloured, or black, and people would give them green or dry fodder, or even millet to eat. They would nibble the green leaves and leave the hard stems. The calves would poke their noses into the sides of their mothers, trying to steal a few drops of milk—a sight that gladdened my heart. Happily, as I turned homewards to tell them how clever I had been, I suddenly recalled, what Bhaia had once told me:

> *Vachcha chunge gao nu*
> *kade na dasiye!*
> *Aap gal kar ke kade na*
> *hasiya!*

(Never tell when you see a calf sucking milk!/
Never laugh at what you have said yourself!)

Bhaia had thrown a bundle of fodder into a corner of the courtyard, raising a little dust. I ran in to get some soft green fodder for the cows. Bhaia's kurta was soaked with sweat and he was wiping his face and neck with the cloth he usually wore wrapped round his head. As I went towards the bundle, he scolded me, 'Khabardar! Don't pick even one swathe; this idle group has made it their trade! Smear oil in your hair, mark your forehead with three lines of saffron vertically or horizontally, and set off from the cowpens of Jalandhar, with the herd. Who can say whether Ram was a cowherd or not? He spent his life in the forests and kept fighting over his wife till the end of his life.'

'Just two handfuls for the cow which has an extra leg stuck on its back!' I begged of Bhaia glancing at the extra leg of the cow that kept surfacing at different places on its back!

'They are fooling you so that you can get people to give them money. If these cows are Ram's, then why are they so odd with an extra leg or tongue? Tell me!—Anyone?' Bhaia declared as if he was exposing a deep conspiracy and needed others to support him.

'The whole country worships the cow as mother and you're teaching this young boy something entirely different!' Ma, who must have overheard us, remarked coming out into the courtyard, her hands still covered with the flour she had been kneading.

'You don't know how devious they are! At the Bhogpur-Adampur meeting, Lahori Ram Bali told us that in ancient times all Brahmins ate beef. It is written in the Hindu scriptures, that one can earn virtue by serving Brahmins with beef on the occasion of shraddha.' Bhaia was bursting with information he had himself got from others. He chuckled and carried on, 'And there is more worth hearing. He said that the scriptures say that he who does not eat meat during the shraddha, is reborn as an animal for the next twenty-one births!'

'You're mad, and now don't misguide these boys! Cow's milk is very healthy, thirty-six different products are made out of it. That's why the Nihangs at Tanda Mandi cut the cows free and let them run away so that the butchers cannot buy them!'

Ma said with some warmth, 'Why are you doing this? The world functions on this system of right and wrong!'

'By us giving alms to the Brahmins? This beggar caste has never worked with their own hands; they enjoy life at the cost of those very people who are not permitted to go near them! When did I say that cows are not our mothers? Our families are nurtured by them,' Bhaia was making his views clear. I was astonished at the extent of his knowledge, which had lain like thorns in his heart. These were the very things that often made him sad and dejected.

'Have they ever asked you for alms? Why are you twisting everything?'

'What do we have to give them? Lice? If nothing else, they take fodder from us.'

'What blasphemy ... ! The boy only wants to give a handful of fodder to the cow, what difference does it make?' Ma commented looking at my woebegone face, but Bhaia refused to budge.

'They have divided society into castes. It is these crafty people who are blasphemous. As if men have any castes! *They* worship stones and animals, and take us to be even lower than them. ... They want us to keep away, because our touch will defile them. If someone were to ask them, do you have anything we do not have?' Bhaia's sweat had neither dried yet nor had he stopped perspiring. As I listened to his words of pain there was a turmoil within me and many things seemed to sink into my mind, the way water sinks into the sand on the western fringe of the village.

'Yes, they have extra organs. Go and look at the statues at Gurdas's! Shiva has four arms, one Devi has four arms, and another, six. Ganesh has an elephant's head. Narsingh also has something ... I say, that if you do not know this, then don't criticize others!' Ma remarked, trying to stop his criticism.

'Who can believe in this fraud invented by the Brahmins? They say Valmiki created Kush out of straw. Hanuman was born of a whiff of air in Anjani's ear! An eight-armed woman has not yet been born on this earth! Had there been a woman with four legs, then I would have accepted that Hanuman was born of a gust of air. Now, you tell me how were Gudd and Birju born? No man can go against nature! Do you understand?'

I felt as if Bhaia had revealed many mysteries with his various arguments, as he opened the swathes of fodder.

'Your discussions will never end! We have many other things to do,' Ma tried to bring the argument to an end.

'There is more to hear, if you are not yet satisfied. ... And teach this shirker something, he is always trying to avoid work. Children of his age are always running about, doing something or the other, and this maama here only struts about! He is growing up, but does not do a whit of work. And he will be in the fourth class in about four months, the rascal! Look at the elder one, he goes with you to Baksha's, to help you clean up, gets kindling, fetches the fodder. And this fellow roams about the whole day, listening to all and sundry! I ask you, will he earn anything merely by listening to people?' Bhaia suddenly ground his teeth, and stood up. I trembled and thought of the thrashing he had given me a few days ago.

'He is still a child, and innocent, why are you after him now? This is the time for him to play, after that he has to work all his life, like us!' I was happy at what my mother has said.

I don't know whether Bhaia felt some remorse or whether he was annoyed with me, for he stared at me and said, 'Son, enjoy yourself at our expense, as much as you can! How long can the prayers of a mother save her child!'

I was taken aback by the word 'enjoy'! A procession of the various chores that were my daily lot passed before my eyes. I saw myself carrying buckets of garbage to a corner of the village, collecting dry leaves, sugarcane skins, and twigs to light fires, taking lassi or tea for my father and his friends while they worked in the fields, feeding the animals. But the train of my thoughts snapped with the sounding of the conch again.

Empty-handed, I joined the other children who were following the herd of cows, which had by now turned towards the lane of the Dhaddas. They stopped at the water near Inder Singh's well. I thought of the complaint that Inder Singh had made to my grandmother about my uncle Gulzari Lal, but Dhyan was shouting for me. The cows had moved ahead and I hurried after them. Sucha, Dhyan, Rampal, and I took turns to put our ears to the newly installed electricity poles, listening to the sounds generated, and telling each other, 'The motor has gone up now; it has come down.'

The cows had by now gone far ahead, and we came back. I thought of the days when these electricity poles were being put up. About twenty men of the electricity department would pull at the ropes tied round the poles. Their rippling muscles showed how strong they were. Their legs would tense as they pulled at the poles, and their torsos were bent forward. It looked as if their toes were rooted in the ground. The poles would gradually go up, and now all the pressure would be shifted to their heels. They now bent backwards. They sang—one of them would sing one line, and the others would sing in a chorus of 'hysha',

*In the middle of Model Town of Jalandhar ... hysha!*
*Two plaits and a long neck ... hysha!*
*Broken cot, rotten twine ... hysha!*
*The baby does not let me sleep ... hysha!*
*Sleep little one, I have to meet my lover ... hysha!*
*She goes running, when the lover calls ... hysha!*
*At the husband's calls she demurs ... hysha!*
*O husband, I don't want to live with you ... hysha!*
*I have seen nothing of your earnings ... hysha!*
*The lover has given me ornaments ... hysha!*
*The best is one of gold ... hysha!*
*The best lace is the lace of gold ... hysha!*

Having heard these lines over and over again, a picture of Model Town, Jalandhar had arisen in my mind. I saw large coloured houses, double storied and palace like, similar to the houses of the nambardars' in the village, and I also saw the people living in those houses! It then occurred to me that the girls with two plaits must be symbols of the progressive views of these people. I had once heard opinions being expressed by the Communists in the village at the meeting. My mind flew from the broken cot, to the rotting twine syndrome, to the rich and poor, living standards, education, and illiteracy, and then they settled on a woman. All such remarks are directed at a woman ... sometimes poverty turned to woman, and then woman seemed to be symbolizing poverty. Many of these things I could not comprehend. I thought that the lover mentioned in the song, must be very rich, like the nambardar of the village, and the one who was told that, 'I have seen nothing of your earnings', must be someone like my father who would either be working as a farm labourer, or on the roads, and his wife must be jeering at him. Despite all the hard labour he put in, Bhaia's helplessness and problems broke my heart.

I suddenly stopped in the midst of my thoughts, in the manner a train halts at the Bhogpur station when it does not get the go-ahead signal. This happened because I had heard Baihank the drunkard singing as he tended his goats near the cremation ground of our community:

*Make some tea for the drunk,*
*Get some milk from the goat!*

Baihank was called Bole—a he-goat or a stud—by many, as he was very tall, strong, and well built. He always carried a hookah close to his heart, his sole companion. Many teased him, 'Don't worry, if one son of a Jat gets married, then this means they all are married. One of your brothers is married!' And Baihaink would smile at this.

The whole gang of children ran towards him and I came back home. I told Bhaia about the electricity poles, and he said, 'Only if the darkness in our homes lifts will we know that something has been done! All this is for the rich! For us, even the coming of freedom has made no difference. I am no astrologer, but I can tell you something, that the son of a grass cutter if he can get an education should not remain a grass cutter. Therefore, study hard whatever way you can and you will not have to slave all your life for the landlords!'

I could understand many things that my father said, but had to keep pondering over others to get at their real meaning.

'Gudd, listen!' Ma called out, signalling to me. Then she explained as I went over, 'We have not told your father about the morning's incident, you also do not tell him, or it will upset him badly.'

I assured her with a nod of my head. The atmosphere was now calm and normal again. It seemed as if nothing unpleasant had happened to Daadi. But the event lay in some corner of my heart, causing an ache, as if an arrow had pierced a bird in mid-flight, bringing it to the verge of a collapse. My thoughts came to an abrupt halt as Dhyan called out, 'Gudd, come let's get some corn parched.'

Quickly filling the lower end of my kurta with multicoloured corn, both of us set off talking, 'Look, how different coloured corn is found on the same cob.'

'Just like us! You are fair and I am dark! They say that a child resembles his parents, and I and Birju look like Bhaia!' I explained at some length.

'The corn on a single cob is often of different colours, and sometimes, there are dark multicoloured corn,' Dhyan remarked. 'That is why such corn is called Brahmin.'

'Even dried shit is called Brahmin!' I retorted and we laughed. An image of the golden cob flickered in my mind, of the pollination of the plants, the soft cobs, the parrots nibbling at them, the crows pecking them. The parrots and crows seemed to me like the zamindars of the village, their sons and nephews, and the tender white cobs were the young girls of my mohalla. Again a question raised its head in my mind: how are the rows of corn so neatly arranged on the cob? I had learnt about pollination, but could not see how it was done. Dhyan's voice intruded into my thoughts, 'What is this crowd between Ratta's shop and Mala the Bhatti's?'

We lengthened our strides.

'He says I can't wash dirty utensils … as if he is the son of a nawab!' Diwan was complaining loudly about his son Pashu. He spoke a different dialect, Majhi, and we would often mimic him. He had come from Batala to our village.

'I have been washing utensils since the morning, and now even the last prayers have been said, the guests have all eaten, it is almost evening! Whenever I want to sit down to eat, someone or the other says, "Wash these few utensils first, a guest has just arrived, and he is leaving by the evening!"' Pashu's words were pellets, and he spoke in a harsh tone which did not frighten me at all. On the other hand, his whole demeanour gave me courage.

'Is that why you have broken the bronze tray into two! To humiliate me? What will our guests say?'

'I have not eaten since morning, what else could I have done? Every now and then they bring a few utensils and say, "Just two more utensils to clean!" I tell you, I am hungry, and made to starve because this old man has died! And people have gorged on *jalebis* and *zarda*!'

To me it seemed that Pashu was saying the words jalebis and zarda to satisfy the hunger gnawing at him. After a moment, he again said, 'I am not going to wash dirty utensils after today! What will we lose if we don't do this sort of work! One container of grain after the summer harvest and another after the autumn harvest! … If they have four guests, we have to cook for them! We cook and wait on them during their celebrations and sorrows! And it is we who fetch all they need for the feast, from Bhogpur!'

'I say, why are you making a spectacle of yourself? This is our work, the work of the Jhiwar caste. Come to your senses now. Come and eat something,' Diwan coaxed his younger son, Pashu.

'This is no bloody life! It is so difficult! Winter and summer … fetch water for people first thing in the morning, and only then can we go to school! From today, I am not going to school. I tell you once and for all. *I am not going to school!* If you get a kurta, you don't get a kachcha, and one has never been given a pair of shoes. I will set up a handcart, but I will not wash dirty utensils,' Pashu was jumping from one side of Mala's furnace to the other.

It occurred to me to tell Pashu that Birju and I did not even own a pair of rubber chappals, leave alone a set of books! I possess only one kurta. It is washed every eighth day, and as long as it does not dry, I go about naked. But all my good intentions of consoling Pashu turned to ashes as Malan took a large part of my corn in return for parching it. My face fell and shrivelled in the heat of the furnace.

I hardly felt the presence of Dhyan walking beside me, as the image of Bade Baba at Sohalpur flashed before my eyes. He had tried to yoke a strong ox which had not been broken to the plough. Baba had caught hold of the ring in the animal's soft nose, pulling it to force the ox's neck under the yoke, but it would keep moving forward and backward, and escape. Baba had hit its strong and muscular body with a goad. After it had finally been yoked, Bhaia had caught its nose ring and walked it round the field a couple of times. It would suddenly stop and refuse to move forward, then Baba would stick the sharp end of the goad into its muscular buttock. It would jump and start walking again. Baba would angrily exclaim, 'It doesn't matter, son, it is only a matter of few days! You would also walk obediently like others; it is only a matter of your getting used to the plough.'

We had now reached our homes. I looked at the bullock, tied near the path, which was bellowing hungrily. To me he appeared to be the starving Pashu. Then, I felt that my brother Birju had become a *hali*—a bullock which is used for ploughing. I am like the calf which is still not used to the yoke, and Bhaia is impatient to put me to the plough of responsibilities. To accustom a calf to the plough and make it a hali, it is beaten with a goad, and I shivered at the very thought of the sharp end stuck into my body. … It seemed to me that I was walking barefoot on the sandy dunes on the way to Bhogpur. My feet were being scorched like the corn in Mala's furnace. Wherever I saw a grassy patch, I ran to stand on it. My eyes fell on the clusters of rushes, reeds, and cactus on the edge of the path. The short clumps of cactus along the mud ridge suddenly turned into men and women of the mohalla. I felt as if this desolation was a symbol of the bleakness of their empty lives, and the long, sharp thorns, the numerous problems crowding their lives. When my eyes fell on the flowers blooming on the cactus, I felt that Pashu, Rampal, Sucha, my older brother Birju, and I were these flowers, which people like Bhaia wished to keep happy. This thought warmed my heart and gave me the sense of a feeling of well-being, even in those days of distress and pain.

# 5

# The Thorny Path

*O god let it rain,*
     *And thus give us grain!*
*Black are the bricks*
     *and the stones,*
*Let it pour, let it rain!*

These lines learnt at school were on our lips as we ran through the lanes and bye lanes of the village. We ran on the earth, and the clouds scattered in the skies raced with us. Whenever we looked up, we could see the clouds nudging and jostling each other, trying to outrun one another. For a moment, we would forget the words 'black are the bricks and the stones' and also forget ourselves. Often we would stand near the overgrown shrubs in the graveyard, which, after the migration of the Muslims of the village was now a wilderness, and tell each other, 'The clouds may not have heard us! Or else they would have surely dropped all the waters they are carrying right here …!'

'Just look, how heavy the clouds are with water! In fact, they give water to the clouds that are ahead of them! They will come back with more water!'

'Right now they are taking water to far-off places! Our turn will come later.'

A rainbow would appear on the horizon. We called it 'the old woman's seven-coloured swing'. It could either be seen in the east or the west;

watching it, we would shout the names of the colours. First of all violet, then indigo, blue, green, yellow, orange, and then at the very top, red! We had often wondered how these colours had climbed right up to the sky! Then someone offered an explanation, 'The old woman probably had only these seven colours!'

'They are the sun's colours.' I told them what I had heard from Phumman. They had laughed in disbelief. 'Phumman says that all these colours are created out of one colour—sunlight,' I repeated.

'We don't see any colour except sunlight!'

'They say that only if you look through a thick triangular glass, will you see all the colours,' I informed them.

'You are talking all nonsense! Come, let us go up that mountain.'

I would be dejected at this attitude, and tell myself that perhaps Phumman may have given me wrong information. But then I would recall how trustworthy he always was, and therefore how right. Whatever he had told me had to be right. This thought would restore my self-confidence.

We would look towards the northeast intently from a high spot. The bluish edge of the mountains seemed to be melting into the sky. The peaks shimmered brightly, assuming shapes and forms of beautiful fairies flying in and out of the fluffy clouds. The snow-laden peaks glimmered, and I thought that the highest of them must be the tallest peak of the Himalayas, the one that was conquered by Sir Edmund Hillary and Tenzing Norgay in 1953. They were the first to conquer the peak. The thought that I knew my lessons made me very happy ... and we would all run back home, yelling and singing,

*O god send us some rain,*
*give us some grain,*
*Black are the bricks and*
*also the stones,*
*Let it pour, let it rain.*

One day, while we ran about and sang these lines, the wind dropped suddenly. The clouds merged, their shapes changed. They hung low in the skies, shutting the sun out. Though it was only late afternoon, it grew very dark. Man and bird retreated to the safety of their homes. One could only see the houses and trees when lightning flashed, illuminating the dark skies.

Then, the rumbling of the clouds also ceased. It seemed as if they were about to fall. A real downpour! Large, heavy drops began falling with great force. The day soon lost itself in the bleak dark clouds. In a matter of moments, everything was awash and full of water. It was now raining heavily and the shadows had deepened.

Bhaia stood at the front door looking around as if trying to reassure himself about something. The roof had begun leaking from various crevices and holes, and he went about placing pots and pans under them. He was tense, as if waiting for something. The night passed somehow. But in the morning, the coming of the sun brought the rains again with greater force. This set Bhaia off on his morning session of grumbling, 'Let them bury more dolls, let them distribute Khwaja Khizir's porridge ...'

There was a sudden noise of a crash, *dhramm* ... , which cut him off in mid-sentence. Who knows what else he would have said! More than half the kitchen wall and courtyard had collapsed outward, obstructing the water as it rushed into the lane. The water in our courtyard was ankle high, and the difference between water from the gutters and the lane had already blurred.

'Quick! Get up, the wall of this room may also collapse!' Bhaia exclaimed as he rushed out into the lane.

Many had come out of their homes. One had a sheet covering his head; another had made a raincoat out of torn piece of oilcloth. Bhaia began clearing the mud and slush of the fallen wall, and throwing the lumps of clay into the courtyard. The area had, by now, become a small pond, full of cow dung, dry turds of cats and dogs, and pieces of straw. A little later, a helpless moan escaped him, 'The clay is being washed away!'

I felt as if *his* strength and determination were being eroded with the clay which the fast-flowing water was washing away. He was tense with worry and spoke loud enough to be heard by the people standing nearby, 'This is the reason why they say, "Camel nettle, camel thorn, and the cart driver, never ask for rain even though the world may die."'

'A holy man had once related a story of king who could not tolerate continuously rained for twelve hours, and thinking about his people, had asked god for twelve years of drought,' said someone from the group.

As they stood talking, a woman called out, 'Sadhu Kewal is buried under the fallen roof ... save him, someone! Please save him!'

The rain had now turned into a drizzle. Bhaia and other men, women, and we children, all rushed to Sadhu's house, shouting, 'Kewal where are you ...?'

'I am here ...' a sad but strong voice came from under the debris of the roof. The rubble was quickly cleared away. Kewal stood in a corner, his body and hair covered in layers of dust. ... Stepping out of the corner, he shook his head like a wet lamb! He had abrasions and cuts all over and some bleeding; he was trembling with shock and fright!

'God has given my son a new life!' Banti gratefully bowed her head, folded her hands, and then pressed Kewal's head.

Happiness radiated from the faces of everyone who stood watching this touching scene. Then, we all moved homewards. Taya Banta said in a suppressed tone, 'Even god troubles only the poor!'

'Drought or rain, hunger, deprivation, worry, and stress, all this is only for us!' Bhaia added.

What possessed Bhaia as soon as he came home, no one knew, but he rushed up the mud steps next to the kitchen and went up to the roof. I followed and watched him walking with slow and measured steps along the edge of the roof, trying to fill the holes by pressing down the wet mud with his toes. I looked around and saw that many of our neighbours were also there, trying to repair the damage. As far as I could see, the paddy was under water, and maize and millet plants stood with bowed heads in face of the rain's onslaught. Only the sugarcane stood erect and proud, vibrant with life. The trees stood motionless, but with heads held high, and appeared to be watching in silence. When all this was going on, I could see the bent bodies of men and women in the fields, and they looked like paddy shoots. The village was full of water: nothing had escaped unaffected.

The dirty and dusty sheet of water had invaded all the lanes and roads to the nearby villages—Rastgo Manakdheri, Sikanderpur, and Dhadha Sanoura. The shrill whistle and 'chuk-chuk' of a train diverted my attention. The engine belched out a dark cloud of smoke as it raced past. I wanted to turn and climb either on to the roof of the nambardar's house, or that of the Brahmins, and watch the train steam past, because the tall sheesham trees obstructed my view from where I stood. I was still playing hide and seek with the train, when I saw Khushia with a couple of boys in tow who carried sticks. When asked, he loudly answered, 'We are off to fish. The lake at Manakdheri is flooded. Come with us!' But they continued walking.

I wanted to run after them, and watch the fish splashing. The very thought of holding the slippery fish in my hands filled me with joy. But the sight of the deep water everywhere upset me.

Coming down from the roof, I saw the people of the mohalla standing about in groups. A dark shadow of grief and worry lay on their faces and I heard someone say, 'She died at night. The cremation ground is flooded. The cremation can only take place if the water recedes by the evening. But the eastern side is higher, and even now the water level is lower there.'

'That part of the cremation ground is for our use,' Joginder declared in loudly tone so that he could be heard over the sound of the rain. Joginder was from the cotton corders' community. Taya Banta showed his dirty stained teeth at this.

The fact was that the cremation ground for the dalits was common to all, but the path to Rastgo passed through it, dividing it into two. On the basis of population, the larger portion of the west was accepted as belonging to the Adidharmis, and the eastern part to the cotton corders. But, over a period of time, this distinction had been all but forgotten. Yet, now and then, tradition reared its head. It had now.

The sun and the clouds were still playing games with each other, but this also did not last long. The clouds regrouped again, darkening the sky and it started to rain, steadily and heavily, disheartening the people.

A few houses had collapsed by the evening. The large dome outside the gurudwara, built of small bricks had started disintegrating. The thatched roof of Tai Taro's cowshed also came apart. The young virgins of our community buried gram under the flowing gutters of our homes. Dolls were burnt at the crossroads, grains of urad dal tied up in piece of red and black cloth, and spells and charms were intoned on it, all so that the rain might stop. One could hear the frightening 'trr … trr …' of the large yellow frogs swimming in the inundated fields. The dark clouds looked as if they were part of a conspiracy against the poor.

The faces of many were marked with deep worry, but I and the other children were excitedly racing about, looking for frogs. We happily bisected the earthworms, and saw how the two pieces would start crawling in different directions after being cut up! We threw pieces of broken pottery into the water and gleefully watched them float away ...

... And like in other homes, our hearth also was cold. The cow dung cakes, twigs, and kindling were all soaked. Bhaia took out two wooden planks from the roof of the small room and chopping them with an axe told Ma, 'For now take this to cook. We shall see in the morning what is to be done.'

It stopped raining that night. The water, however, still flooded all the roads to and from the village. It was difficult for people to go out in the morning to answer the call of nature, especially the aged. Those whose houses had been damaged, were busy repairing their homes.

'The rains have made up for the last year! The water level in the well will rise by more than two or three hands! It will not run dry for at least two years,' a zamindar said happily, as he walked up and stood near the group under the banyan tree.

Mohani of the Ghora's family came along at that moment and remarked, 'Say Jat bhai, have you made a round of your fields? The rains have done a remarkable job, one can see only water!' Then, without waiting for an answer he continued, 'How is that bull you had bought? Is he good on the left or right at the plough? He added, 'Ever since we sold our bullock "Sawa", our white bullock is very depressed!'

On hearing all this chit-chat, Bhaia wrinkled his brows in disgust and walked away muttering to himself, 'They are very happy that that the water level has gone up in the wells, but it is we who are facing floods right now. He is enquiring about *animals*! Has anyone asked me about my house which has collapsed?' He added bitterly, 'It is rightly said that the village is alive and the calf will not lack for milk.'

Our community had faced such heavy and devastating rains earlier too. During the monsoons, such miracles occurred practically every year. Whenever it had rained continuously for a few days, the walls of most of the houses in our mohalla began crumbling. The outer layer of mud plastered on these walls would swell with water and peel off, and the ants which had made their homes in these walls, would run about with their white eggs, looking for new shelter. As the walls collapsed, rodents, centipedes, and other insects scampered about looking for holes to hide in. The scene was good to watch, but Bhaia's worry and tension had cast its effect on all of us like a pall. I felt particularly concerned about this ...

The layers of mud plastered on to the walls had peeled off, but it would now be collected, and within a week re-plastered on the reed structures of the walls making it difficult for anyone to make out the damage the rains had wrought on them, the way a body heals without scars to show where the wounds had been. The repaired and re-plastered walls looked better than they had earlier. Slight smiles would appear on the faces of the poor. Their conversations often referred to earlier monsoon devastations that the rains had wrought, and which they now recalled as a bad dream. Once again they sat under the banyan tree in groups, and their discussions and conversations became lively.

'This time the people from Rastgo, the Gugga people, have not appeared yet!' Taya Mehnga remarked handing over the pipe of the hookah to Taya Banta. After a brief pause, he added, 'Gugga navami is either tomorrow or the day after.'

'They may have been busy in repairing their houses or may even have gone in the other direction to beg!' Taya Banta answered and then mimicking the call of the Gugga people, said, 'Oi ji! Oi ji!'

We heard the sound of cymbals and singing from the direction of Jagar, the watchman's house ...

*Gugga is born, O the elevated one,*
*Illuminating the home and all around,*
*O Jaimal! My husband,*
*Oi ji! Oi ji!*

... The Gugga devotees struck their camps under and around the banyan tree. One of them walked in front bearing the flag of Gugga decorated with multicoloured handkerchiefs, peacock feathers, coconuts, and cowries.

They stopped singing, to smoke the hookah, inhaling deeply. The leader of the group narrated the tale of Gugga. Gugga Pir's mother's name was Bachhal, and her sister was Kachhal. She had two sons,

Surjan and Arjun, both hostile to Gugga. Gugga's wife, Rani Siliyar, was a beautiful woman, and Surjan had wanted to marry her. When he and Arjun fought Gugga over her, Gugga had killed Surjan.

The devotee narrating the tale wiped his tobacco-stained moustache and face with on his shoulder-cloth, and continued, 'When Bachhal heard this sad news, she broke off all relations with her son. Broken-hearted, Gugga entreated Mother Earth and sought shelter within her, but the Earth refused because he was a Hindu. Gugga embraced Islam, and it was after this that the Earth relented and gave him asylum and he descended into the Earth, seated on his horse and reciting the Qalma.'

After the story had been told, the small drums were beaten and the devotees sang in their melodious voices:

> *Arjun and Sarjan were in the lead fighting with the bridegroom,*
> *We will not let you take the beautiful Siliyar,*
> *Oi ji! Oi ji! Oi ji!*

The storyteller stopped again and puffed at the hookah, as a few members of the group went round collecting whatever people gave them, ghee, oil, jaggery, grain, and flour. Then, picking up the flag, they set off towards the lane to the village which was their next halt, and we children rushed up, surrounding them, and mimicking their song in one voice:

> *Gugga had nine children,*
> *Gugga Pir knows all,*
> *Oi ji! Oi ji! Oi ji!*

We imitated the beat of the drum by beating the mouths of our bowls and katoris, which we had covered with oilcloth. Taya Banta said loudly so that the others could hear, 'Sometimes they beg in the name of a blind horse, and at another time, they beg in the name of Gugga ... as if Gugga was their aunt's son!'

'They also are poor and helpless, like us and have no money! This way they can hope to earn a little!' Bhaia said, sitting down beside my uncle.

'Because the one-eyed Fakir of Rastgo is your friend, your drinking pal! But till today neither have we visited their home, nor smoked the hookah or drunk water at their home! And you are very concerned about these beggars!'

'As if the Jats let us near them! They make us sit on the ground in their courtyards. We are treated worse than their dogs!' Bhaia retorted.

'The Jats are men of substance and landowners. Just look at these Ramdasias! They are our people, and merely because they have accepted Sikhism, they act superior to us! At one time they drew water from our wells, but now they have their separate well! They say that the land near and around our well reeks of tobacco from the water of the hookahs! They don't say it outright, but they are no longer the same as us!'

'Our mother still calls Munsha Singh's mother aunt,' Bhaia reminded him.

'She says that she was Sita Ram's aunt,' Taya Banta declared, taking the pipe of the hookah from his mouth. He chuckled and went on, 'What else was I telling you! That it was one community, closely related. But it all changed some thirty-forty years ago. Sant Ram was from the same family, but he became an Arya Samaji! After that he did not look at them!'

Taya paused and then went back to his earlier complaint, 'The crux of the matter is that those who are ours are no longer with us, and you should not think of us as one with the scavengers! What affinity do we have with them? We have nothing to do with them and share no kinship with them! Don't give these barbarians so much importance!'

'At least, show some respect for your own white beard ... what would have happened had we been born into a family of scavengers? Had it been in my hands, would I have taken birth in a family of Chamars?' Bhaiya exclaimed as he got up from where he had been sitting with them, and began walking homewards. As he walked away he said loudly, 'We are not going to get rid of this! All these problems have been created by the Brahmins! It is they who have divided us so that they may dominate us and make us slaves of them.'

Bhaia's chain of thought continued again, 'What sort of life do we lead? We neither belong to this side, nor do we fit in with the others! They call us Hindus. Tell me where do we stand in the scheme of Brahmins, Kshatriya, Vaishyas, and Shudras? We have neither a religion nor a caste! If only anyone were to ask them how are we Hindus?' Bhaia seemed to have run out of breath. He drew a deep breath and began again, 'I have often thought of becoming a Sikh!'

'Who has stopped you? ... I see no difference in Sikhs and Hindus ... we all believe in the same God,' Ma tried to edge her way into the conversation.

'What you say is right! The Sikhs suffer from the same disease of caste as the Hindus.' Then, he thought of something and said, 'This is why I say that one should join a group, whatever it may be. Become a Sikh or whatever you want to be, but don't remain a Hindu! One must get out of this hell!'

'A few days ago, Lahori Ram Bali was addressing a public meeting, and he said that Dr Ambedkar had advised the poor and the low castes to become Buddhists, because the Buddhists don't believe in varna or caste and all are treated equal. God alone knows why the Hindus are so arrogant! They assert that they are higher than this or that group. Shame on them, the oppressors! They deserve to die for all the cruelties they have perpetrated on the dalits! They are killing those who are already dead!'

'Why are you getting so worked up? Just let it go,' Ma said, her tone conciliatory.

Bhaia recollecting something, went on, without any urging, 'This Inder Singh threatened me the other day. He told me to advise my brother-in-law (Gulzari Lal) not to drink straight from the pipe carrying water from the Persian wheel, but only from a lower level, or else he'd teach him a lesson ... this from the man who's spent his whole life playing the cymbals and dholak in the gurudwara!'

The scene of the herd of 'Ramgai' drinking at the pond in which the water fell from the Persian wheel came alive before my eyes. It hurt me to think that we were considered worse than animals! Even stones and dumb animals are accepted and considered better than us! Or at least considered more valuable and important! They are even worshipped. A moment later, I imagined that the water from the pipeline was a boiling cyclone!

'Why are you raking ashes? Don't blow on a dead fire, you will only hurt yourself.'

'My whole being is on fire, and you are telling me to be calm! Had there not been a division of the country, brother Gulzari Lal would have never come here from Lahore! As if things were better here!'

This set off a storm in my mind. My uncle Gulzari Lal was a tall, fair-skinned well-built man. He looked very handsome in the smart clothes he always wore. How could it defile Baba Inder Singh if Gulzari Lal drank directly from the water hose?

My thoughts spun like the Persian wheel and the clear and pure water of the pond turned into a mirror. Various images shape and disintegrated. Huge mountains, and then a volcano, belching flames and smoke! As the hot searing flames approached me, I shuddered! Who knows how long I would have stayed so if Dhyan had not shaken me by the shoulder and said, 'There is going to be *sawain*-eating contest! This time it will be at the well with two Persian wheels!'

On Gugga navami, all the women of our mohalla, all my aunts, would light mud lamps and worship the banyan tree at Gurdas' place. Sprinkling milk mixed with water on the tree, they would then distribute sawain carried on thalis to the children milling around them, holding their katoris and bowls.

The two-wheeled well stood on the eastern edge of the village, and only the women of Jat, Brahmin, and goldsmith communities went to this well with their offering of sawain. They carried trays with lacy white covers, delicately balanced on the outspread palms of the left hand, with a glass or lota or milk and water in the right. Dressed in beautiful new clothes, they walked confidently, compelling me to calculate and permutate, multiply, subtract, add, and divide all sorts of things. The pitiable conditions of the women of my community with their dirty, tattered clothes flashed through my mind. Their listless faces flickered before my eyes. Their diffident walk held none of the confidence and arrogance of the high-caste women. Barefoot, a hoe in one hand, supporting a bundle of grass or clothes on the head, collecting garbage, dry dung pats, or beating their children with the other—that was the picture.

Whatever it may be, the children from our mohalla did go to the two-wheeled well. This time I went with Dhyan, Ram Pal, Sucha, and a few others. We walked through the central lane of the village, with our bowls in hand. When the sawain was being distributed, it was quite natural to try and edge the others out. But when someone taunted me for my caste, I stepped back and stole away from there. I was badly upset and my mind churned. That was the first and last time I went there for some sawain.

The event saddened me and for a few days I was deeply depressed and shaken. Then something happened to lighten my mood. There was the sound of drums and the children from our mohalla flew like a swarm of bees in that direction. Pushing and nudging, they ran as if they were racing each other. Some of them were naked above the waist and others below. In no time, they reached the place where the drummer stood, and started dancing the bhangra to the beat of music, unconscious of the sweat streaming down their bodies!

The drummer was Achchroo, from Binpalke village, about four kilometres from Madhopur towards the south. A middle-aged man of medium height, he had small light eyes, a scraggly beard, and pock marks on his face. He wore a locket on a black thread round his neck, and a turban at all times, with one edge sticking out at the back. Though the turban was either white or pearl-coloured, it was always dirty. He was in a kurta and dhoti, and wore chappals. As he beat the drum, he walked swiftly, as though he had to cover a long distance. As we children danced around him, he wouldn't stop but continue playing, marking the beat with his right foot, appearing to be one of us.

We danced right round the outer lane of the village, and the happy news of the contest of gymnastics would reach the neighbouring villages, some twenty days or a month before the actual event was to be held. The *baazigars* had divided the villages to hold contests and games, and our village was allotted to Achchroo's group.

The meet was often held in the afternoon under the banyan tree of the Sialkotias. Young and old, men, women, and children would all assemble under the shade of the wide and extended branches of the tree, to watch the exploits of the young baazigars. There was an air of excitement, which had been created by the vigorous music.

A few days before the contest, a spot would be selected and prepared for the games. A sloping path of mud would be set up at one end of the spot, graded to be a fair high in front, and this was called the adda—the venue for all the athletic feats. Right in front of the elevated end of this, a ten-foot long plank of teak, would be buried. The whole area which had been dug up, was swept clean and carefully weeded out time and again, smoothened over and flattened. All the pieces of pottery, glass, old nails, leaves, and any other object that might have been lying around, and sure to injure the athletes, were carefully removed. This was where the participants would practise their jumps.

The smart, agile, and lithe young athletes were in tight country shorts. Their muscular bodies rippled and gleamed. Before running up the slope from the west to the east, they would first slap their biceps and then run up to the plank, and placing the left foot on it, jump up, turn a somersault in the air, and then get ready for the next turn. Some of them, mere boys, their moustaches as yet only a shadow on their faces, would run up and standing on their hands placed flat on the ground, form a neat circle and with their upraised bodies execute a dance enacting the revolving Persian wheel. Many old men watching these skilful displays would burst into, 'The boys are really very agile and supple!'

'God! They are delightful! One can maintain one's body only through hard work! Our boys drink the whole day long and bloat out of shape!' One zamindar expressed his unhappiness with the boys of his own community.

Suddenly, the music would get louder and faster. Excitement would run high. The contest would now get serious and we children would stroke our non-existent muscles, in imitation of the young athletes!

The athletes would turn different types of somersaults. The frenzy in the atmosphere grew, and whenever a young man walked on his hands, flailing his legs in the air, the drummer and many of the old men in the audience would burst into song to encourage him, repeating the couplet,

*Dark are the clouds in the sky,*
*The peacocks dance in ecstasy!*

The athletes would run up from some distance, and taking off from the top of the plank, jump up and turn a somersault in the air. Often they would jump backwards and twist and turn in the air. The crowd would go mad cheering them.

'Dharam naal, the boy has done an excellent job of a triple somersault,' an elderly man would express his admiration and hand over a couple of rupees to Achchru, who would make a sign to the drummer to stop, and turning to the crowd, call out, 'Sardaro ... enjoy yourself! May you always ... prosper and flourish!'

As a few athletes prepared for their next feat, a young man would enter an iron ring and lie flat on the ground. Another young man would first pass his head and then his torso with great difficulty into the same ring from the side where the first one's legs were. In this process both their bodies would be full of welts and marks. The drummer would ask them in a loud voice, 'Say, young men, should we call an ironmonger to cut the ring?'

'No, not at all,' the two boys would answer, in low and strangled voices. An old man would pass his body through a small ring, and then clap, and repeat the following lines in singsong:

*Try and try as much as you can,*
*The parrot will fly away.*

And then came the turn of the game of fire. Long supple branches of mulberry were made into a ring, and this would be tied at one end of the pole, covered with rags and moistened with kerosene oil. Two young men would hold it up chest high, and when it was lit, the flames would shoot up. Two athletes would then run up, arms out stretched, bodies upright and taut, as if running into a well! With one leap they would fly through the circle of fire, but at times their lower limbs would be singed badly, and even bleed.

In the same manner, a young man would be blindfolded and a *kripan* with burning rags tied to both ends placed in his mouth. Clenching it firmly between his teeth, he would jump high into the air and somersault.

I was overawed by these feats and yearned to do them myself. Then it would make me important, and people would ask about me, applaud my performance, and admire me! How happy I would be!

The last act, a high jump, was a treat to watch! A cot would be placed in front of the plank at the top of the bamboos for safety's sake, should a gymnast miss a step. When all the athletes had jumped by turn, the plank would then be raised. Excitement would run high for the next feat.

'Sardars, give us a tall and robust young man,' the leader of the athletes would call out in a loud and confident tone. 'Where is Mahinder of the Nobas? Or, if he is not present, ask Iqbal Singh to come forward,' someone would call out.

Mahinder Singh, Iqbal Singh, or Bhajji of Bara Singh, all three were over six feet tall, healthy, strong, and handsome. They were neither arrogant nor envious of anyone. The three would climb on to the cot at the top of the ladder, taking turns to hold a winnowing tray. The athlete would, with great concentration, jump through, without touching the basket and turn three somersaults in the air. The thudding of the drum would rise to a crescendo and applause and noisy screams would greet this daring feat.

People from the neighbouring village would now start leaving. Some of them would go to their local friends for a cup of tea. Gradually, the crowd would disperse bringing the mela of the baazigars to an end.

In no time, there would be a heap of grain near the athletes. Jaggery, rice and pulses, *desi ghee* and mustard oil, would also be gifted, besides some cash. Jat women would present material for clothes to Achchru and his beautiful wife, Banti. She had flower tattoos on her arms and sold combs and needles in the village. The faces of these two reflected their happiness. Their grown son, Joginder, or their nephew, Billu, would quickly cover the heap of jaggery or ghee, or swish off the flies from these heaps.

One of the zamindars remarked, 'This is good, Achchru Ram! You have been able to collect at least four maunds of grain and will now have a comfortable year. You can even sell some of it! And you have not done anything much to earn all this! You have only been beating the dhol for about four days!'

'Sardara, what you say is right, but I have invested a lot of money in this, and you also know that everything has become very expensive. I have worked very hard for the last month or more!'

I would have sat staring at the heaps of grain and the flies swarming around the ghee and jaggery had Dhyan not shaken me by the shoulder and exclaimed, 'Gudd, just look up and watch the pigeons performing their tricks in the sky!'

Watching the pigeons gambolling, I felt as if I was one of them flying high in the clear sky. But the flight of my imagination was cut short in mid-air, and I came back to the earth with a bang, as I recalled the words of the zamindar, 'What have you done? Only beaten the drum for four days!'

As I recalled the sarcastic comment, another thought occurred to me and my father's dark visage flashed before my eyes. It was not my imagination, but a reality. When I reached home, Bhaia tried to advise me, 'The athletes have twisted around and hurt themselves, but these zamindars have not given them even a word of praise! They say that the low castes must entertain and serve them! I say this stigma of low and high will never end in this country without a violent struggle. If only we had a few acres of land, then we would have not bothered about these mean zamindars! You can see for yourself how much they hate us! But one has to tolerate many things to survive. What else can one do? We can only fret and fume about all this!'

After a brief pause, he suddenly lost his temper, 'Maama! You must study or else you too will have to endure this enslavement. They all dole out a bare handful to you after you've worked hard the whole day! It is not even sufficient to subsist on!'

Whenever he lost his temper on such occasions, I bore the agony of his anger. His advice struck home, but I could not understand why I should be the only one to be scolded. Whenever I listened to him, I felt that he and all the low castes were one, and were bound to each other by a deep bond of empathy, desperately trying to improve their lives. Wounded and bleeding by the thorns that littered the path they were travelling on, they were yet determined to go on, though they did not know how long they would have to travel and how far they might have to go.

# 6

## Sunshine through the Clouds

'Gudd, you and Roshi (Roshan Lal) go home and cut some fodder and chop it up!' ordered Master Sodhi, suddenly coming out of his opium haze. Taking a pinch of snuff from a long, round iron box, and sniffing it, he added, 'Go quickly! The buffaloes must be hungry and bellowing away. Wash them also.'

Like obedient students, we neither made any excuses, nor did we refuse. Handing our school bags to our classmates, we set off for Master Sodhi's home, which was about three kilometres from school in village Sohalpur, in the southeast.

We had just come out of the courtyard of the school and stepped on to the outer mud path, when a series of thoughts began their march, like a file of schoolchildren, sticking to me like a shadow. I thought of Master Sodhi's field of millet which I had seen a while ago. It had rained heavily a day earlier and I had seen a row of fat fair-skinned women squatting along the edge of the field, answering the call of nature. Their dupattas covered their faces and heads. The recollection of that sight made me feel as if my feet were bogged down in the filth lying about on the ground, and the stink of excreta seemed to overpower me. My thoughts came to a sudden halt as if I had put a full stop to them, the way I used to, while taking dictation at school.

'He sends us every third day, but he never tells the Jat boys that they should fetch and chop the fodder for his animals!' Abruptly, and for the first time, I showed my resentment.

'He surely doesn't want to get his nose bashed in by *them*! The Jats think Sodhi and the Khatris to be the dirt under their feet!' Roshi, who was a couple of years older than me, commented. Taking a few more steps, he added, 'What do the Sodhis have? Sikhism? But the Jats have wealth, and also lands! It is not for nothing that they storm about and shout in our lane!'[1]

Roshi's comments clarified many things that had been puzzling me. Craning my neck to look at him, I saw the flush of deep anger on his face.

Roshi was my uncle's son, and knew many things which are only known to grown-ups. He had left school when he was in class one and gone to the village. Dhadda Sanaura, to work for a landlord, Sardar Madanjeet Singh. The zamindar's wife, Bichinti, was involved in the liquor trade and knew many drunkards. Whenever the police raided her house and took her away to the Bhogpur police chowki, it was Roshi and her sons who looked after the animals and did the household chores. He had worked there for three years and then come back to the village and become my classmate.

'I want to tell both Bhaia and Taya that Sodhi should teach us also. We are made to sweep the school in the morning, and then we are sent to tend the animals!' I told him what was in my heart. I thought that my suggestion was rather good.

'Stop for a moment, if I don't pull your plait out, then I am not the son of a Jat! These Chamars cut grass only from my field.' The harsh angry voice of the nambardar of Sohalpur cut through our conversation. The thread of our discussion snapped, the way the thread of Bhaia's loom did when he worked on it. The nambardar was walking with quick purposeful strides towards a group of women who were digging grass at the edge of a field.

At this moment, we heard the braying of donkeys, from under the clump of sheesham trees belonging to the 'Buddhas', the people for whom my family worked in many different ways. This sounded like the

---

1. All the ten Sikh Gurus were Khatris—Kshatriyas—and the last five Gurus were from the Sodhi clan. The Jats have always been the backbone of Sikhism. They also happen to be a rich, landowning class, powerful, and politically important.

blowing of conch shells! But we kept on walking and talking, 'It is the humiliation every day and at every step! Why don't we have some land?' By this time we had reached Master Sodhi's house, and his wife handed us a pair of sickles.

We went to the field reluctantly. It was afternoon with the sun at its hottest! Trying to save our feet from both fresh and dried shit scattered about, we would roll the bloodied rags with our sickles, and fling them some distance away, where a couple of pups would snatch them up and run in different directions, playing with them and also with each other. Watching them was pleasant, but the afternoon was very still and the stink around was so overwhelming that it was difficult to breathe. Feeling sick, I wanted to run away and wash my legs and feet. But we went on cutting the stalks of the millet. Then, Sodhi's wife, her dupatta tied across her face, came out to tie up the stalks into bundles. ... Roshi and I both worked at the chopping machine and his wife kept putting the sheafs of the fodder into the machine. By now we were out of breath and sweating profusely. I was abusing Sodhi in my heart, and the words, though unarticulated, echoed in my ears.

As we went towards the hand pump after finishing our work, Sodhi's wife said, 'Stop, I'll give you water to drink'

She made a sign and we went to the back near the gutters, and cupped our hands, as she poured water from a jug, held above our heads. As soon as we stepped out, Roshi exclaimed, 'First our brothers were serving these masters and tending their animals, and now we have to do all this—Sodhi won't change nor will he die! Stupid fool! Addict!'

The donkey could be heard braying as we ran towards the dera-camp of the 'bhaiyas'. Small tents had been put up, as also some huts; a goat could be seen at the door of a hut, as also some kids. We saw some men and women and a few donkeys straying about.

We went forward and saw that Bhaia was seated with these people— those whom we call 'Purbias' or easterners. He was speaking to them in a mixture of Hindi and Punjabi and smoking.

'... There, we have to name our children according to the names of the day they are born on, such as Somu, Manglu, Buddhu, etc., or after animals, or birds; for example, my name is Machchar Das, he is Totaram, and that one standing there is Chiddi Ram.'

'... And these two are Haggi Ram and Mootru Ram?' Bhaia interrupted them as if affirming the social difficulties that the 'Purbias' faced.

'Our names are all rotten and filthy things.'[2]

'... Then you should change your names. There should be no problem in that!' Bhaia made a simple suggestion.

'Names like the ones used by Thakurs or Rajputs! Names of gods! ... My parents named my younger brother Udai Singh, and all the Thakurs came with sticks to beat us up for using their father's name! They said that we were trying to become their fathers! What right did we have— how dare we take names like theirs! They threatened us saying that for our own good, we should not use such names,' said the Purbia bhaiya sadly.

'... Then did you accept what they said?' Bhaia wanted to dispel his own doubts, as he took out a bundle of beedis and matches from his pocket.

'What else could we do? We didn't want to get beaten up! That day, my brother's name changed from Udai Singh to Buddhu ...'

Bhaia was lost in some recollection of the past which left him depressed. He drew a picture on the sand or wrote something, and then erased it with his own hand. I could not understand what he was doing. But his eagerness to know more about the conditions in UP was clearly evident.

'... What can we tell you, Thakar Das! The conditions in eastern Uttar Pradesh are deplorable—the *doli* of the bride still goes directly to the Thakurs. They send for our daughters and daughters-in-law whenever they feel like ...' One of the men from the east was relating his woes.

As he heard this, Bhaia sat up and broke his still smoking bidi into two. His whole body was tense and he flung a glance at us, but was silent.

'Shall I tell you more?' The old man who had spoken earlier, asked, and then stopped. His voice had become hard and yet it trembled, and hopelessness seemed to descend on him. He appeared to be piecing

---

2. Names like, Haggi or Mootri, mean one who shits and the one who urinates. Machchar means mosquito insect.

his words together, the way a child does, and spoke, as if gathering up his courage, 'Don't ask what happens during the Holi festival—the Thakurs come in the evening, drunk and armed with lathis, and order our women to entertain them.'

I felt that he had used all the words he had. He choked and there was fear in his eyes. His neck drooped like twisted neck of a chichen. I was greatly upset by all this.

It then occurred to me that a shared sorrow had demolished all differences of language and geography. Bhaia's eyes reddened. Suddenly, he said with some eagerness, 'It is better that you people live here, than undergo the humiliation you have to on that side.'

'All our relatives are there … What should we do … We can't think of anything … We want to stay here in the Punjab, where things are not as bad. There is less rigidity about untouchability also … We have been living here for the last three–four years and have observed things.'

'Women everywhere are beyond untouchability …' Bhaia remarked. 'The Jats have often bought women from outside, there are many from the east here—there are some in Sohalpur who talk in the peculiar style of "hum ko, tum ko" and then a poor woman is like us. She has neither religion nor caste. You can mix water in anything, and it will take on its colour from the thing it mixes with.'

The bhaiya nodded in agreement.

'Yaar, I just remembered what a friend once told me. When, he was a truck driver in Mumbai, women of all castes were working as prostitutes there, but the rate of Kamla Vashisht, Bimla Verma, Sharma, etc., is much higher than of the others,' Bhaia told him. 'There is such a difference even when they are in the same profession! I was astonished at what he had said, that even in the sex trade, people are concerned about caste!'

'Perhaps, this is so because they are fair-skinned …'

'Let it be … what can we say about these things?' Bhaia tried to wrap up what he had himself started.

Another man who had been sitting with them, took out some tobacco from under his tongue and threw it away, then turning away squirted a stream of tobacco juice before spitting.

My mind was in a turmoil after I overheard the conversation between my father and the bhaiyas. There were many things I had not fully grasped and though I struggled to do so, I failed to understand them; but I wanted the conversation to continue so that I could listen more carefully. Suddenly a small girl, dark, naked and runny nosed, who was sleeping in a basket nearby, let out a yell and began crying loudly. The conversation stopped and we all turned to her. Her tears fell as would drops of ice from a melting kulfi.

Her mother, who had been grinding red pepper on a grinding stone, stopped work, and arranging the edge of her sari on her head, picked her up and tried to quieten her. The girl's dry and matted hair was like a bird's nest on her head, and deep lines of tears ran down her cheeks, even though she ceased yelling after some time. A stream of red water ran across the grinding stone and then slipped over the edge, drop by drop. It seemed to me as if the pungent red pepper had affected all our souls. Perhaps, for this reason my arms which had been across my chest, now slackened, and on their own, slid down to hang by my sides. I felt a strange sensation in my hands, a desire to do something.

After some moments, Bhaia again picked up the thread of the conversation, 'Yaar, sometimes, I wonder what we have in this country? ... Listen to this, every now and then, they come with chains and tapes to survey, and putting a mark in the centre of our courtyard, they declare that all the houses of the Chamars are on the common land.'

'You are talking of land, I believe that even our daughters and daughters-in-law are common possession,' the Purbia interrupted Bhaia. Scratching his short hair he went on, 'You are better off than us ... what if you don't have any land! At least you have your honour!' His voice become harsh and seemed to echo around us.

Bhaia looked at him in astonishment. Looking at their wilted faces, we also grew sad. I was very upset.

'Who knows for what we are being punished ... perhaps for the sins of many births!'

'Forget births and sins, think of some way to get rid of these oppressors. You people also think of some way to place your demands before the Congress, the way we do. Otherwise, by bowing and crying you will not get anything in this crooked country.'

Bhaia had the air of a wise man as he suggested this. If he is so wise, then he should not lift this hand at my mother and abuse her, I thought to myself. But in a moment, that thought had vanished.

The shadows had lengthened as the sun sank a little lower in the west, as if in sympathy with the tale of anguish and humiliation that had been narrated. The wind was blowing harder and the leaves of the sheesham trees were falling all around, some on our feet. The sand from the water canal was in the air. The wind, gathering momentum, turned into small whirlwinds all around. The Purabi women picked up their children and went into the tents. We stood still and by closing our eyes tried to save them from sand.

Bhaia got up, and dusting the backside of his kurta, said, 'Achcha bhaiya Machar Das, this wind is not going to stop now, and the boys are here, I have to take them home.'

After a moment, he signalled to us with his eyes, and said, 'Study hard like good boys! Tomorrow, I shall take care of that addict Sodhi and the other teachers who keep sending you to cut and chop fodder, or with the mail to Jandira, or to the flour mill of to Bhundian (a village some five kilometres from Madhopur) all the time.'

'Master Gurbanta Singh is visiting the school tomorrow,' we told him.

'The community has already decided to ask for lands from the Congress,' Bhaia talked to us as if we could understand the whole thing. He explained, 'Earlier Gurbanta Singh was also a teacher and he would say, "Is the land like a strip of rubber that it can be stretched and you people given a share?" He silenced us with this argument, at Bhogpur some time ago. But no one told him that some of it could be taken from those who had more than they could look after, and given to those who have nothing except their own houses! Surely they too should have some comfort in life! No matter, our time will also come.'

Speaking in his grating voice, Bhaia turned toward the fields of the 'Buddhas' and we took the opportunity to drive the donkeys forward. When we reached the embankment where their panniers were being emptied, we jumped on to their backs and digging our heels into their sides, goaded them back to the pits, the way we had seen in the pictures of rajas and maharajas. We went on playing with the donkeys and mud for a long time. The shadows lengthened. We started back for the village. The whirlwinds had already changed into hard-blowing winds.

We were very tired, and Roshi and I did not talk much as we walked back. The things that Bhaia had said in the afternoon were still echoing in my mind, the way the sun keeps peering from behind the clouds.

# 7

## Our Home
### *The Home of Woes*

'The whole village just went under water, and whatever was left, was swept away by the floods,' Daadi would raise her right hand and then bring it down in a fluid motion to demonstrate how the whole catastrophe had occurred. We were all shaken.

'The village is still there! And Bhaia still goes there to Devi Ma's temple to fulfil whatever vows he takes,' I retorted.

'So it is! But earlier the village was situated where the hillock stands today. Now it is on the other side,' Daadi explained. After a brief pause, she went on, 'That whole family was Nathu's, who was of the same gotra (subcaste) as your grandfather. Your grandfather had a sister.'

'… And your parents-in-law …?'

'I've told you many times not to be so inquisitive,' she scolded me so that I would stop asking questions.

'Ma, what was your father-in-law's name?' I insisted, my tone somewhat placatory. But she felt that I had some ulterior motive in asking this question. Even at this advanced age she was reluctant to say out loud the name of her father-in-law, now dead for many years.

'Do tell Ma,' I pleaded.

'Saudagar,' she took the name with hesitation! 'But one must know about one's ancestors. Your great-grandfather was in the army.'

'Army?'

'Of course, he was the orderly of an important British officer,' she replied, adjusting the string which had replaced the broken shaft of her dirty spectacles, and setting it properly on the bridge of her nose.

'Then?'

'He was given a marraba of land but he could not pay the revenue, the matter could not be settled and the land …'

'What happened to the land?'

'Some relatives of your great-grandfather and some of his family cheated him. They got him to sign some documents,' Daadi would wind up the story abruptly. But I was fascinated by the story and wanted to know more.

'This house, then?' I asked about our house.

'This belongs to your grandfather's mother's family. His maama, mother's brother, had no children. He didn't want to be called a childless man, so he brought your grandfather home, when he was still a child. It was after this that the village of Baqarpur Pandori (a village in Hoshiarpur district on the Hoshairpur–Tanda Road; is known as Pandori Maill Patti Baqarpur in the revenue records) was submerged.'

I calculated that this natural disaster would have occurred between 1860 and 1866. Rainwater from the Shivalik Hills flows in this direction, and consequently, whenever there are heavy rains, the fast flowing water plays havoc with the embankments of the overflowing hill streams, and many villages of the Doaba get inundated. There are many streams in the area, and a popular saying is, 'Twelve miles and eighteen streams' (*Baran koh te attaranh choh*).

Our house is built on a plot of land measuring about three and a half marla, that is about hundred square yards. There is no house at the back, nor is there a wall into another house. There is a mud track leading to the house of my grandfather's uncle in the west, and in the northwest, the central lane of village.

In accordance with the social system which prevails in India, our mohalla is also on the western side of Madhopur village. Except for the house of Baba Chajju (the son of my grandfather's maternal uncle), all other houses in our mohalla are made of mud. Our house lies to the south of this house, and is the first at the crossing of the lane which goes to the mohalla of the Jats, and that is why the Jats keep nagging us about the work that is to be done in their fields.

'Thakar ! Listen!'

Bhaia would hurry to the front door. Often the caller would be a boy of my age, and possibly even a classmate. All the Jat youngsters, boys and girls, called my father by his name.

'He is either Jaib of the Babas or Meeta of the Sadhus! But it cannot be Bamb!' We would try to guess the identity of the caller as we sat in the room.

Bhaia would come back and tell us who it was, 'It was Baksha of the Mantri! He says if we have finished harvesting the peanuts of the Pakkawalas, then tomorrow we should start working in their fields.'

Daadi sat looking in the direction of the front door. I would talk to her to learn more about my grandfather. But she refused to speak, and Bhaia would take care to clear up the awkwardness, 'I have a very faint recollection. Our father was very dark, tall and strong; he had a small beard. They say he had the gift of the gab, and a great sense of humour.'

'Ma, you also tell us something,' I would interrupt him and plead with my grandmother.

'She was always bossing him! How can she say anything now!' Bhaia would remark.

'She bossed him because she was fair and healthy, like an Englishwoman!' I remarked seated by her.

'You fools! You sit by me and make fun of me!' Suddenly she lost her temper. Adjusting her glasses, she picked up her jooti. By this time I had escaped!

... And it was in this house that Daadi had given birth to seven children. There were three sons and three daughters—all older than my father who was the youngest. It was here that she had welcomed her four daughters-in-law, and had seen off two daughters as brides. A third daughter had died young.

My aunts had many children and courtyard full of them; one may say that it was overcrowded. We could no longer live together, and a piece of land had been bought close to the house of a Jat, and the home of my Daadi had fallen into my father's lot.

There was a small room at the back of our house, with four racks. It was always dark, and the wooden beam and roof were made of reeds and rushes. Mice had made the roof their playground. They scampered in and out the whole day long, and when we tried to shoo them off, they would disappear into their holes. Mud often fell from the roof. Many a time, it seemed that they were playing games with us.

Occasionally, one of the buffaloes would poke that wall with her horns. Bhaia had placed the old roller of his room against the wall, to protect it from any damage. It was this that the buffalo butted. Bhaia would scold her even at midnight, 'I will skin you, you bitch! Stop it now and let us sleep!'

Surprisingly, the buffalo would obey him! When she did not, Bhaia would get up and thrash the animal.

It was in this room that Daadi slept in winters. The animals were also tied here. The courtyard stank with the smell of their urine, and there were goat droppings all over the floor.

In summertime, when the heat of the sun became unbearable, it was very comfortable to sit in that cool room. My elder brother (my uncle's son), Maddi, and I would loll around on the clothes on Daadi's cot. We would have our meals here and tell our mother, 'Seebo, put some salt and pepper on the roti!'

'Fry some paranthas! They are always hungry! I tell you roast some potatoes in hot ashes and let them fill themselves up!' Bhaia's scolding was routine.

Ma gave us onions or gur, also some pickle or lassi with rotis. Many a time, we would snatch the roti as she took it off the griddle, and would not even let her put it in the basket to cool. She would shout at us, 'Be patient! You will burn your fingers. What's the hurry? In no time you will clamour for more.

Like most of the members of our community, we also called our mother by her name. The words 'pure' and 'impure' did not exist in our dictionary.

There was acute scarcity of grain during the winter months, right up to March and April. We were left with no option but to drink the impure scum that collected as 'cream' in cane juice boiled in the making of jaggery or brown sugar. Either my elder brother or I would fetch this impure juice from the cane crushers of Mantris or Tajrabias; sometimes the two of us went together. These crushers were at some distance from the village. Some stray dogs had made this area their home. When we placed our buckets for the juice near the furnace, the dogs would keep pushing each other to crawl close to the furnace. The man minding the boiling juice would first throw a bowl of impure juice on the ground before pouring it into our buckets. The dogs would rush to lick it! We often met Sahib and Sohan of Channu at these crushers.

We carried the brimming copper and iron buckets carefully, so that it would not scald our legs or feet. The dogs would follow us. We often turned to shout at them and to drive them away. At times we would stop to catch our breath; they would slink away.

I was ashamed of being seen carrying the scum, which was called, *maila* or 'sludge'. I would yearn to fly home and not be seen by anyone as I trudged home. On the way, if I happened to meet a classmate, I would turn my face the other way and move as fast as possible.

I had expressed my feelings to Bhaia and Ma. Bhaia would scold me, 'Maama, you want to eat a big share of it! You're not the only one who has to fetch it! The whole of Chamarli does it! We also have carried *chattis* full of it on our heads for our relations who lived in Bassi Muda and Bajwaara, 35 km from Madhopur.'

Ma would intervene, 'Why are you scolding them! In a few years they will grow up and start working.'

'Who knows whether these bastards will be here to even urinate on an injured finger or not! This maama is spoilt! You may send the elder wherever you want; he will go without a protest and will not answer back, and quietly do whatever he is asked to.'

Then one day, my elder brother hurriedly called out to me, 'Bring your thali here. Maama has come!' The two of us hastily hid our thalis in the cattle trough at the back. This was in 1964 and I was then in class four. One of my mother's brothers was an IAS officer and had come visiting in his car.

The following year, there was a severe drought. Then, war with Pakistan broke out. There was no grain to be had. The nambardar and sarpanch became more important and sought after.

Karam Singh was the nambardar; but real power was his wife Jai Kaur. Her influence was accepted by the whole village. She helped the people of our community with money. She would talk like a man and her word was respected. She would give grain on credit to those who were hard up. Even after the famine was over, we were compelled to drink maila for years, though I was in the final year of school.

The children of Jats and others of our age, called us *maill peene*, the 'drinkers of impure juice'. Whenever there was a squabble, they would also taunt us with remarks like, 'The friend of the Chamar's mother!' None of us could protest effectively.

The room at the back was cool in summer because its walls were of mud; there was also a big mound of mud piled at the back to support the back wall and make it safe from the water of the gutter from the village, which ran behind the wall. Lush green grass covered the mound, and it was as if someone had planted a lovely lawn. The walls of our room were always damp during the monsoons, and the stink of this damp was sickening.

The roof would also turn green with the moss. Small plants would sprout on the roof and creepers would spread all over the roof. If you looked at our roof from another roof, it looked as if two large beds of berseem had been planted, for though the roof of the room and the hall was one, yet there was a small wall dividing it.

Ants had made straight and permanent tracks through the walls, travelling up and down them. Whenever it rained heavily and continuously, the roof would leak. We would put all our pots and pans under these leaks. But even that would not suffice and the continuous drip would make a hole in the ground. All this water would collect near the only door in the western part of the large hall. My elder brother and I had the job of scooping up the water with our hands and throwing it out. Either he or I would be made to climb on to the roof to try and fill up the crevices there so that it would stop leaking. I would look down from the roof and shout, 'Has it stopped leaking?'

'No, not yet,' someone would shout back.

'Take this, and stuff it into the hole,' Bhaia would tell me, handing me a large ball of clay.

'Saale, you have harmed us, enough! Why don't you stop now?' Bhaia would vent his anger on both god and the rain!

'Why do you always say such stupid things! We are in the same boat as all the others! Will it stop raining by your raving and ranting?' Ma would try to pacify him.

'All the houses on the eastern side are *pucca*! How do we compare with them? They can build another room by mortgaging a couple of *kanals*!' After a brief pause, he went on, 'I am thinking of putting up a roof of reed mats over the courtyard.'

'You do that, if that is what you want. If this is written in our fate, what can we do!' Ma tried to console him.

'Saali, goddess of destiny unloosens her anger in the form of famine and floods on us alone! What about the rest of the country!'

Going out of the room, Bhaia would call out, 'The clouds have parted, Seebo, and the rain is bound to weaken.'

I remember a particular monsoon when the reed roof was stretched over the courtyard and there was no place even to sit or stand, and the house was leaking all over.

Bhaia would be dejected when he saw and thought about it. He would sometimes say, 'We were the ones who dug the Adampur Canal, laid the road up to the Amb police station, but I haven't been able to make a four-roomed house for myself!'

Picking up a hoe and sickle from under the cot, he would go up to the roof. His muttering kept pace with the falling raindrops. He would pull out the weeds and abuse them all the time he worked, 'It has spread itself all over the roof in a few days, Mother's lover!'

As the clouds parted and the sun came out to shine gloriously, the wall facing the village would collapse. This happened almost every year. A part of the roof would also fall along with the wall. Though the beam supporting the other part of the roof looked sound, our hearts fluttered and trembled like mercury and knew no comfort. Crowds of ants, hornets, locusts, centipedes, scorpions, and lizards would run out from under the broken roof, looking for holes and crevices to slink into. The villagers were free with their sympathy for us!

'Well, Thakar, the wall can be rebuilt somehow. Thank god there was no one under the roof!'

One year, one wall would fall and the next time it would be another one. The year when the sidewall did not fall, it was the front wall of the courtyard which collapsed. The salt in the land had eaten into it, eroding its lower half, making it thinner than the upper. Bhaia fetched cartloads of mud and rebuilt the wall.

One day, he suddenly cried out in the early morning, even before the sun had appeared, 'Run out! The middle beam is about to fall!'

In minutes, the whole mohalla had assembled.

'Thank god, Thakara, that no life has been lost. Now, get the pillars made so that the beams get good support.'

'It may be difficult, but it is necessary,' someone else advised Bhaia.

Bhaia had paid a visit to Surjit Singh at Bhogpur and had put his thumb impression on the loan papers. Surjit Singh was a moneylender. Whenever his elder sister, Juwali, passed through the lane, the children flocked around her and passed comments like, 'One spin of Juwali's spinning wheel ...' She was not married and after her baptism as a Sikh she was always dressed like a Nihang. When we teased her, she would pick up a stone, but would rarely throw it at us, and say, 'Can't you people say Jwala Singh! Don't I look like a Nihang?'

After the rains were over, around Dussehra time, donkeys would bray under the banyan tree, in front of our home. And the call could be heard, 'Buy clay mud! Clay is available.'

All the old women would swarm around, negotiating the price. It would either be Baroo Chamar from the direction of the mountains, or the potter from across the river Beas, with their donkey laden with clay, who would assure them, 'Sisters, I have just delivered the same clay in the village of Rastgo.'

My mother and all my aunts bought the mud. Ma had already prepared the area which needed to be plastered and would also plaster that portion of the wall which was intact. It would be difficult to distinguish the old part of the wall from the new because she would spread many thick layers of mud to make it strong.

After the wall had been rebuilt, she would rub her hands on the wrong side of the griddle, and put the imprints of her hands on the wall. I would do what she had done and press my hands on the wall the way she did, and feel very happy.

Sometimes Bhaia would come home while all this was going on and stand in the courtyard, watching.

'Now, the task of warding off the evil eye has also been completed!' Ma would say with satisfaction, and he would smile, revealing his small, sharp teeth!

'Saale, every year there is some problem or the other with this room! Who knows when will this problem be sorted out!' Bhaia would sum up the episode of the mud wall which was an annual occurrence.

'Nothing remains the same!' Ma would console him, clutching at straws.

A small tin box of my mother's was kept in a corner of the back room. She had brought this box along with her dowry. It was gaily painted with pictures of peacocks and peahens surrounded by their young ones amidst flowers, plants, and creepers. These pictures were in grey, green, red, and purple colours. There was a smaller box, similarly painted, inside the larger box.

Whenever Ma opened this box to take something out, my elder brother and I would hover around. We would look at the black ghagras that belonged to her and Daadi. They opened out like tents. There was also a big fan made of reeds and cane, covered with embroidered cloth. We would take it out and take turns to fan ourselves. On three sides, it had a pink border and the handle was uncovered. When we fanned ourselves vigorously, the dust lying on the floor would rise. Whenever there was a wedding or any gathering in the village, it would be borrowed by the family concerned. It had been used by various bridal parties coming to the village, and even by people assembled to condole a death.

There were a few large earthen pots and utensils set by the wall. They contained different types of grain, jaggery, sugar, pulses, and pieces of dried rotis. There was a covered pot which contained salt. Often Bhaia hid his bottle of country liquor in one of these pots. Whenever he took a drink on the sly, he would stroke and press his moustache. Lighting a bidi, he would tell Ma, 'What you say is right. Our days will surely change. Once these boys grow up, they will fend for themselves. Seebo, I must say, you give me a great deal of courage!'

There was a bin close to the box used for storing a variety of odds and ends. It was here that Daadi often hid her katori of jaggery, sugar, or molasses that the Jat women gave her. She would put a big lock on it and tie the key to her dupatta. She would often look for her things at night, in the light of a diya.

It was on this lid and under this bin that Bhaia kept his cobbler's kit. The kit included moulds for jootis, a hasp, pliers, a hammer, and scrapers. I often played with these things, and Bhaia would angrily snatch them away showering me with abuse. The neighbours would borrow them from us.

'Had I learnt the trade thoroughly from my brother-in-law (my uncle Gulzari Lal) at Lahore by now, I would now have been an expert. I would have been sitting under a tree earning money. I would not be serving these Jats as I am now doing,' Bhaia often began his tale of woe on a negative note.

In a corner of the room lay a small grinding stone. I had often seen my mother grinding flour for the whole family. She would sing as she rolled the stone,

> My father gives palaces and
>   mansions to his sons,
> but his daughters he sends
>   to strange lands,
> Oh my saintly father.

She would also grind different spices and condiments such as aniseed, ginger, dried gram, and wheat that she would need after her delivery. After the delivery, Bhaia would roast these condiment in desi ghee, into a mixture called *giza*. I liked to claim a share of this mixture at the births of my siblings.

One summer, Bhaia had come home in the afternoon, having worked in the field of a Jat the whole morning. His turban was slung on his shoulder and he carried a hoe. My mother lay on a cot with my younger sister besides her. She had given birth a short while earlier. She had tied her dupatta round her head. I was playing nearby. As soon as he came into the courtyard, his eyes questioned her, 'What is it?'

'A girl', was my mother's answer.

'What a curse!'

'Is it in my hands, to give birth to a son'? Ma asked. Helplessness echoed in her voice. I felt that Bhaia had perhaps wanted a son this time.

Bhaia stored his hoe in a corner and quickly went to the corner to wash.

I liked my tender younger sisters. I would carry them and play with them, lifting them on to my shoulders. I was impatient for them to grow up and play with me.

Whenever she had to wash clothes or cook, my mother would make a sling out of her dupatta or a length of material, and putting the new born in it, ask me to look after her and see that she did not cry. 'I will just put the dal on the chulha and fetch two buckets of water from the well.'

After the birth of my third sister, my mother suffered from post-natal fever, which gradually turned into typhoid. She lost most of her hair in a month. She kept her head covered, either by tying a scarf or her dupatta around her head. She became very weak and there was no sign of the fever abating.

Many old women visited her and ask, 'What does Gango, the midwife say? Do whatever she tells you.'

Bhaia would tell one of us, 'Give this muda to chachi.' He could weave mudas of reed of paddy straw in round or square shapes. Selecting the straw carefully, he would weave it into ropes.

'Karoora had taken her to Chiranji lal of Kandhala Jatta the day before. He said it is small pox. All along we thought it was plain fever,' Bhaia would tell all those who visited my mother. Deep lines of worry showed on his face.

'Your children are small. God will be merciful ... Seebo, take courage. One does fall ill now and then. Regain your strength and take care of your children.' Some woman of the mohalla would advise her, straightening the folds of her dirty and torn salwar to cover her dirty black knees which peeped though its many rents.

The old women consoled and advised my parents, and when departing, showered blessings on them, 'Thakar, don't worry ... god is kind. If it is small pox, then take very great care.'

In desperation, Bhaia would say, 'Saala, god is bent on inflicting all kinds of trouble on us ... who knows how long all this will go on? How long can I go on borrowing from others?'

Sometimes, he would approach Ma with some hesitation, and say, 'Seebo, I know it is a bother, but can you repair this tear in my kurta? Just look how long it is! My kurta is badly worn out with sweat!'

We would feed our younger sister with a spoon. She would gurgle with happiness. Bhaia would laugh and say, 'Look Seebo, she is thriving on goat's milk!'

'Don't cast an evil eye on her, who knows I may have been saved for her sake!' Ma answered with a smile.

When this sister of mine was about five or six years old, she kept scratching her hair the whole day long. My mother thought she may have lice in her hair. She combed her hair with a fine toothed comb, but found nothing. She heated water and washed her hair. She noticed that my sister's scalp was swollen. On touching it she felt that it was very tender. She called to my father, 'What are you doing there? I have been calling out to you!'

'What is it now?' Bhaia answered, from inside the room.

'The girl's scalp is infected with vermin!'

Bhaia washed Baljinder's hair with warm water. He would dig out the vermin from her scalp with a reed. Her scalp was covered with a thin whitish mesh in which the vermin seemed trapped. Bhaia ordered me as if he was a doctor, 'Gudd, get that bottle of phenyl from the shelf, the one I had used in washing out the cow's vermin.'

'Talk some sense, and take her to Bhogpur,' Ma intervened.

Bhaia put Baljinder on his cycle and took her to Moga Sokra pharmacy.

After this, it was I who took my sister to the pharmacy for her treatment. I was astonished when I saw the doctor push a piece of medicated bandage into the hole that the vermin had made in her scalp with a pair of scissors. Though her bandages were changed every third day, even then it took a month for the wound to heal fully. When she had recovered fully, Ma made an offering of roasted grain and jaggery at the dargah of Shah Roshan Wali, fulfilling the vow she had earlier taken.

During the monsoons and the winters, we slept in the corridor. My brother and I studied in the light of a diya placed in an alcove in the wall between the small room at the back and the hall, and slept on a single cot. Once, a few days after Diwali, my elder brother was still studying, when he began nudging and pushing me. But he uttered no sound and not a word passed his lips. I looked at him and then again went off to sleep. Unable to arouse me, he gave me a light slap and told me in low tone, 'A snake has come through the skylight.'

We were both badly frightened, but did not dare to get off the cot. The jet-black snake had wound its tail around the nail in the wall, on which hung a calendar. It sprang with its hood fanned out, and then slowly slid down on to the floor. We clung to each other in sheer fright. It glided into the small storeroom. It was then that we woke up Bhaia.

Hearing voices from our home, the neighbours also got up. My uncle's son came in and removed everything from the store and put it in the courtyard. They looked for the snake everywhere—whacked the beams of the roof with sticks, poked into the reeds of the roof to see if it had slunk into some crevice of hole. But it had vanished and could not be found!

Someone commented, 'It seems that the boys were mistaken.'

'They are not so young, and the diya was still burning!' Another remarked.

Another said, 'The whole earth is theirs! It protects them. Even then, sprinkle some ash at the threshold and burn some incense ... we will know in the morning, when we see a line in the ashes.'

Bhaia spread out the ashes and then said, 'There are many trees and shrubs around the gurudwara. Until the plants and the wild shrubs are cleared, these things will happen. Why don't they realize that?'

There was a thick growth of thorny plants and trees around the gurudwara. This was a very convenient hiding place for all sorts of creatures such as rabbits, hares, snakes, and the like. Sansis from Rajpur, at about a distance of 6 km would bring their dogs to hunt these small creatures. Armed with sticks and hoes, they would incite their dogs, making frightening noises to drive them out from their hiding places in the thick undergrowth. In no time, one of them would have bullied a hare or rabbit out.

The next morning there was no line on the ash sprinkled on the ground. Out of fear, I did not enter that room for many days. If I had to fetch something, I went in with a trembling heart. Things however became normal after a few days. Ma had recovered and would be up and about early in the morning as was her habit. As she churned the milk she would sing,

*Listen, O my mother,*
*Why did you send*
*Your daughters far away?*
*Listen to me, my mother.*

# 8

## Brahma's Games

'I shall thrash him! The good for nothing ...' Bhaia shouted in a high-pitched voice, stepping into the courtyard. The harshness of his voice and the fury in his eyes and on his face were frightening. 'When they thrash you, you dirty wretch, you will cry for your mother!'

I had no idea what had I done to invite his wrath. But I was dead scared, and all life seemed to drain out of me. I looked at my mother lying on a cot. She had just had her third daughter. Three babies in quick succession had left her very weak. Her frail body was covered by a sheet, and a dupatta was tied around her head. Raising herself on her thin arms she looked at us.

Her pale face turned paler at Bhaia's harsh words. There were dark circles around her sunken eyes, which upset me. I ran up to her and stood near her cot, my face crumpling.

'He's going to get us all killed one of these days, the bastard! Does he ever think of anything else except mischief?' Bhaia declared advancing on me menacingly.

Ma intervened, 'Why are you speaking riddles? Why don't you tell us plainly what had happened? Why are you so angry?'

'You are the one who has spoilt him—the fool!'

'The same thing again! You go on abusing him, but don't tell us what the matter is!' Ma reminded him, as she sat up, holding me close to her chest.

'When no one is looking, he pisses into the well of the Haiknos!'

My mother was clearly shaken by what Bhaia had told her. She looked at me with stricken eyes.

'They will throw him into the same well, if they ever find out! He thinks he's a distinguished landlord at this age! He who can't even clean his behind!'

'They are neighbours! Why do you do such things?' Ma scolded me. 'The world worships Khwaja Khijir as a pir ... and you,' she looked at me reproachfully and then turned to Bhaia.

'He says that the Jats don't let us use the well! He's great one to rebel! Why do you want to go to another's well when we have our own? Are you a nambardar!' Bhaia shouted, twisting my arms. My tears splashed like rainfall.

Getting up, Ma took me out of Bhaia's grip. 'Can't he understand without a beating? Why don't you realize that their bones are delicate, and if his arm were to break, then you would be the one running from one village to another!'

'Let me teach him a lesson and teach him how to ...' Bhaia was breathless with anger. Taking a deep breath, he continued, 'As if we are not aware of these things!'

He gave me a couple of tight slaps. I wiped my face with my sleeve and threw a fleeting glance towards the courtyard. My two sisters stood in a corner, scared and weeping. The younger, her nose running, was sobbing softly.

'Do you want to tell the whole village? Thank god that so far no one knows it,' Ma reminded my father.

Turning to me she admonished me, 'Don't you dare do any such thing again. Khwaja Pir would be angry ...'

Saying this she crossed the courtyard and tried to quieten my sisters. She wiped the younger one's eyes with the edge of her dupatta and caressed her. I scattered my tears with the back of my hand.

A little later, there were no signs of further beating, and I was relieved. I was also happy that he had not discovered many of my other misdeeds. I do not know what came over me, and I told him myself, 'I was not the only one to piss. All the boys of our area piss in the well, while we play hide and seek around that place.'

'Damn you, you bad seed ... you will be responsible for our deaths!'
Bhaia's right hand was raised to strike me, when Ma caught hold of his
arm.

My Daadi had come in from outside where she had been sitting
under the banyan tree, for a drink of water.

'What's this racket about?' She asked, 'What's troubling you?'

When she was told of what had happened, she said, 'The whole
Chamarli reports to the Jats all details of who had pissed, or worse when
and where. It's our own people who carry tales to them. If they were
to hear even a whisper of all this, there is bound to be a big fight!' She
stared angrily at me and went on, 'Now he stands humbly, the cunning
one, as if he has no tongue in his mouth!'

'I've learned that this wise Aflatoon has composed doggerels about
many in this village!' Bhaia asked angrily, 'Tell who have you written
about? Quick! Or you will taste the force of my hand again!'

I recited the lines like a lesson,

*Dhanni the goldsmith's wife*
*Ram Pyari*
*Natha Singh the barber*
*Labh Singh Bhai*
*Inder Singh belongs to Gangi.*
*Labh Singh is the widow's.*
*Mala Mala Mala*
*Golden bells around your ankles.*

Once again Bhaia lifted his hand, and my recitation stopped midway,
the way one forgets a lesson learnt by rote. After a brief silence, without
anyone prompting me I said, 'I didn't make up these lines. I heard them
from others ...'

'Then which ones have you composed?'

'Those are about other ...'

'Well done, you bastard ... you are really brilliant and will make a
mark in life ...' Bhaia said sarcastically. He appeared to be getting over
his anger.

'Let it be ... you have given him enough advice,' Ma said as she went
back to her cot taking short steps, as if she had no strength left in her
body.

Bhaia busied himself filling his chillum. But our attention was drawn to the new-born who was crying, flailing her small arms and legs in the air. I was surprised that she could shed tears.

Ma's frail body and pale face had moved me. I thought of her as she had been few days earlier, her stomach bloated. She walked wearily and her eyes looked tired. She had been eating mud from the side of the chulha and Bhaia had scolded her.

I was surprised that this thin, dark man of medium height and ordinary looks had so much power over my mother. At times, he had even beaten her, but she had neither protested against his taunts and jibes, nor was she proud of her beauty and height. As I thought over these things an idea came to me, and I walked over to her cot and said, 'I have seen a picture of man a woman and two children on the outside wall at Ratta's home.'

'So? Say what you want to say?' Ma had been nursing the baby and now she put her against her shoulder to burp her.

'It is written underneath that only two or three children are good in a home.'

As I uttered this, my mother put her hand on my head. For some unknown reason her eyes brimmed. Wiping her eyes with the corner of her dupatta she looked pensively at my youngest sister. He eyes were wide open, but did not shine.

My older brother had come home from school. Furtively, I went out to sit beside Bhaia and Daadi under the banyan tree so that my brother should not know of the beating I had been given.

I saw Gharib Das, the blind sadhu, asking the people gathered under the tree, 'Tell me what should I talk about today? I'll explain whatever you want me to, at night.'

I was thinking of some of the parables he had delivered earlier and how the people had heard him with rapt attention. As he talked he played on the string of his tumba with his left hand and the cymbals with his right hand. In between, he would take long pulls at the hookah. I was impatient for him to go on.

A large crowd had gathered under the banyan tree after the evening meal and Gharib Das said. 'So, good people, you wanted me to narrate the parable of Brahma ji. Now listen!'

Tightening the chord of his tumba, he touched it with his fingernail and sent a wave of music into the air.

'It is said in the Puranas that the universe was created by Brahmaji. He also created man. According to Manu, Brahmaji created the four castes from his own body, the Brahmans, the Kshatriyas, the Vaishyas, and the Sudras.'

With this statement, Gharib Das reached for the hookah pipe. His short and straggly grey beard seemed like a beehive stuck on his protruding chin.

Suddenly, I recalled what I had often heard the peasants say, 'I swear by god and tell no lies, a she-goat gave birth to a camel.'

Many thoughts overwhelmed me. I saw my mother's bloated belly during her pregnancies, and also that of Brahmaji.

The image of my mother suckling my sister flickered before my mind's eye. The chain of thoughts appeared interminable, and also mysterious, like a parable of the blind sadhu. How could Brahmaji give birth to four at once? Who would have assisted him at their birth and helped him clean up, the way Gango the midwife did in the village? How would he have suckled four babies at his breasts? And did his body swell like my mother's, and how had he walked about?

Then, suddenly, my thoughts turned to my various aunts who had babies every other year, but even they had never given birth to four babies at one time.

I thought over this for a long time but could not recollect any man having given birth to a baby. So my thoughts ran when a handsome, middle-aged man with a tight turban and in a new set of kurta pajama, stood up and asked, 'Sir, did Brahmaji not have a wife?'

'He had and her name … yes, yes, I now recollect … her name was Savitri*,' the blind sadhu answered after thinking over the question for a few moments.

'Any son or daughter?'

'Brother, as far as I know, she did not have any children; it is said that it was Brahmaji who gave birth.'

There was a flutter of laughter which gathered volume. The atmosphere changed into one of discussion.

---

* Brahma's wife is Saraswati. Here, the Sadhu appear to have forgotten.

'This mean that he was either impotent or a eunuch.'

'Eunuchs or impotent men can neither create babies nor have them.' Another young man in a shirt and trousers declared.

'We have never heard of a man giving birth,' another asserted.

'Brother, this much I know that Brahmaji had sexual intercourse with his daughter to create the universe. This is written in the sacred granths.'

'This is sheer blasphemy—who can do such a thing with his daughter! No one can believe this!' Bhaia, who was sitting by me, said in low tone.

'Sir,' the man with a tight turban spoke up again, 'is there any temple dedicated to Brahmaji?'

'No, there is no temple,' the blind sadhu spoke hesitantly and in such a low tone that it seemed as if his voice was coming from the loose cord of his tumba.

'Why are you heckling him? Let the narration continue. If you don't like it, why don't you go home,' Massa scolded. After scratching his head under his turban, he went on, 'Just because you've read four books, looks like you've sprouted wings! How do you know the mysteries of the universe?'

'Then you explain to us how Brahma could have given birth through his mouth, arms, stomach, and feet? How can anyone enjoy his own body? And how would he have menstruated like a woman? You tell us—has a man ever delivered a baby? It's all a lie, an illusion, to fool the people!'

There was a brief pause. 'The Russians went beyond the gravity of the earth, ten years ago, and now America is also getting ready to plant its flag on the moon! But, here, our people are yet to come out of this superstition, this myth of falsehood and oppression, about how the Universe was created!' I was overjoyed to hear the middle-aged man's views so passionately expressed.

Massa again interrupted irritably, 'Next you will ask how Ravi Das got the stone to float! The next day you will want to know how Dhanna saw god in a stone! One can find salvation only by traversing this unique path of renunciation, why else would people abandon their homes and retreat into the forests? ... You were born yesterday and today you are advising all of us!'

In the dim light of the lantern I saw that the faces of the people reflected their agreement with the arguments advanced by both sides, and that they were unimpressed by the the news of man in space.

'We cannot listen to this *kanjar khap*,' said the man with the tight turban as he rose and walked away with his companion.

These two were the guests of the Comrades in our village. No one said anything to them, neither good nor bad, as they walked away in annoyance.

I thought of Kabir Sahib's shloka in my textbook,

> *Pahan pujan Hari mile to main*
> *pujan paharag,*
> *Yan te woh chakki bhali*
> *pees khai sansarg*

(If, by worshipping a stone, you hope to attain god/then I will worship mountains/The grinding stone serves the whole world/It grinds so that the whole world may eat)

'They have spoilt the show—it was such an interesting parable!' Massa remarked in his nasal tone to draw attention to himself, as was his habit. There was a note of triumph in his voice, but the crowd was not interested in his views.

There were muttered discussions. Bhaia was impatient to leave seeing the endless discussions. I followed him as he got up. My uncle's son, Mangi said, 'The boys' arguments were really impressive. They didn't let the blind man win!'

'Having heard those boys' arguments, I feel that we are all blind, and accept whatever anyone tells us.' Bhaia remarked with the air of one who had experienced some divine guidance. 'Mangi, it is reasonable to say that if there is God, then he must have had parents. Is there a human being who does not have parents or a tree without a seed!' Bhaia continued to talk as he walked up to our door. Fixing a bidi between his lips, he tried to light it with a match shielding it with his hands. He inhaled, then blew out, and looking at the match, said, 'It is all imagination, all speculation. Who has seen the creation of the Universe? No one even pays any attention to nature how it works for us day and night, the way we workers and artisans labour. Trees and men grow and flourish. New leaves replace the leaves that fall off—the ways of nature are strange and mysterious.'

The issues that these two men had raised set off a chain of doubts and queries in my mind. As I lay on my cot in the courtyard, the words of these strangers shone like the light emitted by glow-worms in the dark, flickering, yet bright.

The meeting and what Bhaia had said gave me a new direction. I felt rejuvenated. I could see the lantern which had illuminated the meeting place. It seemed as if I had broken free of a trap laid by these tales of Brahma, the way the man in space had vanquished the earth's gravity.

# 9

## Hunger Knows No Caste

The clouds and mist seemed to be competing to shut out the sun. It was almost noon, yet they showed no signs of either lifting or dwindling. A bitterly cold wind was blowing which left many of the children shivering. The sudden clang of the bell startled us. We all wondered why, and there were many opinions. I thought that Mohan Lal must have brought some important news for us in his postbag.

All the five classes sat in neat rows, the way we did for the prayer meeting in the morning. The headmaster, Chet Ram Sharma, addressed us, 'I have some very sad news. Yesterday, on 10 January 1966, Shri Lal Bahadur Shastri, the Prime Minister, passed away, shortly after he signed the Indo-Pak Tashkent Pact.'

The news deepened the gloom of the misty noon. Both students and teachers stood as if turned to stone.

'As you all are aware, Shastriji came from a very poor family. He lost his father when he was just a year old. He had to swim the Ganga to study in Varanasi, because he was too poor to afford the ferry charges. A serious and hard-working student, he joined the Freedom Movement at a very young age. He had an abiding faith in *ahimsa* and believed in simplicity. He headed various ministries. Shastriji will always be remembered for his achievements and abilities. I will now raise the slogan that he gave us. All of you repeat it after me, "Jai Jawan, Jai Kisan"—Long live Shri Lal Bahadur Shastri!'

All of us, students, men and women teachers, repeated the slogan after him, our right arms upraised. The headmaster continued, 'We shall observe silence for two minutes.'

All of us stood silently with bowed heads. It seemed as if a deep silence had descended on everything. Master Ram Kishan took charge, and said, 'Stand at ease!' The headmaster announced a two-day mourning period for the late prime minister.

The school emptied within minutes. As if released from a prison, the students picked up their bags and wooden slates and raced home. Exactly the same thing had happened when the first prime minister, Jawahar Lal Nehru had died.

I, however, walked home all alone. I was upset and bewildered at Shastriji having no money to pay the ferry. It seemed to me that the taunts my class fellows flung at me all the time about my caste were of no significance. Shastri had not been a Brahmin either. How did it matter if I didn't have an extra set of clothes? I had my Bhaia and Ma. Shastri had lost his father! If he could rise to become the prime minister of the country by sheer hard work and determination, I too would be able to achieve many things if I studied hard. But as I crossed our threshold, the chain of thoughts halted. My bua, Karmi, who was visiting us for a few days, was seated in the courtyard and crying. From her reddened eyes it was clear that she had been weeping for a long time. Both my mother and Daadi stood by her. Bua wiped her tears with her dupatta and said, 'Such a day should never befall even an enemy. Sons being killed before mothers; cutting off the breasts of young women! Many killed their women and threw them into the wells—and many were poisoned by their own families.'

Aunt again wiped her tears as they rolled down her cheeks and went on, 'Many of those travelling with us died on the way. ... When I think of the heaps of dead bodies at night, I can't sleep. I still cannot understand how people who had lived together could turn against each other! Had Pakistan not been created, people would not have had to face such atrocities!'

My mother had joined my aunt and was weeping loudly, and I too joined them. I felt that Bua was still suffering from the deep wounds that the Partition of the country had inflicted on her. Whenever she talked of those days, she was overwhelmed by dark memories.

My mother took me in her arms and consoled my aunt, 'Bibi, no one could prevent what happened at that time. It was destiny and it had to happen.'

Daadi had been sitting in silence watching all this. Now, she broke her silence and said, 'Whenever you come, you begin your tale of woe! You should be grateful that your whole family is safe and sound!'

'I cry because the country was divided. But now that it has happened, the two countries should live happily and let each other live. But they want their revenge! Who knows how many mothers would have lost their sons in this war. I was praying right through the war that nothing should happen to my brother and nephew (my father's elder brother, Diwan Chand, and the son of another uncle, Mohan Lal). Thank god, the War[1] is now over.' Bua was still weeping, and her voice, thick with emotion, affected me deeply.

At that moment, Bhaia walked in. He carried a sack of flour, from the ration shop in Bhogpur, which he put down on the floor.

He drank a tumbler of lassi at a draught and handed the empty tumbler to Ma, and remarked, 'The world is going to die, cutting each other's throats! Some died in the riots during the Partition, some of the plague, and some in this war. The rest are dying of this famine. The wells have dried up. Where will the grain come from?'

Bhaia glanced around at all of us and went on, 'People in the town who get to read the newspapers, say that the conditions today are as bad as they were during the 1943 Bengal famine. At that time, whole families were wiped out. People sold their children for ten kilos of flour, and sent their daughters into prostitution. Women were compelled to leave home, and many worked as prostitutes in the cities. Some had come to the Punjab also. That is how Balbir the lame (his family lived behind ours), brought his new Bangalin. ...'

I did not hear what Bhaia said next. An image fluttered in the mirror of my mind—of Bhai Rani, leaning over the balcony of Aunt Aato and talking to her as she stood in courtyard below. 'Bhai Rani' was a tall dark, well-built young woman, always well-dressed and made-up. When she spoke in her Hindi-accented Punjabi, or laughed and talked,

---

1. The Indo-Pak War, 1965.

her white teeth gleamed from behind her red lips like pearls. But this image disappeared when two voices, one male and the other female, were heard outside the front door.

My mother, Bua, and Daadi all looked apprehensive as if afraid that something untoward would happen. A deep silence descended on all those present, and anyone outside would have thought the house was empty. Bua sat with her chin on her left knee and her head on her arm, as if turned to stone.

I went up to the front door, and heard some voices again. Looking out I saw a young man, with a printed turban, tied rather loosely. He wore a white kurta and a dhoti. His wife wore a multi-coloured sari with a woollen shawl wrapped around her. She was beautiful and had a rosy complexion. She wore a silver *tagri* around her waist, thick silver bangles and anklets, and rings on her fingers. She wore yellow jootis and presented a pretty picture. The two of them carried a child each.

My mother came up to the door. The two begged her, 'Bibi just two rotis or some flour—two handfuls of flour! We all are hungry, even these two children. There is a drought and crops have failed. We are not beggars, but just two rotis ...'

Pity welled up in our hearts for this couple. The younger child peeped at us from the safety of his mother's arms, and then rested his head on her shoulder again.

When Bhaia saw Ma and me at the front door, he again started on what he had been saying earlier, 'Look, now hunger has driven these strong and honourable people, who call themselves Rajputs, to beg! They know about our bastis! They never permit us to sit near them. When we go to Ganganagar during the harvest season, and ask for a drink of water, the first thing they do is ask what caste we are! And now they are begging at our door! Someone should now ask them where their honour and arrogance have disappeared! Where has that show of power gone? It is said that a man in trouble will accept even his mother's lover as his father.'

He drew on his hookah, 'No one has the time to listen to our plea that this caste system was not ordained by god, but has been made by man for his own selfish motives.'

The whole family listened to what Bhaia was saying, but none of us agreed with his views. My mother sat down to suckle my infant sister, and said, 'The crux of the matter is that no one can fight fate. Famine has reduced many to penury.'

Bua nodded in agreement. Daadi shoved her feet into her jootis and picked up her stick.

'She is worried about others, but not about us. We go hungry every day. Yet there is neither pity nor sympathy for our children crying of hunger. No one gives us any grain even when they can settle the account later. Does one ever forget a kindness one had received in time of distress? They all say it is the will of god ... Saala ... this God is a complete fraud! If he does exist, then why doesn't he heed our prayers? We are better off without the help of this oppressor!' Bhaia stated his judgement clearly and passionately.

Ma suddenly seemed to recollect something. She beckoned me to her side. As I went up to her, she looked at the bucket and said, 'Go get some impure juice from the Mantris—his ranting is not going to stop.'

The bucket was full to the brim and when I tried to shift it to the other hand, some drops of hot juice fell on my right foot on which I already had some blisters! I was deeply dejected, my heart was full of sorrow, and a sense of shame gripped me. This became acute when my Jat classmates passed snide remarks or said sarcastically, 'You are dark and dirty because you drink this dirty juice! Here is a caste which drinks the dregs of juice, but is still full of pride and arrogance and rampages like a bull ... This year you must have had plenty of meat to eat ... so many calves died during these dry winters ... isn't is so, Gudd?'

I was peeved. My heart seemed to shrivel the way tender plants do at the onslaught of severe winter. I wanted to throw a stone or a brick at the one who had said this and tell him, 'We are compelled to drink this. How are you troubled by our hunger? You overeat and indulge yourself and are bursting out of your clothes! But our bellies are sticking to our backs!'

These thoughts jostled about in my mind, rotating like the buckets of the Persian wheel in school. I felt that I didn't have to bear the caustic remarks of my classmates about my caste for long. I would be going to the Gignowal School and no one would pass sarcastic remarks at our drinking any dirty juice or eating the flesh of dead animals there, and no one would see me collecting dry twigs and grass for kindling the fire at home.

I thought about the bitter truths in Lal Bahadur Shastri's life, and my dejection was dispelled and courage restored. I also remembered what Bhaia had said, 'Trouble or hunger do not ask your caste. We lead this life of indignity because of deprivation and poverty. I want our children to live in dignity and comfort. They should be able to buy a plot of land, or get it after a struggle from the government.'

I was eager to live up to these expectations. It seemed as if slowly but surely, my path was being illuminated and I was encouraged and emboldened to reach for the skies.

# 10

## A Matter of Community

'It is heartening to see that Gudd has become a good worker, Chacha! He has been working in the villages around here—Chamiari, Rastgo, Sikanderpur, Dhaddia, and Sohalpur. Last year he worked for the Babas in our village, transplanting paddy and also mastered the skills of planting and hoeing sugarcane and maize ... and I must say that though he's lean, he is both fit and strong!' This was my uncle's son, Mangi, talking to Bhaia. He smiled when he saw me, with my tumbler tied in the corner of an angocha, flung over my shoulder.

I smiled faintly at him and went into the courtyard. I ached all over and my neck and waist were stiff; while transplanting paddy saplings, I had broken a toenail which was now infected and painful. My feet were numb from standing in the water for long hours and the skin between the toes felt itchy.

The school vacations had come with a load of trouble for me. Troubles do come at a strange time! A blistering sun over one's head and feet immersed in warm water the whole day long!

Many of my classmates were away visiting their uncles and aunts! But here was I waging a continuous battle against deprivation and poverty! The thoughts brought tears to my eyes.

I thought of the time when I was transplanting paddy in the lower fields of the Baria family. Images of dry turds, stinking cow dung, twigs, grass, and thorny bushes of berries swimming in the water, and my own body twisted and bent like a question mark, flashed before my eyes.

Anger and pain filled my heart. I wanted to fling myself on the cot and drift into sleep.

'... In a couple of years, Gudd would be joining us, Chacha,' Mangi asserted.

This remark of his was a bolt from the blue for me. In my mind, I saw my life stretching ahead like the high bleak peaks of the Shivalik Hills and the Himalaya. I wanted to break Mangi's head and Bhaia's also, who was listening to this depressing chatter. I thought of my Bua's son who was a government officer in Delhi ... and also of my mother's brother who was a district collector ... should I remain uneducated? Should I continue to do what the rest of my community was doing? Should I work and slave for others so that they could live in luxury?

No!

Bhaia either did not hear Mangi's comment or simply ignored them. Getting up to refill his chillum with some live coals, he said, 'I tell him that he should save some money and buy either his school uniform or a new set of kurta pajama for himself.'

'You said the same thing last year also, but later you spent the money on two cartloads of mud for the roof,' I reminded him.

'I had to pay off that man, and he had come innumerable times.'

'And this time?'

'Get up! I will give it to you in writing!' Bhaia got up from near the chulha and came towards me. I ran out to hide behind the banyan tree.

A loud and powerful voice could be heard in the lane on the western side of the village. The speaker was unseen as he was hidden behind the haveli of the Haikans. The voice was, however, drawing nearer.

'Brothers and sisters ... world peace is the need of the hour!'

'Here comes Comrade Ram Kishan of Bhundian. He has a barber's shop at Bhogpur,' this was Phumman who was sitting with Daadi.

Comrade Ram Kishan was leading his bicycle with his right hand, holding a bullhorn in his left. He went on, 'We can fight poverty, only when there is peace in the world. We can put pressure on the government to enforce land reforms, to fix and raise wages, and ensure that these laws are strictly enforced. We can also agitate for increasing fertilizer and grain subsidies.'

He stopped, and then fixing the cycle on its stand, wiped the perspiration on his forehead with the back of his right hand. Then he began again, 'Friends, there is greater possibility of development when white flags fly on your frontiers. I want to tell you that with the amount spent on one tank or a warship or a missile, we can build many schools, hospitals, and run various welfare schemes. We are planning to organize a world peace rally soon ... you all must join it in large numbers. The day and the date ...'

'Inquilab Zindabad! Inquilab Zindabad!' Phumman shouted, raising his right hand.

A group of youngsters and grown-ups had formed a semicircle around the comrade by now. They were clearly strongly influenced by his enthusiastic speech! The young men puffed out their chests, tensed their bodies, tightened their muscles, and clenched their fists.

'The eastern wind seems to be blowing strongly,' someone remarked. 'It must have rained somewhere! If winds from across the Hindukush blow this side, things would change dramatically! The trees would be laden with blossoms!'

Another said, 'Will the war stop merely because we say so?'

'America is at the bottom of all trouble! It always urges Pakistan and sells arms to it,' Comrade Ajaib Singh informed the audience. 'As long as Russia is with us no one dare harm us! If there is another pact with Russia, it would mean real progress and development for us!'

'Our conditions will improve only when corruption is either eradicated or at least brought under control,' my uncle Rama expressed his opinion.

'This is all idle talk! Who is going to ask us if they want to start a war?' Mangi said.

'It is a matter of creating enough pressure! One must create public opinion against war,' Comrade Meeta added.

'What the comrade from Bhundian says is right and true ... whatever anyone else may say, we must discuss things with him at length,' Bhaia declared loudly for others to hear.

By now, the slim and energetic comrade, whose moustache was dark and striking, had mounted his bicycle and set off. My eyes followed him as long as he could be seen.

Women had drifted homewards. The wage earners went back to the fields. Dhyan called out, 'Gudd, come now ...'

Knotting my tumbler in the corner of the angocha, I carried, I flung it over my shoulder and went off towards the nambardar's fields to plant paddy saplings. My limbs were stiff, my dark complexion had turned darker because of the hot sun, and my skin was as coarse a buffalo's hide. I would see the young sons of landowners strutting on the edges of the fields, scolding the labourers, showing no respect for their age, and be upset that our men did not even protest! It occurred to me that if I was unable to complete my education, I would have to face and bear all this all my life! This thought troubled me, and it seemed to me that some weevil was eating into my vitals. But simultaneously, and strangely, I felt like a log of the sheesham tree and believed that no woodworm could harm me.

'Ooh …!' The intense pain in my toe made me groan. I had again hurt my already infected toe and waves of pain swept over me.

'Why don't you look where you go? You were looking elsewhere as you walked!' Dhyan admonished me. Looking first at my face and then at my foot, he advised, 'Urinate on the wound, it will heal in no time!'

I immediately followed his advice. Then we hurried to the field we were working in.

One day it occurred to me that though the seasons changed rapidly, our days would never change. But at the height of winter, hopes ran high, and I felt happy.

'The people who are campaigning for the elections, know no rest,' my uncle Mehnga commented as he saw a tempo, overloaded with people approaching. A voice sang out,

*O the tricolour*
*No one is going to vote for you!*
*O the tricolour!*

This was Phumman giving voice to a deep and intense anguish. He had a *toombi* in his hand and played on it as he sang. He made short speeches and shouted slogans enthusiastically in praise of Shaheed Bhagat Singh, Rajguru, Sukhdeo, and other martyrs who had made the supreme sacrifice for the motherland, and interspersed all this with shouts of 'Inquilab Zindabad!'

'He will win.' This was Rai.

'Comrade Kulwant will win!' This was the crowd.

'Where will you put the mark?'

'On the hammer and sickle!' The crowd shouted.

I had accompanied Phumman a few times, riding the tempo to the neighbouring villages. Many a time shouts of 'Stop the tempo, stop', would be heard and it would come to a halt, to unload all the children who had climbed on it for a free ride.

We would often reach home late, tired, and spent. Bhaia would come rushing to me like a raging bull and say, 'You have to sit for your eighth class next month (March 1969) and you do not even touch your books! You read foreign books that you get from the library! How will you help us, if you turn philosopher yourself! And now you go after the comrades—as if they will give us any lands! ... Kulwant has three hundred acres of arable land, why doesn't *he* give a couple of acres to the landless? Or if not that, he should at least transfer his property to some of his servants!'

'The Party asks what difference would it make if one zamindar were to give his lands to the poor. Our purpose is to work for land reforms in the whole country. They say that only a revolution can establish equality in society!' I repeated what I had heard from the comrades.

'They talk glibly, but when it comes to implementation, let alone giving lands to the poor, they are no better than the Jats even in their attitude. They are as high-handed as the Jats, while they spout very high principles!'

'I had overheard them saying that as long as Kulwant is working for the Party, it is good propaganda for the Party ... the Party has no money ...'

'Landlords and capitalists seek power wherever they can get it! Though there is none like Kulwant in the whole area, what can one do about people who are adept at making mountains out of molehills, and are bent on establishing that there is no one is more honest and truthful then them!'

I can't remember when Bhaia stopped talking, as I drifted into deep sleep.

*Your acts will decide*
*your fate;*
*No one will ask you*
*your caste!*
*Three and a half yards*
*Are all you need*
*Though you may own*
*Large estates!*
*You can find god*
*in poverty*
*Yet the world is full*
*Of arrogance.*

The folk song being sung in the lane by a travelling sadhu, in a voice filled with pathos, woke me one morning. Immediately, I stuck out my head from under the *jhool*.

Jhool? Yes, jhool!

This jhool, which we brothers had been using as a quilt for the last three winters, had been found by Bhaia on the road side one evening, as he was coming home from the sugar mill at Bhogpur where he was working on daily wages those days. It looked new and perhaps some zamindar had got it made for his much loved animal as protection from the severe cold of the winters. He must have been carrying it home and it must have fallen off his cart, which was a common occurrence when the carts were overloaded.

When I saw it for the first time, for a moment I had a feeling of having turned into a calf, wrapped in this jhool, who would then either be put to a cart or a plough, exposed to the harsh cold of winter or the sweltering heat of the summer sun.

The sadhu was still singing in the lane. I got up with a start. I must have dozed off. But as my elder brother got out of the bed, his nudge woke me, bringing my dreams to an end. The sadhu's words could still be heard outside,

*No one will ask your caste*
*O man be not proud*

*It was he who made*
*Namdev's shed,*
*Dhanna's cows He tended.*
*O, innocent one, think*
*O innocent soul, think*
*Only of Him.*
*He alone will help you in*
*Your distress.*

I had often heard such folk-songs. But the sweet melodious voice of this sadhu moved me deeply and I was overwhelmed. I went out and opened the front door to stand at the threshold, and looked up and down the path. The sadhu was coming towards me, out of the mist; his soothing voice sending out waves of warmth. As he came he raised his right hand in the manner of blessing me. This made me happy.

I noticed that he had fastened a length of cloth to the handles of his harmonium which he slung across his shoulder and neck. He was dressed in saffron. At that very moment, Kalu, the Haikanas' dog, arrived on the scene on a run and began barking loudly. The sadhu ignored him and went into the Jats' lane, singing to the music of his harmonium. Thoughts jostled in my mind, faster than the blood pounding in my veins. Perhaps God was not aware of the bleakness and deprivation of the lives that Bhaia, Ma, and their ancestors had endured for centuries, or He would have helped us in our hour of distress, the way He had come to the rescue of Dhanna. If God can be found in poverty alone, then He should have at least made some effort to meet us and ask about us. We have been living in terrible conditions for centuries, as the sadhu had described in his song. There were enough reasons for Him to come to our rescue.

I thought of what Comrade Malkit Chand Mehali had said while speaking at a village meeting a few days before, 'The idea of paradise in the life hereafter is a deliberate attempt on the part of man to delude man. This idle group curses the hard-working society in which it lives. It exhorts all to renounce love for possessions, affection, wealth, but is itself steeped in it. … This is arrogance, a fraud. There is only one way of getting rid of your poverty and that is through revolution and by establishing a cooperative society. The revolution is round the corner and it is imperative that you all unite!' He had then shouted, 'Kisan mazdoor unity, zindabad, Inquilab Zindabad' (Unite and be strong, O farmers! Long live the Revolution!).

The veins on his neck were taut as if filled with air. His dark face grew darker, and his eyes turned red. He looked different. Every time he raised his right arm and bent forward, he seemed like a mechanical toy, wound up to perform his acts in a precise manner.

It was evident that this enthusiastic and emotional speech had profoundly affected the listening crowd in the open courtyard of the school. I was surprised to see that this dark-skinned, pock-marked, ordinary looking man of average height, was such an effective and impressive speaker. He was also absolutely fearless.

These images that flashed in my mind left me agitated. The sadhu's voice still lingered in the air. I turned and went in again and got under my jhool.

'Don't the Jat zamindars hear this? We only need three and a half yards—the large estates are all yours! Had they heeded it, then surely they would have been concerned about us, and not despise and abuse us, who are helpless, not treat us like serfs, and give us land because we have been serving them for centuries!' Bhaia raved, getting up from his cot. He wanted all of us to hear him. After a few moments, as if recollecting something, he said again, 'How can reciting God's name help us, or for that matter how will destiny help us? We work hard the whole day long, do a lot of good, but has anything good happened to us? If someone were to ask me, then I would say one should believe in one's own self and be independent.'

Bhaia heard the two of us whispering under the jhool and called out, 'Birju, you are a great help to me, but this good-for-nothing does not help me one bit. The only thing he knows how to do well is eating!'

I thought of what my life had become. Walking a distance of 4–5 km to the middle school in Geeganwal, and on my return, I would often carry two bundles of fodder for the animals, and sometimes a load of millet or barley. I would also help Bhaia and my elder brother scrape the sugarcane, and also fetch twenty kilos of flour from the flour mill. What more could I do?

I tried to think of various things that I could do, so that Bhaia would shut up and not keep lashing out at me or hitting me.

The winter appeared to have become very long, like the unending speech of a comrade! It had gripped me in its harsh clutches! Barefoot, with only one set of the blue-coloured cotton kurta and pajama to protect my body from severe cold winds which cut through me. Going to school was painful for I was always apprehensive of what master Kishan Chand might say. ... After prayers he would often call out, 'All those not in uniform—stand up!'

About a dozen of us, boys and girls, would stand up. I would be on the verge of tears, my long, thin neck bent with shame. I wanted to sink into the earth! But then I would thank heaven that I had reached school, though shivering, and had not fallen down anywhere on the roadside, the way a calf of the Burhas had, because of the harsh cold. When I thought of his carcass on the ground, its left eye still open, it sent shivers up my spine.

'Those who have only one set of clothes will continue to stand, the rest, sit down.' Master Kishan Chand was a man of medium height and advancing years. Fair complexioned, he had a grey moustache, wore a turban, and was dressed in kurta-pajama.

My thoughts floated like wisps of mist, coming together in patches of clouds—my low caste, the desperation of extreme poverty—all this may not have been known in my new school. But, within a few days, it had become common knowledge because of this almost daily occurrence concerning the uniform. A storm of anguish raged in my mind, and my self-esteem was shaken to its very roots. I tried to console myself that when everyone in this school knew everything about each other, even the teachers, would these personal details be news! This realization helped me overcome my depression. My courage restored, I felt better.

Winter changed into warm sunshine. The trees took on an autumnal hue. The leafless trees looked as if they were my close relatives, the toiling people of my community, their bodies naked and exposed to the extremes of both winter and summer. These trees shared their shade with all who sought it, even under difficult conditions, and provided shelter from the rains. When their canopies grow and spread out, their branches are trimmed. In my mind these trees, so brutally chopped, seemed to turn into my father, his elder brother, and his sons.

It could soon be winter again. A frightening thought. The Communists of the village were busy with their political manipulations. They wanted to make a sugar mill at Bhogpur the focal point of all their activities in the area. The slogans about kisan-mazdoor unity (Peasant Power) were becoming louder. The result was that more people courted arrest under the leadership of the newly elected MLA, Comrade Kulwant Singh.

I wanted to be as knowledgeable as the comrades. I also wanted to be able to speak as impressively and passionately as the comrades did when I grew up. When I heard people talk about social equality, and the rapid development in the USSR, I was filled with a warm feeling of a bright future.

... People talked about arrests that were taking place in connection with the sugar mill. The Jats would pointedly remark to my father and others, 'Ishar, Daulati, and Munsha Singh have no sugarcane, then why are they in prison, trying to get higher price for cane, and want twenty-four hours power supply? They seem to have been incited by the comrades!'

'We people are supporting you today ... tomorrow your people will be with us! Isn't it so? What do you say?' Bhaia asked Watan Singh, as we finished the work for the day and set off home.

Watan Singh, laughed slightly as he pressed his long white beard, which looked good on his handsome imposing face, but did not say anything. Then, he wiped his jootis with a piece of cloth which he carried and turned to *bumbi*, the tubewell. My uncle's sons, Mangi and Sohanu, looked at him silently.

Bhaia looked at Watan Singh's receding back and then remarked, 'These people are ungrateful! They have no consideration for anyone's feelings. Our people are in prison, losing daily wages for their sake, and yet they cannot resist taunting us! That is why they say that Jats have no sense of quality, as iron does not know the weevil!'

There was plenty of talk about those of our men who were sympathetic to the Communist cause, even though they had been by now, released from prison. One said, 'All this is being done to establish the hold of the Party over the people.' Another said, 'They have all been influenced by the big landlords.'

When it was time for the paddy saplings to be transplanted, irrigating the fields, and hoeing the maize crop, all the workers of our area assembled under the banyan tree, and it was decided to ask for an increase of a rupee in the daily wages. This news spread like wildfire in the village.

In the morning there was a palpable change. The atmosphere was heavy with silence. It was clear that the differences between the Jat zamindars and workers had widened. Young Jats could be seen standing about carrying lathis, keeping an eye on our lane. They did not want us to go to their fields, even to relieve ourselves, and women and children were the worst sufferers.

Men of our community visited the neighbouring villages to ensure that the wage earners from these villages would not come to work as substitutes. The situation changed rapidly and became tense. Many families had to send their animals to their relatives in other villages. Many were hopeful of an improvement in the situation, though others were dejected.

After five or six days had passed, there was another assembly in the courtyard to decide upon a future course of action. My uncle Rama said, 'The zamindars have sent a message that the demand for higher wages should be dropped, or they will take a harsh view of the whole affair.'

'How long can they delay calling us? Don't they see that the crops have to be harvested soon? Hold on to your demand, they will come round.'

'I think we should talk to Comrades Ajaib and Meeta—they may help us to sort out the problem. Our people are in touch with them, and have courted arrest with them,' someone suggested.

'I have been to see them. They say that though they sympathize with our cause, how can *they* raise the wage? It is a matter which concerns the whole community and they cannot go against the community. They have to go to these very people for votes when it is time for elections, the sarpanchs, therefore ...' this was one of the comrades who was openly sympathetic to us.

When those assembled there heard this, their hopes fell. It was a sudden and severe blow. A storm of criticism against the Jats raged at the meeting. They were pronounced devious. Though they lived and ate well themselves, they were harsh to others. They distilled country liquor for sale, but themselves drank foreign spirits! They were high-handed, oppressive, and given to all sorts of debauchery. They had fun at the expense of the dalits and a raise in wages for us would not have made much difference to them! The cost of living was rising. Everything seemed to be going up; not only cloth and other necessities, but even something as basic as tea was beyond our means.

'The other day Mehali was vigorously shouting about the unity between the peasants and the workers, and that we should help each other, support each other! Now, we could ask him when he visited next—what use was that idea of kisan mazdoor unity and support? What is the purpose of this Khet Mazdoor Sabha (Agricultural Workers' Union)?' Bhaia comments were acidic.

'Brothers, don't worry, we will think of some way!' Comrade Munsha Singh Charra said, pressing his hand on the yoke of his plough slung across his left shoulder. Hope shone on his face. 'It is not easy to change their hearts. Perhaps the young ones may change, after education.'

To me it seemed that Munsha Singh was trying to put all the blame on the deep-rooted attitudes which had always plagued the lower castes, and that by seeking to assuage our hurt feelings, he was trying to exhort our people to get ready to wage a long drawn war against socio-economic oppressions.

It was later that I realized that if we tried to overcome the barrenness of our lives, we had to make a more strenuous effort and with greater unity, and carry on our fight continuously and vigorously against this exploitative system. The tale of our woes is hundreds of years old. Yet it has neither been heard, nor have our woes even been sensed, by society at large.

# 11

## Monsoon without Rains

'Birju, do listen to me carefully. At least finish your tenth class, even if it is difficult … your uncle is a district collector, and he can get you a job somewhere … it will be the making of your life,' Bhaia and Ma had both pleaded with my elder brother, time and again. Bakshi (whom we called Birju), had decided to stop studying when he reached the tenth class. This was in 1970, when I was in the ninth.

The word 'district collector' rang a bell. The images of that bright day in 1964 came to me, when most of the people in our lane were seated under the banyan tree working on their looms. The clothiers from Jalandhar, Hansraj and Bhagwan, had set up their mobile shop under the tree and were displaying various materials that they knew were popular. Hansraj and Bhagwan were related by marriage.

Ma came hurriedly out of the house and going up to Bakshi, held out a postcard, asking him read it. Everyone fell silent, their eyes fixed on Bakshi who read out, 'I have become an IAS.'

No one understood what the words IAS meant. Taking the postcard from Bakshi's hand, Hansraj read it and then remarked, 'Send for laddoos, only then will I give you the good news!'

Faces shining with happiness, they all looked at each other. But Bhaia was impatient and said, 'Lala, tell us what is written in the letter!'

'IAS officers become district collectors! Sister Seebo, congratulations, your brother has become a big officer.'

Bhaia ran off to Jairam's shop and brought a thali of laddoos and distributed them to all the houses in the neighbourhood. People came out to congratulate us. But these images receded to a remote corner of my mind, I returned to the present to see Bakshi's set face ...

Bakshi seemed to be stuck on that one word, 'no' and would not let go.

'I am not going to study anymore,' he declared.

'Then the matter ends here; from tomorrow onwards you are going to come with me to work,' Bhaia had announced, still hoping that the thought of the hard work he would have to do would persuade Bakshi to change his mind.

'Come with you tomorrow? Have I not been going with you for the last four or five years, even when the daily wages were only three rupees, and I handed over all the money I earned to you? Or have you forgotten?' Bakshi reminded him.

'Your wish!' Bhaia said rather reluctantly. He was very unhappy about all this and the strain showed on his face. He put the hookah pipe into his mouth, and smoked for some time in silence, and then sighed deeply and said, 'All my hopes and expectations lie smashed.'

My uncle Rama walked in at that moment and saw me and my brother sitting on our grandmother's cot. He said with a laugh, 'Birju and Ghirju both hit the thanedar with an axe!'

Uncle Rama had given us many names—good as well as bad. Instead of coughing to signal his entry into our home, giving Ma enough time to cover her face with her dupatta, he would say something funny about the two of us.

Uncle sat down near Bhaia and taking the hookah pipe from him, put it into his mouth, and pulled at it furiously. My uncle would sometimes let out the smoke through his nostrils and sometimes through his mouth. And at times it was difficult to know where the smoke had gone, because he would store it in his mouth for a long time.

He asked casually, 'Why this long face? Looks like you've just buried your daughter! What's the matter?'

'What are we going to tell his Maama? That he doesn't want to study, or we cannot afford to educate him? What is he going to think about us?' Bhaia answered with a string of questions, which perhaps contained the answers he was himself looking for.

'Finish your studies. ... You can then get a good job. Think about your future.' Uncle advised.

My father looked tired. He stared at the floor as if he was looking for something that he had lost. He suddenly looked older and more haggard, and the stubble on his face had more grey in it than before.

... Bakshi started going to work with Bhaia and the others. Slim, active, and strong, this dark young man lifted heavy weights and bricks and worked hard in the fields. He himself had chosen this back-breaking path. However, after sometime, I sensed that his desire not to study further had waned. He would often pull angrily at the hair which now sprouted on his face, as if wanting to come to terms with his future. The pimples which now appeared showed that his life was no longer plain and straight as it had once been.

My parents still worried about him and Bhaia would often say, 'He will be like this his whole life! I say, why don't you talk to your brother, the collector, and ask him to get Bakshi a job in the police? You know that the policewallahs beat people up and then extort money from them!'

Listening to this, I thought of the day my Maama, had visited us last winter. He was a tall, handsome young man, open-faced and sporting a fine moustache. I also recalled the conversation between Bhaia and my Maama.

Bhaia was telling him about our family problems, 'Sir, if you could put in a word with the general manager of the sugar mill here, he may give me a permanent job this year. The family would then be more comfortable.'

'Bhaia, I'll talk to him ...'. Maama had assured him.

'The children would be able to study properly, and they may get good jobs.' Bhaia had continued after a brief lull in the conversation. He had pleaded with my uncle because of their close relationship.

'Thakar Das, don't worry I will talk to him, and soon inform you,' again Maama had assured Bhaia of help so desperately needed and sought.

Bhaia thought that if he got a permanent job in the sugar mill, it would mean a better future for the whole family. He did not hesitate to remind him time and again and say, 'If not this season, then perhaps the next. ...'

'I have been working there for the last fifteen seasons; even those who had the smallest recommendation have been made permanent, those who could bribe have been confirmed. Only about eight or ten of us are left, who either have no recommendation or cannot bribe. ...' Bhaia fell silent. Perhaps he remembered what my aunt had told him about Maama's helplessness.

Maama sat stroking his tie, as if trying to straighten out unseen wrinkles.

Seasons came and departed. When Maama had been appointed secretary to the cooperatives department, both Ma and Bhaia, had been overjoyed. Suddenly, a light had appeared to illuminate their dark lives.

Bhaia's colleagues in the mill, who were also our neighbours, now declared, 'Your work is as good as done, Thakar. You will now be made permanent and be able to break the shackles of the oppressive Jats. Surely he can do this much for you!'

Bhaia was excited by all this talk and felt encouraged to overcome his instinctive reluctance and made an effort again, 'Sahib, it is now in your hands. Please, if you could only ...'

'Thakar Das, what you say is right, but I have never asked any favours for a labourer. Yes, if it was someone who was literate, then it would be a different matter,' Maama was very clear and did not bother to hide his thoughts.

This put an end to all Bhaia's hopes.

Strange though it may seem, Bhaia had still not stopped hoping that having worked for fifteen years, he had earned a right to a permanent job. Now, he started visiting my elder Maama, who was a sarpanch. The situation, however, did not change despite all his efforts.

The train of my thoughts came to an abrupt halt, when Bhaia told Ma, 'Forget my case, and see if he is willing to do anything for Birju. Even the smallest effort on his part will go a long way in helping the family. We can live the way we do, but when I look at these children, my heart sinks. Their whole life is before them. Tomorrow, they will get married. If the Jats ask about the lands a family owns, then, in our community they want to know about the job a boy has ... they ask a hundred other things.'

After a brief pause, Bhaia continued, 'Go and ask him. He may help. Even though Birju has not passed the tenth class, at least he has studied up to the tenth.'

Bhaia had come to terms with the situation he was in; yet had taken the right decision in a desperate attempt to improve our conditions. I felt that he was deeply perturbed about Bakshi's future.

Bhaia often taunted Ma about her brothers. Sometimes he would abuse her, and throw things at her when his temper ran away with him. And Ma … she had steeled herself to patiently bear all the humiliations heaped on her. She would only say, 'What is in my hands? I can only ask and implore.'

After Ma had asked him many times, Maama had sent for Bakshi, to arrange for him to be taken into the police. My uncle's message had come like a cool monsoon shower, over a dry and parched land.

The whole family bloomed and blossomed, the way plants and trees do during the rainy season. Happiness was in the air. Bhaia's complaints and taunts had all been washed away.

Maama had sent a word of advice, 'The job of a conductor in the roadways is far better than that of a police constable. Tell Bakshi to get a conductor's license.'

Bakshi had managed to get a license with great difficulty. He had to make many trips to Jalandhar. He had also trained in first aid at Pathankot, which was about a hundred kilometres away. It had been arduous for him, as he had no money to spare for transport. Yet, he was very happy and his hopes and thoughts ran ahead of him. There was talk of good times that lay ahead, with a great deal of curiosity, the way people had talked of the Americans landing on the moon and what they had discovered there and brought back to earth. The educated had declared it to be a wonder wrought by science, and the old dismissed it all as mere rumour.

'Gudd, let me tell you the truth! I whistle to the driver in my dreams! I pick up and drop passengers at Bhogpur, Kala Bakra, Kishangarh, and various other stops! It is great fun when the driver starts or stops the bus when I whistle!' After a pause Bakshi said, 'Now I will get a permanent job—you can study as much as you want, there will be no dearth of stationary or books. Become a big officer like Maama …'

This confidence displayed by my brother suddenly made me feel taller. I saw myself boasting to my friends in so many different ways. I imagined I had passed out of college and was handing over my first pay packet to my mother. Sometimes the tight leash I had kept on my feelings seemed to fall slackly out of my hands.

But the happiness which kept the family going, soon drained away like the ebbing of the tides. After persistent questioning, Maami told us, 'My husband says that he will not ask the person who can give the appointment, for he is too senior, and the other person he doesn't want to ask as he is too junior. But don't you worry ...'

I felt as if the beam of the roof of the inner room had cracked a second time; and that Bhaia was the only one who could stop it, and he was busy looking for another log to put up as support for the roof. His robust optimism was proof of that.

A pall of silence engulfed us all, but Bhaia then told Ma, 'Had my mother-in-law been alive today, she would have listened to your problems ...'

My blind Naani's dark, wrinkled face swam into my mind the moment I heard this. I could never remember a time when she was not sightless. She would sit in the large open courtyard, waiting for her sons and daughters, grandchildren and guests. I thought of those moments in 1964 when she had felt me all over to see how strong and tall I had grown. She showered blessings on me time and again, and putting her hand on my head and said, 'Give me a kiss, son. If only I had eyes so that I could see my grandson! Gudd is now nine years' old, isn't he, Seebo? May god give him a long life and keep him happy ...'

I was still sunk in my memories when I heard my uncle Rama's voice at the front door.

Throwing a glance at all of us, he wanted to know why we were so gloomy. Bhaia related the whole story.

'You are always advising others that they should try to be independent and self-reliant. Then why are you so mixed up and indecisive yourself?' Taaya asked and took the hookah pipe from Bhaia. Then, as if he had been reminded of something, he said, 'Let me tell you something, Gudd's maama is a good man ...'

'He helps others also ...! Perhaps he wants to maintain a distance from us. Whoever becomes a big officer, forgets his roots ...'

Taaya cut Bhaia short, 'You should not listen to what the others say. … People say many things, that the officers have formed a separate category of their own and are ignoring even their closest relatives. Gudd's maama has maintained his relations with you and keeps visiting you.'

Bhaia looked crestfallen. Deep wrinkles furrowed his forehead. Giving a thought to what his brother had said, he commented, 'Seebo, I think …'

I had a feeling that Bhaia could not forget the time Ma used to clean out the cowsheds at Surjan Singh Jat's haveli. Either Bakshi or I was always with her. I was repelled when I saw her collecting all the muck and dung with her bare hands, and wanted to run out into the open, to breathe in the clean fresh air. Then, I would curse myself for not being of any help to her in her work because I saw myself as her protector or her saviour.

'What are you thinking about?' Abruptly Taaya asked Bhaia.

'I was thinking that if only Birju could get some work, then we could also hope for a few days of comfort. …' He could not say anything further, as if the hopes of the future held his tongue.

Then he went to Ma's dowry trunk, which lay in a corner of the room, and took out some letters which had been carefully stored there. He placed a bronze thali on the floor and then put the postcards on it. Taking out a box of matches from his pocket, he set them alight, and remarked, 'I will mix oil in these ashes and use the paste as an ointment. They say it is the best cure for eczema or rash.'

He was quiet for a few moments, and then added, 'Life goes on … I wanted to put an end to this.'

No one said anything.

'Gudd's Maama is a man of principles. He eats the salt of the government. It is because of this that he says, '"When they have not studied how can they get jobs?" He is not far wrong when he asserts that first they should study hard. Isn't it important for us that he is Gudd's Maama?' Taaya declared with great confidence.

It seemed that Bhaia had not heard anything that Taaya had said.

'It seems as if they are going to trouble us again at night and won't let us sleep!' Bhaia said and he went up to the cot which stood against the wall and beat it with stick. As bed bugs fell out, he crushed them with his jooti. I ran forward to help him as the bugs retreated under his assault, 'Here is one … there goes another …'

He went on beating the cot at both ends with the stick and crushing them. Sweat poured from his forehead, and he was almost panting. Wiping his forehead with his right hand, he went up to my Daadi who was sitting under the banyan tree, and remarked, 'This is the season of rains only in name. Who knows how long this dry spell may last!'

As I walked behind him, I pondered over what he had said.

# 12

## Daadi's Saga

'May you die! ... Stop! ... Let the ones who gave you birth come home! You will get a beating you will remember all your life ... I'm going to eat you raw!' Yelling such gory sentiments, jooti in hand, my grandmother would often run after me. Once something set her off, she could seldom restrain herself.

The neighbours would race out to watch this frequent occurrence. Most of the Jats used to walk past our home.

'Let him go, old woman, he is a foolish boy,' someone would tell her hesitantly, afraid of becoming the next target of her tongue.

But this word of advice was enough to enrage her. She would shout back, 'Other youngsters bring home two glasses of milk from school, but this fool spilt the milk he got! Let him come back. I'll cut him into pieces ... Isn't there a saying that the more you beat a hoe and a boy, the better they become!' And then muttering to herself, she would go home.

Those days, tins of milk powder were being given to schools, where it would be diluted with boiled water, and distributed to the younger students. Most of the poor children took the milk home.

I would loiter around for some time and then come home, but she would still be annoyed. Once, she was so angry that she had flung a brass tumbler at me. I was not wearing a shirt, my stomach had taken the force of that throw, and for years I carried a circular scar on my body.

She always had pieces of jaggery in her pocket. I often sat by her and stealthily snuck a piece or two and slipped away, to eat it at leisure. Whenever she was in a good mood, she would be very affectionate, I would tease her and try to catch the dangling flesh of her upper arms, which shook as she moved her hands and gesticulated, but my small hands could not hold her quivering flesh. I would then look at my frail body and say, 'Ma, give me some of your flesh.'

'Eat all you can. How else are you going to grow strong!'

When a woman from the carpenter's family in the neighbourhood entered and said, 'Mai, please come with me,' we all understood the nature of her work.

At times she took me along and I would clutch the chicken by its legs and bring it home. The carpenter kept chicken for eggs and whenever a bird was ill or died, we would be summoned to bring it away.

Once Daadi asked me to cut up the chicken. Bhaia was not at home. Picking up the scythe like an obedient child, I put the head of the bird on the leg of a cot and tried to sever its head. I held its body down with my left hand and hit it three times, but could not cut it. By now Daadi had started shouting at me, 'Stupid fool! You are grown up, but still cannot even ...'

That was enough for me. I took the neck of the chicken in my right hand, and putting my left foot on its body with one stroke of the scythe, I severed the head from its body.

By the evening this incident had made me sad. I could not sleep till late at night. Images of the chicken's severed neck, its fluttering body, flashed before my eyes, again and again. My elder brother, lying next to me was in a deep slumber. I don't remember when I drifted into sleep.

Thinking of losses suffered, she would suddenly talk about the division of the country. She would remark, 'We do not even get the things that we use to eat before the country was divided. The Muslims from Rastgo would bring basket loads of meat to sell in the market, the way bananas and apples are sold now. We could eat as much as we wanted.'

'You do not know about these things. When the calf of the Naukras died suddenly, its meat was distributed to all the households ... it was a real fat calf. ... The silly fools started fighting over what they did or did not get!' She would recall such events and I would mentally store all these anecdotes.

'Where did we get grain those days? We had to go to the zamindars, cut their millet crop. Then the grain was dried, pounded, and ground. Only then could we get grain. But we ate well, because of the meat. Many animals died during those winters and we would dry the meat. Even bones would be dried and stored on the roof or hung from hooks.' Daadi would narrate many such episodes from her life, some with relish and others sadly.

I was a little older. We had often starved, but as far as I know, the flesh of dead animals had never been brought into our home. That was the reason we took such interest in Daadi's anecdotes.

'Before the Partition, the whole of Chamarli had tins of animal fat. They all used it as ghee, and smeared it on rotis or used it to season the dal,' Daadi would tell us. I was surprised at this, and would try my best to keep the atmosphere happy so that she would not lose her temper.

'Who used mustard oil or kerosene for lighting diyas those days! We used animal fat!' Daadi's statement would be endorsed by our neighbour Khushia, who would explain things in great detail, and say, 'You ask your Bhaia. Chajji, Dheru, Maghi, Shinha, Minha, Fakir—they all used to eat meat.'

My heart would sink at this description of eating the flesh of dead animals at the cost of one's health. Even rajahs and maharajas ate the flesh of animals they hunted and killed. Primitive man had survived on the produce of forests and animals that he killed. Civilizations have developed and attained great heights. Yet, our people were still compelled to live in these primitive conditions. Words like civilization, culture, and national freedom sounded very hollow to me.

I had never seen Daadi working. But she would always criticize daughters and daughters-in-law of other houses, 'Bitches! They get up late in the morning! We would have finished grinding ten seers of wheat by this time. Who went to flour mills those days?'

She washed and repaired her own clothes. She could not bear the extreme heat of the summers and usually sat on a charpai under the peepal tree near our home. She seldom wore a kamiz, and wrapped her body with her dupatta in such a manner that it looked like a sari. She was the oldest inhabitant of the village, but whenever an aged person stopped to ask after her health, she covered her head with her dupatta. She always held a reed fan and did not wear too many clothes even in winter. She used a *khes* woven by Bhaia, and a pair of jootis on her feet. Occasionally, she wore my police-Uncle's cast-off jersey.

Daadi would scold and taunt my mother whenever she bathed us with hot water during winter. She would say, 'Don't use all the wood to heat the water! Couldn't you have put it in the sun for some time?'

Summer or winter, Daadi always had her bath in the afternoon. A bucket of water would be put out in the sun very early in the morning. Daadi and my mother bathed in a corner of the courtyard. A cot would be placed on its side and a piece of cloth flung across it to create a cover of sorts, and they would bathe behind this improvised screen. This corner served as a urinal at night, and it always stank of urine even though the ground had been dug and the two sides of a grinding stone set into the hole.

Daadi would start her critical commentary whenever she watched Ma bathing us with soap used for washing clothes, 'Now, she is using soap to bathe them—as if she is the daughter of some king. We washed our clothes with saltpetre and used curds or lassi to wash our hair! But there is no end to the foppery of this new generation!'

Despite all this, my mother would never retaliate. She was afraid of my Daadi's harsh tongue and would neither argue with her nor say anything against her. At times, it appeared as if she had lost the use of her tongue.

Once in a while, a Jat woman would come and softly call Daadi, 'Come home for a while.'

Daadi would pick up her stick and walk behind her without a murmur of protest. But in a few moments, she would be back. The wrinkles on her fair face looked like the soft ripples of sea waves. As she crossed the threshold the door would swing back soundlessly the way a child balances and takes a turn on its toes. She would shout, 'Where has everybody gone?' Put out a cot for me!'

One of us would hasten to obey her. Quickly, she would take out the pieces of rotis from her dupatta and spread them out to dry. These were the leftovers of a wedding or an engagement or a bhog ceremony. These dried rotis would be then be soaked in jaggery and water, and we would eat our fill. Sometimes, they would be cooked in cane juice. The appetizing aroma of this mixture made one's mouth water! They were really tasty!

My Daadi never went to the gurudwara, though it was just a lane away. But, yes, when the rains failed and there was a drought and the Jats distributed porridge in the name of 'Khwaja Khizir', Jagar the chowkidar would then go round our mohalla calling out, 'Everyone go and get the daliya from the gurudwara ... take the prasad, ple-e-e-ase ...' He would stretch out the last bit and then walk on.

Daadi would then go to the gurudwara and get a thali of daliya. She would pour some desi ghee on it and eat it. But she did not go to the gurudwara on sangrand, or to listen to any katha or kirtan. She never lit a lamp at the mazar of a pir, or any diyas on Diwali.

She did not like observing the various religious traditions just to parade her piety or to conform. Often she would say, 'Man should depend only on his own earnings, not criticize others, and lead a good and honest life. Then he need not run after God!'

Her eyesight was now badly affected. She would use her hands to shade her eyes and peer, and only then could she recognize a person. Many years ago, her left eye had been operated upon and bandaged for some days. She had not rested even on those days. The only thing that had changed was that she now had to use a stick. But the effect of her commanding presence and her influence were the same. Whenever a child irritated her, she would scold it, 'Which child-eating mother gave birth to you? Go and shout in your mother's presence! You bastard!'

If a Jat woman (or any other woman) passed near her without wishing her, she would say loudly, 'Wonder which arrogant bitch just passed by!'

This would draw the attention of every single person seated under the peepal, and also of the children playing marbles near Daadi.

'Who was that bitch?' Daadi would angrily ask those sitting with her about the woman, and describe the face and features of the woman who had had the audacity to ignore her!

The poor woman would have a hard time. Daadi would complain about her, taunt her, and pass abusive remarks about her. Matters would be settled only when the offender apologized, 'Ma, I was in a hurry. Come take this jaggery. It is still warm and fresh from the mill.'

Daadi was given all the things that she needed—cane juice, gur, dahi, vegetables, butter, and cane—some of it she would pass on to us, and some to her other grandchildren.

'Ma, pairi paini hain (I touch your feet in respect)!' Some woman would call out as she went by. These words always gave my grandmother great solace.

'May the Guru bless you!' She would shower blessings in return. She would discover all the good qualities in her and say, 'This Kulwinder, granddaughter-in-law of Gangi or Lal Munhi who is Gujar Singh's, they never forget to pay their respects whenever they pass by. They give me all the respect and honour! Why should I say otherwise ...'

Many families respected her as a recluse. They would send her food on festivals. Some Jat families would send her kheer on the day after Lohri, which we ate for two whole days. On these occasions, I liked Daadi very much. Whenever there was no gur at home for tea, she would always give us two large pieces.

My Bua would occasionally visit Daadi. She was an inveterate talker. She also smoked, but behind Daadi's back. Bua would signal to me and say, 'Son, go and get a hukki from Nanti's.'

I would quickly put fresh water into the hukki, and pull at it. While doing that sometimes I would pull too hard, and my mouth would be full of water, making me choke and cough. Bua would at once understand, though she would be indoors, that I had got everything ready for her. Daadi hated the gurgling sound and the smoke of the hookah. She would often scold Bhaia and say, 'You always have the hookah pipe in your mouth! May it burn your mouth!'

Daadi's authority was unchallenged. One day, Taro Tai (who belonged to a Jat family) and Chaachi Chhinni were on the swing on the peepal tree when Daadi saw them, and no one knows what happened but she shouted, 'Is this the only work left for these wanton women? They are not bothered about their husbands and are not concerned that they worked hard the whole day and are tired! Loose women! Bad ones!'

The swings stopped. It looked as if the sun was impatient to sink into the horizon, even though it was a bright afternoon. The brightness faded. The onlookers slunk away. Frowning, Daadi took a couple of steps in their direction, but by then the women had scampered away.

Tai Taro was very friendly with Daadi and would always send her whatever delicacy she cooked at home.

Tai had two sisters-in-law. Whenever these three went out, they would leave their keys with Daadi, who made it a point to tell all and sundry who passed that way, 'These daughters-in-law of Chanda Singh always leave their keys with me! Mine don't even bother about me!'

Once Daadi and Tai quarrelled. By that time Taya Udham Singh, who was called Shah by the whole village, had passed away. He was the one who drove the cart with Bikar Singh of the horse. Daadi had raved and ranted. Standing in the lane she shouted, 'You are responsible for many women being widowed, but despite being a widow, you are no widow!'

These harsh and bitter words shamed everyone who heard them.

It was Tai Taro who diffused the situation; with a disarming laugh she said, 'Are you forgetting the time when I came here as a bride? At that time, your father-in-law moved about bare-bodied, wearing only his underpants! And now you want to fight with me, you devious one!'

I still remember that many Jats of the village would come to Daadi asking for her advice about weddings and other such celebrations. They would also do whatever she advised them. But she would not stand in their presence even when old men came to see her, the way my Taaya Rama did. He would make the Jat visitor sit on the charpai and then seat himself on the ground. This was the accepted mode of behaviour and show of respect and honour. When Bhaia and Taya visited the homes of the Jats, let alone neglecting to ask them to sit beside them, the Jats would not even ask them to sit.

I can never forget a certain episode. There had been no rains and the dry spell had created many problems for us. The village women were playing Holi by mixing cow dung with mud and water as a way of appeasing the rain God, Indra. Seebo of the Noba family threw a bucket of this mixture on Daadi. This was enough to set her off.

'You low wanton woman! At least show some respect for my white hair, you beater of children!' She went up to Seebo's house, shouting abuses at her, but came back immediately, for there was no one there who could carry on the quarrel. The whole thing came to an end only when Seebo came over to apologize to Daadi. After that she did not was past our house for three months, though it was her usual route.

Daadi's obdurate nature did not change, even with her advancing age.

The whole family wanted my mother to wash Daadi's clothes. But whenever Ma asked her, Daadi would answer abruptly, 'I don't want to be dependent on anyone; better to die.'

She was still good looking. If we listened to her, she would tell us many things about the days gone by.

'The girls find it difficult to walk two steps today! But I could walk up to Lahore.'

Whenever anyone talked about the British rule, she was sure to comment: 'Elizabeth II has just become the queen!' It was from her that I had first heard the name of George Pancham (V) and Edward, and the coins that had been struck in their names.

Daadi's health was fast deteriorating, but her eating habits did not change much. She ate makki ki roti with butter and spinach, drank cane juice or its scum, and lassi, as she had done her whole life through. She would put some spinach on the roti, or even in a katora, and pour some butter into it before eating it. If there was no butter, she would put some curd into it. She always fed the sparrows by throwing crumbs of roti at them as she sat eating. About thirty or forty sparrows would hop on to her bed. It was a very touching scene. She always fed stray dogs, because to her dogs were recluses with good souls. In her last years, a couple of dogs were her constant companions.

Daadi's powerful and commanding voice weakened with age. Children would run around her, whistling and playing. Whenever she was irritated and upset by an adult or even a child, she would say, 'May you also become this old!'

When the tone of her voice altered, it surprised all of us. I still remember some of the abuses she showered on me and other mischievous children! Most of them were related to meat and meat eating, 'I will make mincemeat of your liver and eat it!' 'I will cook and eat you!' 'I will eat your brain!' 'I'll turn you into a kebab and eat you!'

My mother would turn emotional whenever Daadi fell ill, saying, 'There are not many like her; a widow for over forty-five years; brought up her children, settled them, yet never been beholden to anyone.'

The whole family was worried. 'She may not last this winter! She is almost hundred or just a couple of years short!'

During the winter her charpai was put in the room at the back, where the animals were also tied. During the day, the cot would be brought out into the open courtyard, into the bright sunshine.

Many elders, men and women, would advise her, 'Haro, now take the name of God.'

Winter passed and summer was on us. The wheat crop was being harvested. Bhaia and my cousins would worry, 'What if it happens while the harvesting is on?'

She would lie on the cot. It was my mother who washed and changed her clothes, combed her hair, and took care of all her needs. People would praise my mother, 'Seebo, there is none like you. You take such good care of her. God will bless you.'

Daadi's attitude towards my mother changed. She showered blessings on her, 'May God give your sons all that they need. Your children are good. I may not live to see it, but the world will see your good days.'

She would advise all those who cared to listen. Someone would come and say, 'Haro, take the name of God. Now it is the time for you to think of God. He may relieve you.'

'I think of Him, but he doesn't take me away,' she would answer with a toothless smile.

During her last days, she had begun cutting new teeth. Whenever she was fed, the tips of her new teeth would rattle against the spoon.

'Ma, tell us what would you like to eat?' We asked her once.

Pat came her clear answer, 'Meat soup!'

Bhaia got some goat's meat. In the evening, a bowlful was given to Daadi. She took a roti and drank all the soup.

Next day, she seemed to revive. She talked to my mother. That day, 2 May 1976, was her last day. Half the village collected around her. As her body was laid out, there was praise for her on everyone's lips.

'Haro was always full of life.'

'She was respected by young and old alike.'

'She was fairer than a white woman.'

'She had a commanding presence.'

I felt that Tai Taro was paying her a deep and heartfelt tribute.

My mother was weeping. All of us were sad. A large crowd followed her bier to the cremation ground. The balloon tied to the bier flew in the air, upright and high, a testimony of her self-respect.

# 13

## The Banyan Tree of the Chamars

'When we were small, the distance between the peepal and the *bargad* was wide enough for us to pass through,' Bhaia told us. My eagerness to hear the details increased rapidly.

'Just look at the way these trees cling to each other, it is even difficult for the air to pass through!' He remarked and then stopped. The silence stretched like a small rivulet before us. I was impatient for him to say something.

'These two have embraced without word or thought. And, here is man, who doesn't want even another *man* to come near him!' Bhaia said coming out of the silence which seemed to have engulfed him. The wrinkles on his face had deepened. I felt that he had been trying to balance various things in his mind. I watched the leaves flutter as the burgeoning buds glistened on the twin trees.

'Let me tell you, it was my father (Ram Ditta, my grandfather) and Thakar, the grandfather of Ram Singh Jheer, who jointly planted these two trees.'

On hearing this, I instantly began calculating the age of these trees. Taking into consideration the death of my grandfather, the ages of my grandmother and father, I came to the conclusion that this must have been some time between 1876 and 1880.

'As you are eager to know more about them, listen. The sixteen marla (484 square yards) of land under the bargad was bought by our community from Kartar Singh of Neevan Vehra. The whole transaction was by word of mouth, and no document was signed. Bhai Harbans Singh of the Puccawalas himself measured the area. Those days they law did not permit Churas and Chamars to own land, or build houses, let alone for cultivation, even if they could pay,' Bhaia was assailed by his own memories, and I did not want to interrupt him in any way.

The members of other castes, such as Jats, Brahmins, carpenters, barbers, kahars referred to the tree as the bargad of the Chamars. If a Jat asked another Jat where was he coming from, the answer would be, 'I had gone to Chamarli and have arranged for four Chamars to work for me on daily wages.'

Many Jats would use expletives for the tree. After the departure of the Jat, Bhaia would curse him.

During the harvest season, many Jats would visit our mohalla to arrange for workers for their fields, at a time when most people would be eating in the shade of the trees. Many of these visitors would be wearing dirty kachchas and dirty shirts or vests. After their departure Bhaia would sarcastically remark, 'Who knows when these Jats will show some sense! They should wear at least a dhoti or a cloth around their waist when they come here. They should know that our families live here.'

Our people knew everything about the Jats, the crops, and the nature of the soil. Most of them did not want to work in the fields located on the sandy dunes. 'Which fool would like to toil in sandy fields?'

Arrangements about meals and tea would also be made. They were given three meals and tea twice during the day. Bhaia and my cousins would say no to many a Jat, saying that they had to go elsewhere. And at his departure, they would say, 'He even weighs the fodder he gives us— his intentions are bad, and he nags and pesters the workers all the time saying we waste too much time smoking, but we need to take breaks. Our skins burn, working under a blistering sun the whole day.'

Screeching peacocks would sit on the peepal, at dawn and dusk. Then, flying off, they would descend on our roofs, and begin dancing. We would throw grain at them. They were not scared of us. Crows would pick at the fruit of the bargad. Sparrows would fly off and then come back to sit on its branches. I had often seen *mauli*, the sacred thread, tied around the wide trunks of the peepal and the bargad, and had once asked Bhaia about it.

'The banyan tree in the eastern part of the village which is in the mohalla of the Walis was married to our banyan with full rites and rituals, and the villagers had celebrated the wedding.' Pointing to the thick branches of the trees and indicating the deep shade of those trees, Bhaia would say, 'These trees have been a blessing for us, whichever way we look at it. Mauli is tied around their trunks for their protection and welfare, what else!'

The branches and canopies spread out splendidly and the looms of many families were placed under them. These families earned their living through their looms. Weaving was not easy and involved the whole family. First, the yarn had to be tied up in hanks, then these hanks had to be put onto the pulley, and only then would the weaving begin. Bhaia would dig in a few stalks of rushes for the warp. They would be joined at the bottom, in the form of English alphabet 'V': a long slender column. At times, Bhaia would fix the reeds in a double row. He would then weave the wool by passing the spindle through the space between the reeds. When the yarn on one pulley was over, he would seal its end to another hank with saliva. He would weave rapidly till the evening, with my elder brother, Bakshi helping him. The next day Bhaia would weave the welf, and then with a brush, coat it with a starch to prevent the strands from sticking to each other. He would turn and twist each strand making it supple with his saliva. Now it was time to weave the warp and the pipes would be readied. Bhaia would sit, his legs dangling in the pit. He would press the lower part of the loom with his feet, once to the left, the next time, the right, and quickly weave the warp into the welf. He would apply mustard oil on the sharp pipe if he felt it was not moving fast enough. As it was, the pipe made of black wood was very smooth because of constant use, and would often slip out his hand.

Some of our Jat neighbours would sit near the pits my uncle and Bhaia used. One of them was Hari Ram and we called him Taaya Hari Singh. He was also known as the cripple in the village. He and his elder brother, Channu, would call out to me, 'Gudd, run and get a packet of cigarettes from the Brahmin's shop.' Taaya Channu would scratch his hand and laughingly relate the interesting events that had occurred at the Bhogpur sugar mill.

I would run off to the shop and come back in a few moments with a packet of cigarettes. The two brothers, sometimes singly and at other times together, would come to the looms and smoke. Their uncle's son, Reshu, had a radio and would sit with them till twilight. I laughed at the perfect circle shaved at the top of his head. I had the opportunity to see it time and again, whenever Taaya spread out his hair to dry. Many times, Gyanu the barber would shave the top of his head or his beard under the tree itself. As far as I can recollect, I first heard Asa Singh Mastana, the famous Punjabi singer's recitation of *Kissa Puran Bhagat* or *Kissa Heer*, on this radio. Taaya was a bachelor, and was often called *chharra*, or single, and even a stud or a he-goat behind his back.

Whenever Bhaia left the pit, either to fetch the pipes or to relieve himself, I would stealthily smoke the hookah. If Bhaia caught me he would abuse me sharply.

Many Jat women from the village would bring their own cotton yarn to be woven into *kheses* with geometrical designs or white sheets. They would summon my mother to their homes, weigh out the yarn, and pay her for the labour in kind, by giving either wheat or maize. Many times I insisted on going with my mother on these visits to their homes.

After the whole transaction had been completed and the lady of the house helped my mother to lift the bundle of yarn or cotton wool onto her head, she would say, 'Seebo wait, let me give some gur to the boy to make him happy!' This would be enough to make me happy and my mouth to water, wiping my ever-running nose with the upper part of my kurta and run home before my mother.

It was at these looms that towels for the army were woven, as also fabric with zigzag patterns. The silk or linen material would be 110 yards wide and the roll 30 yards. When the silken yarn being woven on the warp sagged in the middle, Bhaia would fill his mouth with water and blow at the sag. This made me laugh! But the fabric would tauten after two or three such treatments administered by Bhaia, who would then quickly begin weaving again.

'What was the bloody return that we got for all our weaving! Five rupees per roll! All the raw material was bought from Muslim weavers of villages in Hoshiarpur—Jaura, Khanpur, Chandial, Khalaspur, and Nainowalia Munshi. We had to travel on foot carrying heavy bundles weighing two maunds (about 74 kg) on our heads, sometimes under the blistering sun, rain or storm, and at other times in bitter cold. Yet we did it all.' Bhaia remarked sadly. I now know that these villages are 7 to 27 kilometres away from our village.

'Perhaps, we are born to bear all sorts of oppression. What a hard life it was!' And his voice was full of heartfelt pain.

'Let me tell you what happened one day! The sergeant of Bhogpur police station had come to the looms. Dharam naal, he was very handsome and virile, that one! He told Dhanna and me to come to the police station the next day with rolls of material. Both of us took a number of rolls, and went to the police station. He selected a roll from the lots both of us had taken. We waited for him to give us some money for what he had bought. But he abused us and told us to run off and not to expect anything from him. By God, we were trembling with fright and rushed out of the police station, afraid that he may slap some offence or the other on us!' Bhaia said. And then he remarked again, 'These looms were full of life! There was plenty of hustle and bustle here!'

My young mind would immediately conjure up an image of the yellow leaves of the bargad tree fluttering in the wind. I felt the warmth of happiness engulfing me as I ran with the wind in my face. I could almost hear the loudspeakers that were often hung on the branches of these twin trees at weddings and various other celebrations.

'Our Diwan (my uncle Diwan Chand) used to recite *Heer*. He had a melodious voice. Half the village would assemble to hear him,' Bhaia smiled.

I instantly thought of the blind sadhu Gharib Das, who used to sing the ballads of Puran Bhagat, Kaulan, Tara Rani, and Dahood, under these trees in summertime. He played the *ektara* with one hand and the *khartal* with the other. During the recitation, he would explain the story in great detail, and interpret it for the audience. In between, he would also smoke the hookah. His moustache was smoke-stained and seemed to be a part of the flowing saffron-coloured robe that he always wore. His long hair was full of lice, and he kept scratching his scalp under his turban. Everyone called him Andha Sadhu—the blind sadhu. He would stop singing to tell me, 'Gudd, please fill the chillum.' He often sang till midnight, and when he was about to leave, someone from the audience would extend an invitation, 'Maharaj, please have your meal with us tomorrow.'

I also remembered another blind sadhu who called himself Aslam. He was well built, always carried a stick with a metallic ring at one end, and wore a green robe and a cap. He visited our village two or three times in a year and stayed in the house next door, as a guest of Bhaia's cousin. He sang *kafi*, qawwali, and other religious songs. He would play on the harmonium or the *sarangi* or the tabla as he sang, and while singing, would grow ecstatic. His voice would rise and he would become oblivious to all else around him. He belonged to our community, but had embraced Islam, seeking a way out to escape social oppression. His discourses had influenced my uncle deeply, and he and his three sons had become Aslam's followers. He had a deep knowledge of the Guru Granth Sahib, often pointed out the mistakes that the granthis made while reciting the Gurubani, and openly admonished them and challenged them, 'Ask me which word occurs on which page; you can ask me to read the Guru Granth Sahib backwards.' The villagers assembled in large number to hear his discourses.

'Once our sants from Mehuna had organized an Akhand Path of the Darbar Sahib under this banyan tree near these looms,' Bhaia told us, making me even more curious to find out about these sants as I had already been thinking of them. Though I was young, I could recollect the fair, smooth face of Sant Ram Lal, with his flowing white beard, well respected in our village because he was so knowledgeable. People of all communities had come to hear him on the occasion of the completion of the Akhand Path. When the time for distribution of prasad had come, most of them had slunk away on one pretext or the other. This incident had been discussed by our people for many days. The common view was, 'if they didn't want to take the prasad, then why did they come?'

Not much weaving was done during the monsoons because my people tended the buffaloes of the zamindars of our village and the surrounding villages, such as Sohalpur, Manakdheri, Rastgo, Sikanderpur, Dhadda Sanaura, either on half and half, or on five to one basis, and these animals were tied under the twin trees. Water was drawn from the wells near the banyan tree to bathe the animals. Their tails would be trimmed, and curbs put round their mouths and necks. My father would also put bells round the necks and feet of the animals. The whole family was involved in tending them. All of us—Bhaia, my elder brother, and I—would fetch sand from the river close to the village and spread it out under the trees. Bakshi would collect the dry leaves from the ground during the winter. At times, we would surreptitiously collect leaves of sugar cane to spread them under the buffaloes.

When the buffaloes were ready to deliver, then a proper price would be settled for them. Mostly, it were the Jats who bought them. And then, my father would hand over the rope of the animal to the Jats after having tended it for over a year and a half. The whole family would be very sad.

At times, the animals would deliver at our home. That would give me a chance to play with the calf and pamper it. It made me happy when the calf chewed up its rope. I would put soft green grass in its mouth and it would try to bite my hand. My eyes would fill as I stroked its small, smooth neck. When the calf was given away with its mother, I begged for it to be kept back.

'We will get another buffalo—a Punj Kalyani,[1] or a Boori,[2] a brown beauty,' my mother would console me.

Bhaia never tired of praising the buffalo that had been sold. Dharam naal, he would say, 'it was so well behaved!' Sometimes he would say, 'If only we had some money, we could have kept it. It would have been useful, and it was a good breed! But our bad luck ...'

It was under this tree that Rulia the barber cut our hair. All the children called him Taaya. He made us sit on the ground in a row and would make us take off our shirts. While at work, he took short breaks to smoke the hookah of Taaya Mehnga or Dalipa. I would get tired of sitting there with my hair stinging me like thorns. He first used a pair of scissors, and then the clipper, and his last weapon would be the razor. He would take it out of his bag and sharpen it on a piece of round leather. He would test it and then dip the fingers of his right hand in a mug full of water and wet the area between the ear and the temples. I would shiver and he would say 'bus, bus' to reassure me, which made the rings in his ears swing. He would pick up a small mirror that lay at his feet and then trim his own moustaches and beard. Tucking his hair

1. A buffalo with five white parts, viz., cornea, all four feet, end of tail, forehead and mouth.
2. A brown buffalo.

under his white but dirty turban, Bhaia would look at the cut hair and say, 'The bastard had spent all his life doing it. Yet he doesn't know how to cut hair. Just look at the haphazard way he has cut it! Just look at it Seebo, the saala has cut the boy's scalp here!'

Once I had asked Bhaia, 'Taaya comes from a distance of four kilometres to cut our hair. Taaya Gyanu and his father, Baba Natha Singh, are in our village and they also cut hair.'

'They are Hindu barbers, and they don't cut our hair,' Bhaia had told me and then got busy. At that time, I did not fully understand the implication of this statement. But I had seen Taaya Gyanu many times, cutting the tails of the animals that belonged to the Jats.

The area of the looms under the trees was clean and open, and therefore something or other was always going on here. It was here that marriages were fixed and weddings were held. The *baraats* were put up here. The area served as an assembly ground on occasions of bereavement.

Our mohalla was the centre of entertainment for the whole village because of the bargad trees. It was here that mimicry shows were held, and *Saal* was organized—an annual feature, it was organized after the monsoon, when everyone prayed for the welfare of cattle. It was considered a part of the duties of the Chamars. Arrangements would begin a month before the celebrations. We, all the young men of the area, would go about collecting supplies for the different rituals and the actors and mime artists who came along to perform. The collection from each household was at the rate of a seer and a quarter (about 1 kilo) for each animal. There would often be scarcity of food grains in many poor Jat households, as also of the Chamars. The result was that many poor Jat households concealed the actual number of animals they owned.

Saal was organized to protect the cattle from the foot and mouth disease and to appease the gods. The head of the group of devotees responsible for performing all the ritual was Kirpa of Kadia. He was tall, well built and broad chested. He was always dressed in saffron and wore a number of necklaces. His daughter, Nanti, was married to a man of our community, and her husband, Massa, was also his follower. He liked being addressed as Massa Singh, but the children called him 'Massa Ranghar' behind his back. When a buffalo refused to yield milk, he made a ball of flour, muttered something, and blew on it. Then, he would grumble about the woman whose animal it was, 'Silly woman! She doesn't feed the animal properly, and then expects milk to fall from the skies!' He would make sharp comments with a smile, 'Here she comes to waste her money!', or she says, '"Brother, my daughter-in-law does not conceive …!" What can I do about it?'

The beginning of the Saal would be performed near the mud wall behind our home. There was a small mound of earth, which would be plastered with cow dung, after which shlokas recited in honour of Baba Sidh Chano. On every sangrand—the first moon day—and amavasya—the moonless night—the people of our area would distribute rotis and churma amongst the children as an offering for the health and well being of our cattle. The rotis would be made from a mixture of wheat and maize flour with jaggery.

Baba Sidh Chano or Baba Sidh Wali is a popular and powerful deity of the Chamars, and revered and worshipped as a protector of animals. An *akhara* or assembly would be held in the morning and evening in honour of Lord Krishna and Baba Sidh Chano. One of the devotees would recite shlokas while playing on the harmonium and two of the participants would wrestle. The devotee would narrate the following tale of Lord Krishna, the great statesman and warrior. 'One day, Baba Sidh Chano had the honour of facing him in a wrestling match. For eighteen days they wrestled, but Krishna could not defeat Sidh Chano. Then, on the last day, Krishna created an illusion, with his foot, of a prolonged day with no sunset and thus succeeded in defeating Sidh Chano who was resting at that time …'

The last day and evening of the akhara was celebrated as the Saal. People from most of the villages attended the assembly and one saw crowds and rows of men, women, and children all over the ground. Worship with lights would be performed and ardass-prayers would be said. Guru Ravidas would be eulogized and one of the devotees, who was called 'Bhaunra' would swallow live coals, crushing them with his teeth, and then blow out flames through his mouth. The other devotees would continue with their singing, *'Bhaunra aag khaye ga'* (Bhaunra would eat fire). People would be astonished at this terrifying scene. As soon as the ceremony ended the musicians would begin singing, 'tha thaiyya, tha thaiyya', and a male dancer dressed up as a female, would jump to the centre of the area, close to the singers and start singing,

> *Though I wear a muslin kurti,*
> > *Yet I am sweating!*
> Or
> *Don't measure my waist, O tailor,*
> > *But stitch me a one-piece set!*
> Or
> *The Jatti is like a luscious fruit,*
> *The black snake has swallowed*
> > *her.*

This was a signal for the assembly to pay the performers. If a person from a village or from a group of the village gave five hundred and one rupees, then the process would become long and tedious. Currency notes would be tied to the point of a stick a spear, a club or an axe, and held up high in the air. The dancer would put his finger in his mouth and whistle, and the musicians would slow down for a moment, and there would be cries in support and praise of the donors. Occasionally, a drunk would grab the dancer dressed as a woman, and the dancer would also act coy, eyes downcast, but all the while using his hands to extract notes from the pockets of the drunkard.

Mimics from Manikdheri in Hoshiarpur district visited our village. The people of this village had not allowed these *Mirasis* to leave for Pakistan during the riots in 1947. The devotees of Saal and the mimics were all members of the Chamar Community of the village Pipplanwala in Hoshiarpur district. The mimics and *bhagats* (devotees) would mimic a Jat and *seeri* (a labourer), and the dialogue would go like this:

JAT:      Bhai Dhanna, would you like to take up a job?
SEERI:   Yes, Sarkar,
JAT:      What wages would you want?
SEERI:   Food and drink would be on you.
JAT:      Food and drink would be on us.
SEERI:   Clothes would be on you?
JAT:      Sure, clothes would be on us! And ...?
SEERI:   Soap and oil would be on you.
JAT:      Yes, yes, soap and oil would be on us ...
SEERI:   Then, my jootis will be on your head!

Loud laughter would follow this and the Jat would pretend to lash out at seeri's chest with a leather strap. The worker would raise his kurta and wait for the lash!

Most of the night would pass in this manner—laughter and entertainment. The devotee performing the Saal would interrupt to say, 'Khushia, Bheema, wherever they are, should come up to the platform.'

As the end of the performance, Bhagat Kirpa would be made to sit on a charpai. Four men would carry this cot to the western edge of the village, where he would perform a magical rite and exorcize evil spirits from animals. An elephant trunk of sorts would be attached to the charpai to create an illusion of a ride on an elephant. Those who carried him were strictly forbidden to talk to each other. I had accompanied them a few times to watch this ceremony. We were stopped at some distance from the village boundary, so that no evil spirit could attack us children.

'It was a tough task this year! The animals were really in the grip of bad spirits!' This was the comment of these men as they returned home.

'Kirpa Bhagat is heavy!'

Khushia, being the shortest, must have had to bear most of the weight. I understood. At the break of dawn, Jagar the chowkidar would call aloud, 'Bring back the animals from under the Saal …'

All the animals would be brought out from under the branches of Sialkotis to which coconuts wrapped in red silk bound in mauli, were tied. The branches were spread over the lane in the manner of an arch over some royal procession. After this, water would be sprinkled over all the havelis and houses in the village and incense burnt. Some incense would be distributed so that people could use it later for their animals.

During the summer and the monsoons, parties of card players would assemble under the banyan. Many a time the croaking of the frogs in the pond of the Nangas would mix and match the hissing and bubbling of the hookah.

My father's sisters and the daughters of the families in our colony could visit their homes for the Rakhi festival. On Rakhsha Bandhan day, Bhaia and his brothers would keep the rakhis on their wrists for an hour or two, and then tie them to their hookahs for more than a month or so.

Swings would be put up on the lower branches of the banyan tree. For young women, swings would be on higher and thicker branches. Tai Taro, the Jati and chachi Chinni would swing very high, my heart would tremble at the very sight, and I would feel my breath stop somewhere between my ribs.

If our banyan tree provided shelter to the village during the monsoons, it was also a witness to many happy events, bitterness, tensions, and fights. Whenever a young Jat lad passed through the lane on his cart, he would pull at his rope to guide his pair of oxen and sing, and eye our young girls from over the walls of our homes.

'Maama, doesn't the cart go through the outer road?'

'Can't you sit … and drive the cart through?' Would be flung at him, or someone else would say, 'Huh! Posing as if he is Rani Khan! They always threaten us to stop us from shitting in their fields! As if *your* bum is grander than ours, that God has bestowed lands on you! Are we not the same as you?'

Many times, Bakhtawar or his younger brother, known as 'Lamba Sohi', would come to our area, dead drunk, and noisily curse the whole Chamarli. This was enough to create tension between the two communities and lead to clashes between them. Sticks would be brandished in the air, and missiles of abuses and curses fired at each other. But this din would subside after five minutes when Taaya Channan Singh reviled his own sons and told the others, 'Stop this fighting. My children have embarrassed me enough.'

'What has not happened to us under this banyan tree!' Bhaia said with such feeling that we knew he wanted to tell us something. This was at night, after dinner.

'Yes, Bhaia tell us,' I was impatient to know.

'Before the riots of the Partition, Nambardar Sher Singh would often visit our looms, ordering us, "Thakar, you and Khushia, get some grass for the thanedar's mare tomorrow."'

'We were compelled to take the grass to the thana, rain or storm. First we would show the bundles of grass to the nambardar. He would examine them to see whether the grass was of good quality or not. As it is, we were afraid of even entering the thanas. We would stand there till he expressed his satisfaction. If the thanedar's mare were to fall sick, it would mean trouble for us, because we would be blamed for giving it rotten grass. Those were very bad days for us. Dr Ambedkar and Mangu Ram agitated and only then things improved. Even after the Partition they would harass us, but we stopped taking grass to the police station. 'Now, it was a free country.'

'Shall I tell you more?' There was a gleam in Bhaia's eyes.

'Do tell us,' we insisted.

'Once, Achchan Singh, who was the zaildar of village Laroiya and nambardar Sher Singh were passing through here. We were all busy at our looms. Suddenly, the zaildar got off his horse and started beating chacha Chajju with his stick, saying, "Why didn't you hold the bridle of my horse!"'

'Chacha pleaded with him—"Sardarji, I didn't see you ... else I would have held your bridle!" The zaildar cursed the whole Chamarli. Dharam naal, we all left our looms and stood trembling. Ultimately, Sher Singh intervened, "Let it be, Sardarji, Chajju Ram be more careful in future." And remounting their horses, they rode away towards Rastgo. The zaildar had wide judicial powers, and could put anyone behind bars, or let off anyone he wanted. It was said that he could get away with murder, and that is why the whole world was afraid of him! He could take away as many men as he wanted for begaar, the bastard!'

Bhaia's anger seemed about to explode. I felt that he was creating a new awareness of freedom in us.

I had often seen this pro-British zaildar near the Bhogpur thana. I had also seen him later when he was leading a miserable existence. But the plume of his turban and the proud tilt of his head were proof enough of his arrogance.

Bhaia went on, 'This was our lot! You must get some education, you bastards, then alone can you make something of your life. Things are not the same today.'

And then came the day I had not even dreamed about. It was in February 1972, an unforgettable day. An unforgettable experience. My last term in the tenth class was almost over. When I came home from school, I saw that our banyan peepal trees had been cut down. The bruised and massacred twin trees were an unbearable sight. Their long, thick branches lay scattered on the ground. Jagar the chowkidar and his sons were cruelly hacking and sawing away at the vast tree trunks.

I thought of last winter when most of the families in the areas had spent nights under these very trees, during the Indo–Pak war blackouts. We had dug trenches under them. Whenever a bomb fell near the Adampur airport or Bhogpur sugar mill, people would run to shelter in these trenches.

It was under these twin trees that the village folk had assembled to take turns guarding the various points in the village. During those frightening nights, I had felt life pulsating under these trees. A new twist to teasing would be given by Inder Singh's Swarana when he would say with a guffaw of laughter, 'The secret of "thefts" during winter nights will be out before Dussehra! What do you say, Krishna!' We adolescents could all understand the implications of his statement!

Looking at the broken and battered branches on the ground I felt as if the protective shade on our heads had been torn asunder. The loom pits seemed naked and vulnerable. The sole witness to all the oppression we had endured had been felled and destroyed.

The shadow of grief lay clearly across the faces of my family. My Daadi showered expletives on those responsible for this destruction and went on till the next morning, 'May you be destroyed! You have hurt me! God will do the same unto you!'

Daadi had seen those twin trees grow and flourish before her eyes ever since she had come here as a bride. She was deeply upset that the tree planted by her husband, and which had become a sturdy haven for the whole area, had been so cruelly and heartlessly destroyed.

Bhaia was also sad. But he consoled himself with the thought that whatever had happened had happened and was over. At least, now the young Jat boys would not loiter about or sit under the deep shades of the twin trees.

# 14

## An Oasis in a Desert

'Thakara! Thakara! Open the door!' Came the shout in a single breath from someone who was obviously agitated.

'Sounds like Babu Basant Singh!' Bhaia said as he rushed to open the front door, 'So early? The sun is not up yet! He has never done this before ... I hope everything is well!'

'Thakara, Jeet poisoned himself last night! He is asking for you! Hurry up and bring some asafoetida from Ratta's,' said Baba, tearfully as he came in. He was sobbing and wiping his tears with the *loi* wrapped around his shoulder. The news shook us all badly.

'Couldn't you call me at night?' Bhaia asked angrily.

Babu Basant Singh appeared not to have heard this. He repeated in a nasal tone, 'Thakar, come quickly! Malkit Kaur left for her parents' house yesterday.'

I noticed that Baba's rubber shoes had a thick layer of dust on them. There was a deep shadow of helplessness and sadness on his face.

'How stupid of him,' Bhaia muttered to himself.

Baba was gone in a few minutes. I recollected what had happened a few days ago. Taaya Jeet had been ploughing the triangular field near the dam on a rivulet of rainwater between Sohalpur and our village. He had fondly called out to me, 'Gudd!' and beckoned to me to come over. When I had gone up to him, he had stopped ploughing and forcibly stripped me of my shirt and underpants, and hung them on the horn of his pugnacious ox. Then he had told me with a laugh, 'Now you can take your clothes off from there!'

I had wept, trying to cover my nakedness with my hands. The louder I wept, the harder he laughed. His large teeth shone between his black moustaches and beard. Finally, he was wracked by a fit of coughing which turned his handsome face red.

'Here, take them off now,' he dared me. Picking me up in his arms he had teased me. He knew very well that I was scared of his black and white ox, a fierce looking aggressive animal. One of its horns had been broken while he was still a calf, and I remember how the wound had been bandaged for over a month. I was still weeping when Baba Arjan Singh, who was Taaya Jeet's uncle, had shouted in a commanding tone, 'You should be ashamed of yourself, fooling around with a boy like this.'

Taaya had immediately taken my clothes off from the horns of the ox and handed them to me. By this time, Malkit Kaur, his wife, had also arrived with lunch and so had Bhaia, Bade Baba, and Chotte Baba, who had all been working in the adjacent field. When Tai had heard about the prank he had played on me, she had frowned at him and taken me home with her when she left.

The train of my thoughts came to a halt when I heard Bhaia say, 'Oh! You ...'

He had been taking his bicycle out from the store inside, and the pedal-cog of the cycle (which had no pedal) had pierced his leg, a little above the ankle. Wincing, he muttered to himself, 'Haste makes waste!'

Bhaia cycled away, faster than the wind towards Sohalpur, which was a small village about three kilometres, southwest of our village.

There were deep wrinkles of worry on his face. Before mounting his cycle he turned to both of us and said, 'You two, don't go to school today.'

A little later the two of us had our meal and set off towards Sohalpur. Many frightening thoughts troubled me. I shivered as I walked along, and my heart beat faster and louder. When I saw the snake-trail on the ground near the dam, I was scared out of my wits.

Both the Babas looked tired and worn out and their eyes turned constantly turned towards the lane. They hardly spoke to each other. If they did, it was only to say, 'The afternoon is almost over … and Thakar has not yet come back …'

Babu Baba was running between the charpai on which his son lay and the door. He was restless and his nose was running.

After some time, a white car halted outside the door and Bhaia alighted, followed by a tall, stout, fair sardar. They made straight for Taaya's charpai. The two Babas hovered around, hope lighting up their wan faces.

'Sardara Singh, don't worry about the money, whatever it may take. I'll pay, but save the boy,' Baba Arjun Singh pleaded.

Babu Baba looked at their faces by turn; his face was forlorn and vulnerable. He sat down on the floor near the charpai.

The doctor examined Taaya thoroughly and carefully and gave him some medicine. Taaya vomited. After that, the doctor gave him an injection and some powder.

'Sardara Singh, we can take him to Bhogpur or Jalandhar in your car,' the elder Baba implored the doctor.

Taking Bhaia aside the doctor whispered something to him. The two Babas turned pale. They stood, motionless and silent, as if turned to stone. It seemed as if they had no clue whatsoever and the doctor appeared to be a God to them.

'Have faith in Waheguru. I have given him medicine, the rest is in God's hands, and life is His gift,' the doctor consoled them, as he straightened his own shirt. He went out and in the twinkling of an eye had driven off, and was lost in a cloud of dust. I watched the car as long as I could see it. To me, it seemed that Taaya's life hung in the balance of this cloud of dust that the car had raised.

On the other side of the haveli, Daadi Rao, who had been sitting there since the afternoon, signalled to me.

'What did the doctor say?'

'He says only God can give life.'

Daadi sighed and went towards the haveli. She had hardly taken two steps, when she stopped. She could not walk. Clutching her heart, she sank to the ground, tears streaming down her cheeks.

Babu Baba and I got busy covering the piles of shit and vomit at various points on the ground with dirt. His hands shook and he talked to himself, 'His insides are all torn and he is now dropping the fat in his body. His life is slipping away.'

'Thakara, save me, I did wrong!' Taaya pleaded as he writhed on the charpai. We all looked at him. Tears streamed from Babu Baba's eyes.

'We are all here. Be patient,' Bhaia tried to give him some courage, which he himself lacked. Then, he looked the other way and wiped his eyes with the edge of his turban.

'I will die, Thakara. If you can save me ... but don't let it come near me!' Taaya again told Bhaia, 'If you leave me ... I'll jump into the well.'

'Jeet, have some patience ...!' Bhaia seemed to have no words left and was unable to say anything more. Coming out of the room he told Baba Arjan Singh, 'It breaks my heart to see him in this condition ...'

The horizon had now turned orange, the sun was now almost ready to go down, and birds were seeking their nests.

Bhaia came back to the room after a drink of water at the well outside. He saw Taaya lying on the other charpai with the white sheet on top of him. He asked, 'Jeet ...? Why are ...'

'Thakara, it is the end ...'

'Don't say that Jeet ... God ...'

'Ask Malkit Kaur to forgive me,' Taaya could only mutter these words as life ebbed from him. His hand clutching Bhaia's slackened and then fell limp.

Baba, who stood next to the charpai, burst into tears.

'One is in Allawalpur (Jalandhar district) and the other in England—he was all that I had!' Babu Baba was talking about his sons. He seemed about to collapse, and sat down near Taaya on charpai and waited.

At the sound of the two brothers wailing, Daadi rushed in, crying and beating her chest. She moaned and called out to Taaya, trying to rouse him from his sleep. And as I watched her, I too burst into tears.

The birds were now safely back in their nests. The darkness, descending from the skies, was now impatient to take everything into its fold.

By this time, Chain's Pito and the nambardar's wife, Nanni, had also come in and were weeping loudly. The animals in their mangers were listening to the loud wailing, their heads turned in the direction of the house. Perhaps they could sense a greater tragedy.

'Both of you go home, I'll come later,' said Bhaia.

Baba Arjan Singh said, 'Thakara, go to Kathar as soon as you can and tell Malkit Kaur that Jeet is very ill, and that she should bring her brother along. Tell her brother in confidence that they have to reach here early in the morning for the funeral. Also, inform your aunt Prito and sister Meeto (the two were married in the same family) on your way.'

When we came back after the funeral, I saw that the big lane of the small village was packed with Taaya Jeeta's friends. This sad event took place some twenty days before Diwali in 1965.

Even after the bhog ceremony had been performed, conversations in our house continued to be centred round him. Bhaia would proudly tell us, 'Not every family has a man like Jeet! He was unique! Once we were at the haveli, and suddenly catching hold of my arm, Jeet took me to the cowshed and said, "Both of us are not wearing turbans. Come, put your hand on the cow as I do, and from today, both of us are brothers." And when we went home, like a child he told Malkit Kaur, "From today, if Thakar asks for the cycle, money, or anything else, don't refuse him; if you do I will be annoyed ... we are now brothers."'

Bhaia fell silent, and after a few moments said, 'Once Malkit Kaur came to the haveli and told me, "Bhaia ji, I hear that he is drinking at Baramia Mehndu's house ..."'

'I rushed there on my cycle and asked for him. When he came out, I told him, "Shame on you! Today you are drinking with them here, tomorrow they will also come to your home to drink." That was it—he immediately came away with me.'

'Shall I tell you more?' Bhaia asked.

'Once Takhi Shehbaz Pur reviled me sharply while drinking. Jeet caught him by the collar, "Don't talk nonsense! If you want to leave, then go right now." Sucha of Talwandi also once abused me and called me "Chamar, kameena!" It was Jeet who instantly rebuked him and shut him up.'

Bhaia had many memories of Taaya Jeet. Every night, at dinnertime, he would tell us a new anecdote.

'At Avtar's wedding, Baba Manakdhari was rolling out chappatis and he told chacha Arjan Singh, "Thakar is adding kindling to the chulha."

Chacha retorted, "It will poison everything!" Almost the same thing happened when Gyanu the barber complained, "Thakar is handling the food. Shame on you! If you talk this way we will not even get the bottle of liquor we have been promised." "Thakar is taking care of the whole show," said Daru the Jat halwai from Madhopur. "As you say," Gyanu answered. I had refrained from asking him why he had not objected to drinking the lassi that we had brought in buckets from the homes of the Jats and the Chamars on the occasion of the Akhand Path, just two days before. What was the difference *now*?'

Very sadly Bhaia said, 'The day passes somehow, but when the night comes I feel as if Jeet has returned and I can't sleep at night, and even if I do fall asleep, I dream of Jeet. He is on the lane near the dam, unscrewing the top of the cycle bell and using it as a cup to drink from, and passes it on to me to drink and then tells me, "Let's go, we will shout at the top of our voices! Don't worry, I am with you."'

As I sat listening to Bhaia, my thoughts would fly to Taayi. One could not bear her grief. I often visited her on holidays.

Badi Daadi Ishari, who was Tai's great-grandmother-in-law, would be on her charpai in the courtyard, either with a loi or a quilt around her. When I used to sit by her on her charpai, she would cover me with her quilt, press my head and back, and shower blessings on me, and tell me, 'I have taken you from Thakar for five rupees. I exchanged the turbans of Jeet and Thakar. Grow up fast, my son!'

The thin, dark, aging face of Bhago, the nambardarni of our village, flashed in my mind. She was always dressed in dirty clothes, with torn jootis on her feet, and a stick in her hand. She would always keep some distance between herself and our women, and would gather the folds of her clothes around her when she talked to them. If a child playing about in the lane happened to touch her, she would flick her stick and also shout at the child. She would be polluted by the touch! I would think, Badi Daadi did not get polluted when she touches me. She is also a Jat by caste and owned extensive lands. Our villagers keep going to Rada Tahli (the mand of River Beas) for wild grass and yet they treat us in this way.

Badi Daadi pampered me so much that I didn't want to go home. I would think, the same wind blows in our village too and people drink the same water. I would also think of Bhaia's remark, 'Sohalpur is a village of drug addicts! That Khushia of our community—people get poppy seeds from him any time they want. They cannot do without each other, how can they be polluted by touching each other!'

I would come out of my reverie only when Tai handed me a tumbler of hot tea. Tai would give me roti with jaggery or molasses, sugar or butter. She would also give me dal, dahi, and saag. If I wanted pickles, then I would take some from the chatti in the small room next to the kitchen. Nor would she let me wash the vessels I had used.

Tai had always loved me and frequently said, 'Do come to see us whenever you are free. It makes me happy.'

I knew what troubled her. She saw her dead daughter and son in me. When she did her washing, I would ply the hand pump so that she could wash her clothes properly. She liked having me around and I followed her like a lamb its mother.

When it was time for me to go home, she would say, 'Tell your mother to come and see me. After Tar's wedding, she came only at your Taaya's death. Tell her to come soon.'

On my way back home, my feet felt heavy. I would think, 'We should build a house near Tai's home, so that there is no need to go back and forth every day.'

'When her first son was dying of dropsy, everything possible was done to save him, but he was not to live. Then her daughter was born, but she too died. When god gives children he should also give them life,' Bhaia explained to us. 'God will bless her with grandchildren to carry on the family name. The poor soul has suffered enough.'

I interrupted, 'The other day Taaya said something about Bade Baba?'

'He asked for money for a bottle of liquor. He wanted to drink with someone at Dussehra. Chacha scolded him, saying that he did not have money to waste on liquor.'

Suddenly he said, 'Had Dr Sardara Singh come with me when I had gone to fetch him, Jeet would be alive today. But Maama delayed, "Let me see this patient and then the other one." He fussed about like an old woman, and it was afternoon by the time we left. Then he said, "Life is in God's hands." And he thinks he is a good doctor!'

'What can a man do? May God be merciful and kind to them. That alone can allay Malkit Kaur's grief.' Ma could say nothing more.

There was much talk of Taaya's heir after his death, the way we talked about warmth during the bitter winter, and then the New Year dawned.

It was the evening of 1 February 1966, that on his return from Sohalpur, Bhaia told us, 'Malkit Kaur has had a daughter.'

'If God had given her a son ...' Ma said with some hesitation, and then went on, 'It is His will, may He give the child a long life.'

I did not visit Tai for many days, the way I use to play around my mother's bed after her delivery, without going near her bed. The day I did go to Tai, she told me, 'Here is your sister. You'll soon finish your fifth standard and go on to the Government Middle School at Geeganwal to study. Then you can come and play with Debi.' Debi was as soft as cotton wool. When I picked her up she would laugh.

Daadi Rao, seated on the charpai, would tilt her head back and put a pinch of snuff into her nostrils. I would surreptitiously steal her snuffbox from her pocket. When she needed it again, and began looking for it, I would climb up to the roof. She would shout at me, 'Just wait, you good-for-nothing. Give me back my box, like a good boy! I'll set you right ...'

But she would laugh when she saw me prancing about, but I could only see her tongue in her toothless mouth. The wrinkles on her face deepened when she shaded her eyes with her hands and screwed them up to look up at me. She would search for her stick and I would immediately come down the step ladder, one bar at a time, and run off towards the haveli. Gesticulating, she would call out to me, 'Take tea for your Baba, my son.'

I used to put the pail of tea in front of Baba, at the tubewell. He would be waiting for it, looking intently down the lane, like a crow eyeing something it wants to eat. He would soak the poppy seeds in water, grind them and strain the mixture through a cloth, and then close his eyes and drink it in one breath. He pressed his hand over his moustache and straggly unwashed salt and pepper beard. He would tell me, 'Gudd, don't ask me for tea in future and don't drink any as you bring it for me. There is opium in it. I am addicted to it, but I don't want you to ...' Then he would take a sip of tea and advise me, 'Hard work makes all things possible. Isn't it said, "work hard and eat to your fill." It is true that

I am addict, but yet I don't waste my time. I do what I am good at. One must work with all one's capacity and power.'

Babu's clothes were often dirty. He would sit behind the tubewell, picking the lice from his kachcha. His salt-and-pepper hair was short and full of nits and lice. He was always scratching his head with both hands, under his loosely tied turban. He took a bath only once in about six months. He was terrified of the slightest bit of moisture.

Babu had taken me under his wings. He, my brother, and I would all cut the fodder for the cattle. We would work in the fields, planting, weeding, cutting, and harvesting. I never tired of work because Babu would relate stories from the Ramayana and the Mahabharat and about the Gurus. I wanted to write these stories in my book.

He would pull out his snuffbox as he worked, take a pinch and putting it into his nostrils, take a deep breath, draw it in, and then he would doze off. On coming to his senses, he would tell me, 'My son, study hard—only then can you help rid your family of poverty.' I felt as if Babu was repeating an eternal truth. I would look into his tawny eyes and laugh to myself.

People would come to him with problems of spinal pain, which he would cure by exorcizing the troubled spot. He would stop whatever he was doing and tell me, 'Gudd, run and fetch some lilac leaves.'

He would brush the leg of the patient with the leaves and branch I had fetched and intone something under his breath. He would then tell the patient, 'Come to me once more. It hasn't cost you anything. Have faith in God, you'll soon be well. Bring some prasad with you next time.'

Then, while distributing the prasad he would tell me, 'We have this gift, of healing—what else do we have—it is all the blessings of God.'

Bada Baba would call out to me, 'Gudd, come for a ride in the cart!'

I would run and climb up on the shaft of the leveller. He would pull at the ropes passing through the nostrils of the oxen to make them run and also prod them with his stick, calling aloud, 'May God be merciful to you.'

He took me with him to the flour mill or to get the punctured tyres of the cart repaired. Baba would sit on the yoke with the ropes in his hand. Before setting off, he would call out in his commanding voice, 'Check the tool box and lock it carefully so that nothing falls out when we are on the move.'

Whenever he went out, Bada Baba tied up his snow-white beard neatly and looked elegant. His light tawny eyes gleamed. He always wore a white muslin turban. A set of white kurta and pajama made his intelligent face and handsome body look more graceful. His martial bearing was testimony to his life in the army.

The whole family and the whole village, had deep respect for Baba Arjan Singh. He did not say much, and whatever he said was spoken with patience and intelligence. Though he did not scold the members of his family often, they were all afraid of him. His orders were obeyed promptly. I too was afraid of him and would pretend to be good and sensible in his presence.

Whenever Baba sent me home for some work, I would play with Debi. I was in the eighth or ninth class at that time, but I took her piggy back riding round the courtyard, to make her laugh. I would pretend to be 'frisky' and try to throw her off my back and make her cry. Tai would watch all this horseplay and comment, 'Another couple of years, and Gudd will go to Tanda to study. Then what?'

'Dishi (Debi's cousin, her aunt's daughter who lived with them for her studies) is there. They will soon become good friends.'

I would return home from Sohalpur, my school bag slung across my shoulder and a bundle of dried millet or fodder on my head. I would think of Tai and both the Babas, their small talk and feel happy. But I had been hurt by Daadi's comment as I was going out to the field's from haveli, 'With that spade on your shoulder, you look like a Jat.'

The hurt stung. I felt demeaned by Daadi and was upset for many days.

My trips to Sohalpur became less frequent after I began studying at Tanda. Tai and both the Babas would send me messages, but I was busy with my newly found interests—attending poetry readings, or participating in various other activities going on in the college. When my classmates told me, 'There is great fun at the NSS Camp, attend just once and see for yourself?' I too joined the camp, after my BA Part II examination at Munak (Gurudwara Tahli Sahib). It rained very heavily for a couple of days.

'I am going to the village and will be back!' said my friend Dhyan when the heavy rains stopped. He and I were from the same village.

By evening, he was back. At once, he told me, 'Gudd, I met your Bhaia. He asked me to tell you that Chacha Arjan Singh passed away four days ago (26 June 1977). He died of brain haemorrhage.'

The image of Baba seated under the peepal tree and reciting the Japji, the morning prayers, and the Rehras in the evening flashed before my eyes. I thought of his trips to our village with cartloads of mud to help repair a collapsed building, or carrying loads of dried tobacco, in the baithak of Taaya Diwan, drinking rum, and exchanging stories of war, 'Look Diwan, I was shot through my left ankle, here, but I still had my rifle with me—we were crossing the Panama Canal at the time, during the World War I ...'

Taaya would add his story to this, 'We of the CRP also questioned the Mizos thoroughly, but they never give us any information—Phizo's influence is very strong.'

I thought of Baba talking to people as he sat on the charpai, basking in the sun and saying, 'This Behram Sarishta located on that knoll—my grandfather has seen the boats tied near the banyan tree; the River Beas flowed right here.'

Dead, Baba was now even dearer to me than before. Then I thought about the white pajama kurta set he had given me. At that time I was in the class eight and he had bought them for me when he returned from his pilgrimage in appreciation—as I had slept at the haveli with Babu for more than twenty days.

On my return from the camp Bhaia told me, 'Chacha had bought a marla (about thirty-one square yards of land) opposite our home for us. Whenever I needed money for paying your fees or for some other work, he would tell me, 'Take whatever you need from the cupboard, but put away the rest carefully.'

Having said this, he stopped, and then went on, 'Whenever I talked about all that he had done for me, Chacha would say, "Thakara, it was you who dug all our land some five or six feet deep and turned the soil, making our lands fertile, and helped us become prosperous. Earlier, our fields hardly yielded any crops, and only crickets and insects shrilled and played about here. Now, we sell a minimum of a hundred and twenty- five sacks every year. This all is because of your work. We can never repay you enough."'

Bhaia had an inexhaustible stock of anecdotes about Chacha, 'His tigerish face would brighten up when I discovered some money he had tied up in an oilcloth and hidden in a bundle of hay. Taking the money he would say, "Honesty holds up the sky and keeps the earth going ... though old values have been all but forgotten. That is why I tell you, Thakara, that it does not matter if a poor man takes a little more than is his due, at least he will never cheat you. You work for us the whole day long. When you are with us we seldom think of our children—it is you who looks after us. All this talk of mine and yours is meaningless and we should not get too involved in it ..."'

My uncle's sons interrupted Bhaia, 'It is good that the old man got the land registered in Babu's name—now they can make whatever arrangements they want. Your relations with Babu are very cordial, this we must acknowledge.'

'Babu is also on his last legs. Who knows what may happen and when,' my cousin Manji remarked.

'He is heartbroken and is also getting on,' Bhaia said. 'We have had a very pleasant relationship, have no complaints or grudges, and have always got whatever we wanted from their fields. If we had to go to some function or wedding, then we were given plenty of fodder to leave at home. If we were harvesting the wheat crop they never once came to check, we could bring away as much as we wanted.'

Bhaia smoked his hookah for some time and continued, 'That is why the Jats and even their own relatives are annoyed with them—and say that they have given me control over everything. It is true that I look after his accounts, and pay the carpenters, ironmongers, water carriers and all the other artisans and also look after the lands.'

He stopped and then went on sadly, 'If we had some land, we too would have had a better life, with a storehouse full of wheat, the way Jats have. People like the nambardar would have also come to us to ask, for sugar cane, or fodder or something else.'

As I sat listening to this conversation, images of Bada Baba or Babu watering the wheat fields. I remembered that they had never stopped us from playing in the fields. I and Deba, the sons of Lashkar Singh Patwari (son of Babu Baba) would fight on the berseem. Deba was stout and flabby and he would some times, threw me down and straddle me. We were classmates and his elder brother Binder and my elder brother were in the same class. This trail of images broke when Bhaia called out, 'Gudd, fill the chillum.'

'Look at this! I sent a message to them … that Gudd had got a job in FCI and they haven't sent me even a box of sweets!' Tai said when one day I touched her feet and presented her with a box of sweets.

'May there be greater successes to your name. Don't forget what you were, and look after your parents.'

Daadi Rao also added her comment as she raised her stick and said, 'So you did think of us!'

I felt that in her eyes, I was still a child, the way I had been when I used to steal her snuffbox.

'What nonsense are you talking! Give us some tea,' Baba Babu was impatient.

'I will continue to visit you, Daadi.'

'Good, I had taken a vow to visit the Bangla Sahib Gurudwara in Delhi, on five consecutive amavasyas. Take me along … Birju now lives there.'

'Daadi, you can come with me whenever you want.'

Tai interrupted her, 'Look Gudd, Debi is shooting up like a sugar cane plant!' Debi, who was studying in the seventh at that time, looked away and laughed faintly in an embarrassed way.

I visited Tai once every few months. Our regular conversation always included the family of Sohalpur. Bhaia would be worried and say, 'It would be nice if Patwari comes back. His return would be really helpful. There are only old women at home, and there must be a man there. The Patwarin does occasionally visit them to ask about their welfare. They say that by God's grace, Binder is doing well in England.'

He would pull at the pipe of his hookah, and putting it away, say, 'Dishi and Debi are growing up, but we can only say that they may do whatever they wish.'

One day, on 5 August 1980, I had just come home from Bhulath (where the FCI office was located then) when Bhaia informed me, 'Gudd, Babu is no more.'

'Really? What happened?' I asked with a deep sigh.

'It had rained heavily. They tell me that he was sleeping in the verandah near the cattle. The roof of the verandah fell on him. They found him in the morning.'

'Did you attend the funeral?'

'The stream was flooded and no one could reach us.'

'They could have come over the Bhogpur bridge.'

'I went over today. Malkit Kaur was telling me. "Bhaiaji, we told the nambardar and also Chain's family to inform you, but no one did."'

Babu Baba's face, the tip of his nose, slightly crooked, his hand pressing his beard, his rope-like turban tied untidily, flashed in my mind's eye. I saw him seated in the ironmonger's workshop, listening to the radio, before and during the war with Pakistan in 1971; talking to Bhaia in the fields, 'Russia has also warned America that it should not try to grab India through Pakistan or they will enter the fray.' I saw Baba scattering seeds on the ploughed earth. I saw him guarding the fields against birds and animals, or blocking up the holes of field mice to protect the standing cane crop in the fields. I saw him piling up mud and trying to build a protective barriers with his bare hands, around the land. His words rang in my ears, 'Work as hard as you can and your poverty will vanish—and never say "no", but always say "hanji" (yes sir).'

Sometimes, I saw Babu Baba telling me, 'This is the black partridge and that is the black quail—now you know the difference? This is the yellow-black sugar cane rooster. Just see how frisky those red sparrows are! Did you see the nightingales? How fiercely the snake and mongoose fight! Don't ever hit the porcupine with a hoe, it may put one of its quills into you. You two brothers have killed this big lizard, but in future, take care, it can bite you. All these creatures have come down from the mountains because of the dam and the digging of the canal.' And just then a rabbit had dashed out of the bushes near us and scampered away.

I realized that Babu had been giving me a lesson in general knowledge.

The next day, I had gone over to condole with his family, and Daadi had sadly said, 'Son, we both, mother and daughter-in-law are now widows. You alone are our support now.'

'Daadi, we are always with you.'

I felt as if I was lying to her because my visits to Sohalpur were infrequent. But Tai said, 'Son, you and Debi are like brother and sister! Do go to see her when she is married.'

Tai's emotional appeal moved me immensely. Tears sprang to my eyes. I felt that if Debi had had a brother, Tai would not have to plead with me in this way. A son does have his own importance in our society.

It seemed as if Tai's worries about Debi were increasing.

It was during this period, in March 1987, that I was transferred to Delhi.

I was now four hundred kilometres away from my village. Yet I still dreamt of the fields of Sohalpur, the crops in those fields, the silk cotton pods bursting with white fluffy cotton, the roses blooming, the clear bottom of the well of the nambardar, and the dead crows swinging from the electric wires. I yearned for those sights and sounds of my village; was bored in Delhi and longed to go back.

One day, when I visited them, Tai had remarked, 'It is good that you have gone away to Delhi. Bhaiaji was telling us that the extremists had you in their control. Waheguru has saved you.'

Daadi interrupted her, 'Son, I want to visit Bangla Sahib Gurudwara before I die. Because I took a vow, Meeto and I will both come.'

'You can come any time. Daadi, it is your own home.'

Two months later, Daadi and Bua had come to Delhi. After observing the fifth amavasya, she said, 'Now, I can die in peace, son. Now, Death may come when it likes.'

'Attend my wedding before you die,' I answered, and Daadi laughed as she brandished her stick at me!

... Then, suddenly I received a letter from home ... 'Malkit Kaur has passed away yesterday.' It was 25 July 1988.

I thought of the promise I had made a few months ago ... that I would take my wife to see them. But now, this was impossible.

Like a film unrolling images continued to flash by ... sometimes I was with Tai as she visits her sister in Susaan or her sister in Gadhi with Debi in my arms.

Sometimes, Tai gives me a bag and takes Debi in her arms, and at other times, she is telling me, 'Gudd, you and Birju write the name of your Taaya in a beautiful style on the wall of the new home.' Again, she was telling me, 'Gudd, do give her a scolding; she plays the whole day and doesn't study—she is in the eighth class now, by the grace of god.'

When I visited the village, Bhaia had said, 'Who is there to visit and condole with? You have expressed your condolences to us, that's enough. She was ill. But she was not the type to bother about small things. Also, we didn't realize that her time would come so soon.' He paused and then went on, 'They say that Malkit Kaur had insisted that the triangular field near the dam should be given to us for the fodder crop, but could not do much. Though Jeet was not alive, she fulfilled her duties towards us, as he would have.'

Despite Bhaia's advice, I did go to Sohalpur. The house which had been full of happiness and laughter, and whose doors had always been open for us, was locked. The lane outside was overgrown with grass. Then I looked at the haveli, and saw the dilapidated condition it was in. But I also saw that the peepal sapling Babu Baba had planted stood tall and strong.

I was not inclined to go into the haveli, because I saw the tall plants of hemp, carrot, and other plants from some distance, and the courtyard was bleak and desolate, with despair stretched all over it.

Now, whenever I think of the love and affection given to us by this Jat family, it seems to me that their love, which made our lives beautiful and colourful as the spring, had been an oasis in the barren desert of our lives.

# 15

# Hatred of my Name

'All the Chamars have started studying and are growing swollen headed! If they all get jobs, who will work in our fields? Bhaiyas? They are all rushing to this area! Only if you instruct them ten times will they lift a finger and on top of it, they gobble up ten-ten chappatis at any given time!' This was Bhujjar who, seeing seven or eight of us going to college, raised his voice so that we might hear him.

This set me thinking. Our parents had worked hard on low wages or no wages at all; they had borrowed to educate us; and we also worked for daily wages to pay for our education. We did not cheat anyone, and yet these people always resented us and were forever planning to get *their* sons appointed to high offices. I suddenly thought of the time when we had gone to work in his fields and he had recited a ditty, rather sarcastically, as he was pouring tea into our glasses in the afternoon,

*Chah (chai) choori, chah Chamari,*
*Chah neechon ki neech,*
*Pooran Brahma paar the*
*Je chah na hundi beech!*
(Tea is like a Chamar, the lowest of the low/ Had it not been for tea, the low castes would have been able to attain redemption).

I was shocked. Only one who has experienced life in this region would understand this vile verse. Tea was the low-caste's drink while the upper castes drank milk. That by itself made tea an inferior drink. Therefore as long as low castes did not drink milk, they could never hope to attain heaven/Brahman/*moksha*. It was difficult for me to swallow the tea poured into my glass. I felt like throwing my tea back at him and clawing his grisly grey beard, teach him how to speak properly, and also understand that it was the mind more than the body that found such treatment intolerable. But I also remembered what Bhaia had once told me, 'Look, it is with great difficulty that I have been able to collect this money, which is as slippery as a rabbit, and you are now in college. Study, but also work like a man. The money has to be returned along with interest.'

These thoughts helped me to control myself from giving Bhujjar a piece of my mind, and I swallowed my fury which played havoc with my mind and body.

He was called 'Bhujjar' because of his thick salt-and-pepper beard which was more white than black, and which he tied with a twist. Thick layers of fat covered his cheeks and lay around his eyes, and people often wondered how he managed to see.

My heart twisted inside me whenever I thought of his bitter words. My efforts to make some headway in life seemed so hopeless, and I would then console myself with the thought that though others said whatever they wanted, time did not stand still. Time must move forward, and it would.

Those summer days, as I studied in the dim flickering light of the diya, I thought constantly of Bhaia. My eyes may have been on the book, but my thoughts were about the backbreaking labour he undertook to earn for the family he supported. We were seven siblings, of which the youngest two were still at my mother's breast. One was still cutting his milk teeth and the other was yet to shed his.

I had often told my mother very clearly, 'I don't want any more siblings. Our problems are increasing, and I am ashamed of carrying my sisters around.'

My mother agreed with me but sometimes she also would be annoyed. She would argue, 'How can one throw away God's blessings?' Whenever she told Bhaia what I had said, he would chase me with his jooti in his hand, 'Saala, he has become an Englishman—now he wants to advise *me*! ... Should I become ... a renunciate just because *you* feel this way!'

I tried to explain things to him. I would remind him of our financial problems, and the setbacks I faced in my studies. I reminded him that there were ten of us including Bhaia, Ma, and my grandmother, living and sleeping in this courtyard and the small dingy room at the back. During the rainy season it would be very humid. There were five animals tied indoors for a large part of the year. The house was overcrowded and life was painful and a terrible headache, Tauba! Tauba!

I felt my responsibilities intensifying ... and I bought a table lamp with a glass chimney from my earnings. This way, the light of the lamp did not flicker and was now steady. I had a feeling that now no wind could turn the light of this lamp into darkness, by blowing out its flame. The possession of this lamp gave me great pleasure, as if I had acquired something precious. But at night, the lack of a room of my own and the waste of my time hurt me, and I was afraid that this would shatter all my hopes for my future. Then, I had an idea. During the day I would either study under some tree or in the small room off the gurudwara, which had been built with the wood of peepal and banyan trees, and at night I studied and slept in the sitting room of my classmate Rampal.

Studying in college had its own charm, though I had to walk some four or five kilometres every day to the nearest railway station, books in hand. I had the freedom of the college, with newspapers in Punjabi, Hindi, and English to read and the boundless knowledge stored in the library, all within reach. I wanted to assimilate all this in no time and forget the social difficulties, I had often encountered ... just forge ahead ... I went to college eagerly, nurturing a deep desire to do well in life.

It was at this time that the Moga shooting incident occurred on 5 October 1972. All colleges, including ours, closed down, but student organizations became active. Long speeches were delivered with various promises and bits of information. Our blood would boil listening to this rhetoric. But when a student whom I didn't know, handed me an object wrapped in a piece of cloth, my legs trembled. I had no clue what the object was and when he returned after fifteen minutes to retrieve his packet, he looked at my face and remarked, 'You are half dead with fear! What a chicken-heart!' I was relieved.

We did not go to college because the conditions were such. But a few days later, all of us from our area prepared to go to college against the wishes of our families. Bhaia again advised me, 'Don't do what the Jat boys are doing.'

While Bhaia's advice sank into my heart I wondered why he always warned me thus.

Passing through the clusters of bananas, pines, and bamboo and past the well, an incident that had occurred a long while ago streamed into my mind. I was in the fourth class at that time, and Tai Taro had told my mother, 'Take Gudd out of school and send him to work at our well so that my Avatar can go to school.'

The very next day, I was seated on the beam of the Persian water-wheel, working it. Tai had brought some food for me and had told me, 'Gudd, get off the beam. I have to fill water for your Taaya. You can drink water from the lower level.'

This statement sent an arrow into my heart exactly like I had seen her husband piercing the hind quarters of the buffaloes with his goad. My tears did not spill over the way water drips through the holes of the buckets of the Persian wheel into the well itself, but were soaked back into my eyes.

I was jolted out of my reverie when I saw a swarm of bees ahead of us. They seemed to be coming at us from all sides. Helpless, my friends and I sat on the ground and stayed that way for a long time, hoping for a bright future!

The college was still closed and the students still in the streets, raging like mad bulls. One of the so-called student leaders would raise his arms dramatically, flail them about, and say, 'Friends, there has been a shooting at Batala. Two or three students have been wounded, some even martyred. This is a critical moment for all of us. Come, let us all intensify our struggle to increase the pressure on the government. Let us also send in a memorandum, written and signed in our blood. Rest assured, victory shall be ours, 'Inquilab zindabad! Long live the revolution.'

We all enthusiastically put our bloodied thumbprints on the memorandum. We learnt new words. The consequence of all this was that colleges closed for thirty-nine days and then it was winter.

Right through the time I spent in college, I liked the meaning of my name—Balbir. To me, it seemed in tune with the style that the Sikhs used. There was also a hidden challenge in it. More significant was the fact that it had no caste undertones. The latter part of the name 'Chand' however, echoed with Hindu beliefs, a system which still held us captive. There was an odour of abasement and humiliation in it which was all pervasive.

I would often think of the day Bakshi had brought home a calendar with a picture of 'Sita-Ram' on it from the Dussehra mela. The moment I saw it, I had snatched it from his hands, ripped it up, thrown it on the floor, and stamped on it. I was in the seventh class at that time.

Bhaia had guessed my intentions and exclaimed, 'You stupid fool. What have you done! How will this change anything?'

'It is said that it is this Ram who murdered Shambuk Rishi because he believed in God,' I repeated what I had heard, in all innocence, and added, 'Raja Ramchandra and his people are "Arya putras", from alien lands, and they felt that they were superior to us—the real inhabitants of this country. They snatched power from us, and made us untouchables ... they tricked us into slavery ... they were extremely cruel to us. If a fortress was to be constructed, then it were the *achchuts* who are to be sacrificed, if there is any "sacred" work to be performed, then an untouchable is to be made a scapegoat, and all this evil is being perpetrated in the name of religion ...? If we revere the Guru Granth Sahib, how are we Hindus?' I went on with great fervour, 'Have you forgotten the time that a group of Hindus from Jalandhar visited us, advising us in Punjabi, that we should mark "Hindi" as our mother tongue in the census? And it was I who retorted that we speak Punjabi, and that Punjabi is our mother tongue.'

'We also did not accept their suggestion! Were we not aware that all this was being done to create differences between the people?' Bhaia retorted with great confidence.

Bhaia told us many things, when he had heard my arguments that day. He asserted, 'I also want us to strike at the deep-rooted hypocrisy of Hindu society, the way our banyan trees were uprooted and cut into pieces. But one man cannot do anything; it must be a joint effort, and it needs courage and dedication.'

He pulled and adjusted his turban firmly, and looked around with a satisfied expression in his eyes, as if he was trying to see his future in me! I felt that he was not in any way annoyed with me, even though he had scolded me earlier.

The desire to change my name grew in me. I did not ask anyone about this, nor seek any information. But whenever I thought about not being able to change my name, I would be upset and sad.

During this confusion during my annual exams a strange thing happened, which aggravated my problem. We were all in a bus, when this exchange took place, 'You have deliberately stepped on my foot three times,' said a commanding and cultured feminine voice from behind us. We immediately turned around and some passengers looked obliquely at what was going on.

A boy from our mohalla, and also our classmate, was making excuses and looking very innocent, 'It was not deliberate, accidental. I don't know how it happened.'

'You are trying to be over smart. Don't you have a mother or a sister? Take the bus to the police station,' a frail, innocent girl told the conductor. Her face was red with anger and she looked imposing and impressive.

'Let it be, biba, drop the matter,' an old man told the girl, and turning to the boy, said, 'Don't ever do this again.'

As soon as the bus came to a halt, we all jumped down hurriedly. This girl kept on asking people for help.

We had just gone a few steps when the boy said, 'Oh-oh, light brown eyes, sharp nose, fair complexion, a beautiful round chin, her lovely face helped allay my hunger!'

'Allayed or enhanced your hunger?' I asked sarcastically. I took a few steps more and asked, 'Why don't you write all this in the Punjabi exam paper you are going to appear for?'

This incident, however, bothered me for many days. The thought that the girl was right but that no one had taken her seriously haunted me.

We had a few days off before the next paper. I went to the room near the gurudwara with a pen and some papers. Suddenly, the urge to write resurfaced within me. I was impatient to write about the recent occurrence.

I kept fiddling with words and putting them together, writing and scratching them out. Finally, I was able to write a few verses, and a page and half were filled with them. I was overjoyed. I recited the verses in which I supported the girl to some friends.

My verses were praised.

And I began writing poetry.

The question of my name assumed great significance when the matter of my poem being published in the college magazine cropped up. My heart cried when I thought of not being able to change my name, the way a peacock regrets its claws as it dances, its tail spread splendourously. The contempt that I felt for my name increased and I tried to think of ways to give my Hindu name a different form.

# 16

## Literature and Politics

Picking up my books and charpai, I sought temporary refuge in my eldest Taaya's house, occupying his central room. I positioned myself before a window which had no shutters. I arranged some bricks to make a table, and placed my books and table lamp on them. I spread a sheet on the rod at the top of the window, to make a curtain. This was my room! And on its peeling walls, many images flashed and flickered before my eyes—of some sad and many happy faces, of dancing men and women. There was an impression of the lean and handsome face with sharp and neat moustaches of Shaheed Bhagat Singh, in a hat, and there were also flashes of the faces of Lenin and Marx to be seen. I felt that either my presence had refined this dull space or my personality had improved in this room.

But suddenly, my bright mood came crashing down the way a high-flying, gas-filled balloon bursts and falls to the ground. A sudden heavy squall drove the curtain on the window into the room. The lamp fell on to the charpai. I rushed to save my books from the heavy downpour, but a shard of the broken glass of the chimney pierced the sole of my foot.

The reed roof of the room was still dripping water the next day, the way blood had from my foot the night before. A sudden thought came to me, and I told Bhaia, 'If only I could get Hari Ram's room ...'

At this half-expressed wish, Hari Ram handed over his room at Bhaia's asking. The next day, my eldest brother had made some khus chicks for the windows, and fixed them onto the window frames. I felt as if spring had descended into the bleakness of autumn, spreading its pleasant fragrance all over.

I became so attached to this room that I would visit it at least once every day, even in summer, when I was out in the wheat fields, harvesting or planting maize, or weeding sugar cane. As I sat there and read some book or the other, for a while, all my weariness seemed to drop away from me. Gradually, my connection with home became restricted to my meals, or doing some work that I had been asked to do. Bhaia would suddenly descend on my room for inspection. He would ask, 'Do you study or are you sleeping most of the time …? Listen to me carefully … poetry is not going to feed you … First, pass your BA, then you can write whatever nonsense you want to …'

As I heard this warning, I thought of the day I had asked him for money to buy a pair of shoes and had instead returned with some books that I had bought at the Russian literature exhibition at the Panjab Book Centre in the college. I had got involved in this sort of literature, and I would often spend all the money I could spare on Marxist publications.

Maxim Gorky's *Mother* and his biography left me shaken. I read out some parts of it to my family and my uncles and aunts. Sometimes, I was so moved by the books I read that I would cry, and at other times, feel elated at a man fighting so successfully against the heaviest odds.

During those days, I was attracted by the communist ideology and the Party, and was deeply impressed by the initiative taken by the Soviet Union for world peace, and the efforts it made to create a strong support for it in the Third World countries—by organizing rallies, sit-downs, demonstrations, processions, and meetings. I would listen to the long rhetorical discussions of the comrades on various international issues. As my interest grew, I wanted more information … and I would read socialist literature and try to understand many public issues. Ultimately I became an active worker of the Indian Communist Party, when I was about twenty—in 1974–5.

Regular meetings of the village cell and the block level cell were held, and the different problems of peasants and landless workers were thoroughly discussed. I participated eagerly in these discussions.

Problems that had a bearing on all, such as population explosion, rising prices, and unemployment were discussed, but suddenly it would focus on 'your people', 'your community', 'Adi dharamis', and other such words. A zamindar comrade would then intervene, 'Don't aggravate the situation, forget caste ... and talk about class ... when economic conditions are the same, then why talk about caste ...?'

... Land reforms were also discussed. One of the working-class comrades suggested, 'Our senior member should exert pressure on the government for these reforms ...'

'I do not agree with the party line that reservation should be based on caste. They should be based on economic conditions. There is also the need to relate it to merit ...' Comrade Sharma tried to give a new direction to the discussions.

'Comrades, the proletariat, which is the vanguard of the revolution we are trying to create, do not have even human rights ...! What do they have, except social inequality and economic distress? How many of them are educated? How many have jobs? The government has certain rules and norms for selection, and unless they meet those norms (which they can't) they cannot get jobs. Second, tomorrow, if they were to say, keep your jobs and give us lands, and that we should stop taking the double advantage that we take, what will you people do? We do keep discussing the question of social equality and removal of disparities,' I intervened and added, 'Intercaste or love marriages should be encouraged, for that alone may help create social equality.'

'No use churning water, don't waste time discussing what is impossible ... land is a Jat's life ... it is for our leaders to think about land reforms—not for the likes of you and me,' this was one of our zamindar comrades.

'The real question is, how many people are you taking for the demonstration tomorrow for twenty-four hour supplies of electricity and increase in the subsidy?' Our leader would try to wind up the discussion.

The true reality of the social system was revealed within six months of my becoming active in the party ranks. One of our senior and prominent comrades left the Party at the behest of his inner voice. He underwent the Sikh baptism ceremony by taking the *amrit* and began wearing the baldric of his kripan over his shirt.

I tried to woo as many from our courtyard for the Party as I could, as instructed by the Party. I read Russian writers such as Dostoevsky, Gogol, Sholokhov, Chekov, Ahsad Mukhtar, and Chengez Aitmatov, and was deeply impressed by them and the characters they had created. But when I compared these characters and the determination with which the Bolsheviks had worked for the development and progress of their people with the conditions of the landless labour, with the low-castes who were deprived in the name of religion in my own country, a storm would rage in my heart. I wondered at the difference in our two societies—the Soviet government encouraged and made efforts for equal distribution of wealth, setting up of cooperatives, public health and education, and here, there was only contempt for the poor, even after the backbreaking work they did, and curses and abuse showered on them in the name of caste. The lower castes were not even treated like human beings. What was this if not a conspiracy to keep the depressed classes beyond the pale of society?

These ideas were reflected in the poetry that I wrote, which became more aggressive, and my themes were largely concerned with the working class, caste divisions; with people deprived of all rights. To protest against the caste system, I had already changed my name to Balbir Madhopuri.

My interest in literary and political activities deepened. I took part in all rallies, demonstrations and congresses of the Party, held far and near—Bhatinda, Chandigarh, Patiala, Jalandhar, and Delhi—with my friends, and also took sympathizers and fellow-travellers to them in large numbers. This comforted me. It made me happy to see hordes of people waving red flags in their hands. We raised enthusiastic slogans:

'Look at the games Indira Gandhi plays,' one would say and the rest would shout, 'she has eaten the electricity and drunk all the oil.'

One comrade would say, 'When the workers' blood flows,' calling forth the answer—'Then will the red storm rage.'

We, the active workers of the Party at the lower levels, would speak of the Congress and the Akalis in derogatory tones. We called the Akalis 'Communalist' and referred to the Congress as a party of the capitalists, and gave detailed reasons for our views. Many called us the mad atheists.

Sometimes, there were disagreements and tensions. But in the end, we stuck firmly to the party line. Bant Brar and Tara Singh Sandhu of the All India Naujawan Sabha were the instructors of Jalandhar, Bhogpur, and the tehsil level cells.

Differences within the Communist Party of India on issues of supporting Congress policies such as bank nationalization and the abolition of the privy purses of princes, land reforms legislation, and maintaining close relations with Soviet Union, and efforts made for world peace through the Non-Aligned Movement, spread. There was criticism within the Party and the need for introspection was stressed. But I was busy writing poems against the capitalist countries and their leader, the USA, venting the pent up anger within me. One example was:

*Burdened I am with the worries of life*
*The way Diego Garcia is loaded with armaments!*
*My body and soul belong to my beloved,*
*The way Pakistan is mortgaged to America!*

My poems were now being published in papers like *Nawan Zamana*. From time to time, my translation of some literary piece would also get published. I. Serebriakov's *Panjabi Literature* and a collection of essays entitled *Guru Nanak* (Progressive Publishers, Moscow) were a great help in giving a proper direction to my literary efforts.

My literary activities received a shot in the arm when Bhaia refused to pay for my education after my graduation. I somehow persuaded him and joined MA classes in Punjabi Literature at Lyallpur Khalsa College, Jalandhar. I had pointed out to Bhaia that Bakshi was now working in the Police Department for the last three years, and that all of us at home were also working.

The atmosphere in the College was very stimulating. The teachers were all very friendly and progressive in their views, like Prof. Didar Singh of Tanda College, who had written the book *Luna* (1954). They were very encouraging, helped us in our literary efforts, and guided our creative impulses. I, Misir Deep Bhatia, and others were often sent to other colleges to participate in various poetry competitions. A *Kavi Sammelan* (a poetry recital), had been organized by the college at its open-air theatre, and my name featured along with those of other leading Punjabi poets. It was a day I can never and will never forget.

Jalandhar was an important centre of political activity, and I was happy there. Newspapers in all languages of the region, Punjabi, Hindi, and Urdu, were published here, as also were magazines. It had a radio station and a television centre—Doordarshan. There were frequent visits by many politicians and foreign delegations. Russian writers often visited the city, and it was a revelation for me to watch and participate in the public meetings, to hear Comrade Jagjit Singh Anand's translation of their speeches and to witness the response to their oration! I felt that it was worth sacrificing everything for the sake of the Revolution.

On a bright winter day, the people waited for hours on the green lawns of the Desh Bhagat Memorial Hall for Shri Inder Kumar Gujral, the Indian ambassador to the Soviet Union. We were informed that bad weather had delayed his flight from Tashkent to Amritsar. It was an experience to hear about the Soviet Union from this personality with a Lenin-style beard! Democracy under proletarian dictatorship! The views and ideas of intellectuals and writers in the delegation deeply touched my heart and mind, since experiences were a continuous process.

I would often think that we should as early as possible set up an administrative system like the Soviets in our country. Economic equality should be achieved with the wave of a wand, and the dark mark of caste should be forever removed from the social system. Everyone should work, no one should be oppressed, and the exploitation of the dalits and the Untouchables should be stopped. The attitude of the zamindars who came to our area and raised hell should immediately change. We should get rid of those demeaning traditions which have kept the dalits and the workers suppressed and exploited.

I joined the Food Corporation of India in 1978. My literary and political activities had increased especially after I was elected the general secretary of the district branch of its union, by a marked majority. This clearly showed that a large numbers of workers in the organization supported the Communist Party. I was wholly convinced about my wisdom.

I had many bitter experiences of this public sector enterprise, working in its Bulath branch. Trucks would arrive, loaded with wheat, rice, and other food grains, which would then be unloaded in the godown. Huge heaps of grain would be loaded off the trucks in seconds, and the grain then filled in sacks. I was often told, 'Comrade, you relax, and read. The work will be done.'

By evening those sacks would be turned into money, which would be pocketed. I would hear, 'Do something about the comrade. He doesn't take money, doesn't drink. If nothing else send a woman after him.'

Musical evenings would be arranged to forget the tensions of the day and to relax. Jokes, which were mostly about women, would be told. Even the women who were working in the godown were not spared.

It was very upsetting. Sometimes I had suspicions about those women, and then again I felt concerned about their vulnerability and their helplessness. The result was that I would often advise these women how to conduct themselves with dignity.

'Have you finished counselling them? Are they your mother and sisters?' One of my colleagues commented sarcastically as he suddenly came out from behind a cover and laughed.

'Yes,' I answered. 'One must do something to protect them from being exploited.'

'If you can't get them, then make them your mother or sister! That is good, comrade! Do you think that no one knows about the secret doings of your union leader? Let them be a secret, don't be angry with *me* ...!' He took out his hankie and wiped his face and beard with it. Then, he continued. 'You are new here, in a couple of years you would be doing the same!'

On hearing the truth about the president of the union, I shut up, the way the shutter of the godown is pulled down with a bang.

The second stage of such musical gatherings would be when the liquor drunk began to show in their behaviour! Even the behaviour of the best would change drastically and they appeared totally different! 'You have not seen the ways of a Jat!' 'The Jat can break but does not bend!' 'If you defy a Jat, things can be difficult for you!' 'What does the Jat think of outsiders like you?' 'We are here to have fun—I have plenty of land anyway!'

I was getting tired of these pinpricks that were by now a daily occurrence! One day I said, 'Sahib, it would be better if you were not to repeat these words so often! You all are educated ...'

'Comrade, you are right, but I am used to this word "Jat", it has become my second nature!' Sahib explained, interrupting.

But a few days later I got my punishment, in the nature of a transfer to a distant place. The distance from home became longer. It meant cycling twenty-five kilometres one way. I could go home only once or twice a week. I knew no one in this area. My only companion here was a fourth class employee, Bela Singh, an ex-army man. My expenses increased. My family thought that I was spending on undesirable activities.

Finally, one day Bhaia did say, 'People earn plenty of extra money! But you ...?'

I did not say anything. He again said, 'The women of Bagowal are drunkards. They themselves get liquor and kebabs to entice men ... be careful ...'

I managed to spend two months in Chona Mandi. But that was not enough and I was sent to another place which was even further away. As the godown incharge, I was kept so busy that I could seldom find a few moments of leisure—except for quarreling with the workers whenever I learnt of the theft of some rice or wheat sacks.

The matter, however, was not yet over. I was often sent on duty to Kartarpur railhead to supervise the loading of grain sacks on to the train. The railhead was twenty-five kilometres from the village. I had to accept such difficulties as part of employment.

I would often chase thieves for two kilometres whenever I saw someone stealing grain. 'Don't run after them! If you must, chase these people,' a colleague of mine gave me this advice one day, as I came back with the labourer whom I had been chasing. He had pointed at a middle-aged woman who was picking coals between the railway tracks.

'She doesn't have much strength, otherwise there is plenty of coal scattered about ... they can go on collecting coal day and night ...' another colleague had added.

Suddenly, loud voices were heard, as also the sounds of slaps. Someone was shouting, 'They have taken away our Bimla, who was collecting grain from the flow of the trucks!'

A group of eunuchs from South India were shouting loudly, complaining about someone. I felt that these people had come a long way from home to earn their living to assuage their hunger, and the truck driver had committed this heinous act to fulfil his own hunger!

Gradually, the thought that I should leave the FCI and look around for another job in some other department began to take hold of me.

I passed my MA exam as a private candidate during this period, and got myself transferred to Bhogpur where I had like-minded colleagues.

I had gone to Bulath to visit some friends when I met a young man of about twenty-three, Rajendra Yadav by name, at the bus stop. I was troubled to see that the young man had lost both his hands. He looked at me with helpless eyes and said, 'Brother ... I have no money ... if ...?'

He continued with some hesitation, 'I was working on the chopper, cutting some fodder, when both my hands got entangled and I lost them. I had collected a few men and approached the Sardar who agreed to pay four thousand as compensation for the loss of my hands, and six months' wages, but later he went back on his word. He also drove me out of the village of Talwandi Husseinwal, in Kapurthala district. My sister must be waiting for me ... this happened fifteen days before Rakhsha Bandhan ...'

'We can go and meet him again ...'

'It will be useless.'

When he told me that he had not been taken to the hospital immediately after the accident, I told him, 'Come with me, I'll make arrangements for sending you back to Bihar.'

Next day, I took Rajendra to meet my good friend Purshottam Sharma. I had also brought a bagful of clothes from home for Rajendra. We spent the night at Purshottam's house. We asked Rajendra about Bihar. After dinner, he washed his amputated hand and coming into the room, looked at the pictures on the wall carefully. Then he asked, 'Are you a Chamar?'

Sharma had put up pictures of Hindu devi-devtas, the Sikh gurus, and various saints on the wall.

'What's the matter?'

'Isn't that Raidas' picture? Sharmas are not Chamars!' Rajendra asked. After a moment he went, 'Now that I have eaten ...'

'Why don't you throw it up if you feel that way,' I remarked.

'My right thumb is still intact, thank God. I can eat and rinse my mouth and perform all other tasks,' he said, a little shamefacedly, and trying to change the direction of the conversation.

Anyway, we bought his ticket and also dispatched some money which we had collected from various friends to his address.

For many days the thought that this bhaiya, who had lost his hands and was destitute, was still not willing to give up the caste system, troubled me.

I wanted to become a full time worker of the Party so that I could work for landless peasants, the oppressed and exploited people, and help create a new awareness in them, of their rights. But when I thought of the conditions of the Party workers, who went from village to village, door to door, spreading the ideology of the Party, I would shudder. They did not even have money to get their cycles repaired or drink a cup of tea; they did not have enough clothes. I felt a deep respect for their ability and commitment.

... Then, a new window in the vast open sky suddenly opened. The elder son of my bua, Daulat Ram, who was a high-ranking officer in the Planning Commission, sent me a form for the recruitment to some posts in the Ministry of Information and Broadcasting issued by the Union Public Service Commission. He also sent me some instructions and I began translating English texts into Punjabi, and Punjabi into English. When I passed the written test, my cousin gave me tips on how to face the interview. He also told me that if I did not know the answer to any question, I should not hesitate to admit it, and many other such tips.

The result was that I was able to leave the Food Corporation of India. I joined as a class II non-gazetted officer at the Jalandhar office of Press Information Bureau in June 1983.

It was a dark period for the people of Punjab—the peak of terrorism. I had to translate various bits of news into Punjabi, then, I spent the rest of my time, with Comrade Surjan Zeeravi at *Nawan Zamana*. He gave me a new self-confidence. He kept joking and pushing wire despatches towards me commenting sarcastically, 'Here, make news out of these obituary notices!'

I started translating the famous Russian writer Alexander Pushkin's book *When Daddy was a Little Boy* which was being serialized in the

Sunday edition of *Nawan Zamana*. I was encouraged by the letters that I received from readers and the appreciative comments from those I met personally. Also, my articles and book-reviews on Leftist ideology, on the geographical, cultural, administrative system of the Soviet Union, on the probable Third World War, and on scientific and technological developments were now being regularly published both in *Nawan Zamana* and *Ajit*. I got to know many writers and became friendly with many others. Some would call me the representative journalist of the Soviet Union to tease me. With all this I also continued to write poems and letters against the extremists and got them published.

Some act or other of inhuman cruelty occurred every day. Some blamed the government for its failure to take action, or its helplessness and wanted that it should take some stringent steps against this. It was said in some quarters that the government itself had encouraged this movement and also helped it grow, and would root it out whenever it wanted. Others were critical of the way the Sikhs had been divided into two groups—moderate and extremists—and disapproved of their not condemning the massacre of innocents and declared that both the groups were equally responsible for whatever was happening. People were so frightened that the village lanes would empty by eight in the evening and everyone became tense if they heard even footsteps in the lane outside at night.

The Leftist groups took out rallies to appeal for the unity and integrity of the country. Claims of lining up rows of martyrs were made, which was clearly an acceptance of the feeling of helplessness and disappointments. There was a greater evidence of unity in the face of this cruel challenge, and all old grievances of caste and religion were forgotten. Despite slogans such as, 'Sikhs are a separate nation', 'Khalsa is supreme', 'Khalsa Raj', and 'One Sikh will take care of thirty-five Hindus', 'Politics and religion are the same for Sikhs', there was no division between the Sikhs and the Hindus. This show of unity and oneness was encouraging for both the people, and also for the Left forces. The bandhs that were organized by them were always successful.

... Then suddenly, the earth seemed to shift from under my feet one day, when one of my close friends, one who studied with me from class XI to MA, told me very explicitly, 'If Khalistan comes into existence, then Jats like us would become district collectors or superintendents of police! How many Sikhs are educated? We should all work for the establishment of Khalsa Raj. I have no ulterior motive—I already have plenty of land, and my elder brother and his wife are doctors! Who doesn't want to be a high official!'

After this, I did not take much interest in this friend, but one day when I was returning after a visit to my mother's family, my friendship reasserted itself, and I rode my cycle into his courtyard. My friend was not at home, but his younger brother was.

I asked him, 'I don't see Doctor Sahib and his doctor wife! Where are they? Are they not at home … on a holiday …?'

'Doctor? Bhaiji is a compounder and my sister-in-law is teaching in a school …' he intervened.

'Yaar, what news about your job? … But you don't need to worry as you have plenty of land … If you do get a job, it would be good for you.' I tried to change the topic.

'Bhaji, what lands can we Baris have? We are four brothers and it would not come to four kanals for each one of us!'

'Baris?'

'Yes, our caste is not found in large number in this area, but is concentrated in the area along the river bank!'

I was astonished at his simple words said with such honesty. I recalled the day when my friend had told one of our girl classmates, at Lyallpur Khalsa College and in my presence, that he was a Jat and had given her detailed information about his extensive land holdings.

I felt that his desire to pretend that he belonged to an upper caste clan was the result of a deep-rooted sense of inferiority; he seemed to be burdened with the artificial and double life he was leading. I felt that the backward classes had to work with the untouchables. Social change is another name for revolution. There is the need to strike against all those forces which support the social system, which is against any change whatever and are working to maintain the status quo.

I thought of the famous scholar and religious reformer Martin Luther who had revolted against the corruption rampant in the Church. He had challenged the prerogatives and privileges claimed by the Pope and the clergy, their assertion of spiritual leadership, the right to interpret the Bible, and had resolutely rejected these claims through his ninety-five points.

I thought of the superstitious restrictions on intellectual development and freedom, justification of caste on the basis of rebirth and transmigration of souls which prevailed in our society under the garb of religion and spiritualism, and I would wonder who would come forward to challenge it. The train of my thoughts would finally focus on Dr Ambedkar and Ramaswami Naicker Periyar.

An idea that I had been toying with earlier, once again held me in its thrall.

... During this phase of terrorism in which brother was killing brother, another incident disturbed me a great deal. One of our relatives informed us, 'The Sardarni I work for as a sweeper had one day happily told me, "Sister, Khalistan is about to be created. That would be great. The Hindus will all leave, and you people will live with us in Khalistan!"'

We all listened intently to her, our questioning eyes were fixed on her face as she went on, I said, 'Sardarni it would be great for you, but will we also get some land? Then again, why are you insisting that we should stay here with you in Khalistan? For us, Hindus and Sikhs are the same. Do you really love us so much Sardani ...?

'Then?' We had to hear what came next.

'Then what! She said, "We like you, that is why I am telling you! Who will clean and sweep for us in Khalistan?"'

I thought of Jinnah and what he said at a meeting about this problem of the untouchables at the time of Partition. He had said that the untouchable population should be divided into two. It was much later that I comprehended the meaning of what he had said.

It upset me to hear such things every now and then. I realized that there was no concrete plan to fight these extremist forces. All promises of peace rallies, of parades of martyrs, or the setting up of groups of volunteers, were just hollow things. It was ordinary persons like me and my friends who were concerned about the security and safety of the common people, and our dependence on government. The party leaders considered these organizations communal and supporters of imperialist forces, and an obstruction in the path of the Revolution.

Despite high hopes and firm resolve, sometimes we were overwhelmed by despair, which we took care not to reveal. We continued to think about plans to rid Punjab and the country of terrorism. We would compare the activities of extremist organizations with their killings and massacres, crimes against women. The refusal of the communal political parties to condemn these heinous crimes, raised many questions in my mind.

The murders of close friends and companions pushed me into depression. Many workers of the Leftist parties felt alienated by the behaviour of the leaders. One would leave the Indian Communist Party and join the Marxist Party and another would do the exact opposite. I would think of the struggle of the different small communist groups in Russia against the Czarist regime. If only our Left parties would provide honest and serious leadership to our people and be able to rise above their own egos and arrogance.

It was at this time of uncertainty and procrastination that I came across Nicolai Ostrovsky's novel, which had been translated into Punjabi under the title *Kabhu No Chaadon Khet* (*Never Shall I Retreat*) by Dr Karanjeet Singh. This autobiographical novel gave me immense inspiration. A new wave of energy swept over me and I resolved to work and even sacrifice my life for the country. This novel had the quality of creating a new determination in a man who had been drifting into depression.

I shared my views about this novel with my friends. I even bought seven or eight copies of the book and presented them to my friends. Comrade Purshottam Sharma named his newborn son Pavel and his daughter Tania. Misir Deep Bhatia also called his son Pavel.

Whenever I was alone, I would think—the world lives on hope. I would think that our present and future generations should be willing to help realize Ostrovsky's hopes.

# 17

# Departure for Delhi

In the last five or six years, the situation in this land of five rivers had deteriorated sharply. It had changed its hues like the politicians of the region. Men seemed to have turned into monsters and were doing their best to control even nature. At night, even the dogs slunk indoors quietly as did the humans, as if they had forgotten to bark at the winds. They seemed to understand the silence which engulfed the lanes of the village. If anything broke the pall of silence, it was the 'thuk-thuk' of gunfire and the heart-rending sounds of weeping and wailing. If during this howling, someone tried to oppose the force that caused it, he was immediately cut down by the devils who spread fear all around.

This harvest of hate was nurtured and the waters of provocation flowed powerfully. Those who had supported it were now confident of achieving their goals. Those who killed and raped cruelly and with impunity, now claimed to be pure and virtuous. Aliens seemed to be in control, and voices of alienation and separation were being heard. Missiles full of the venom of antipathy and enmity, were fired from sacred places of worship. Walls of differences were being raised within homes ...

As I watched, birds flew freely in the open blue skies in moments of leisure. They perched on one tree and hopped on to the wall of a house. Indifferent to boundaries and borders, they treated the whole earth as one and claimed it as their own. My thoughts would often fly with them, and many a time I felt that I also was no longer on this earth.

People were upset at having to go from village to village to attend funerals. Women, young and old, their heads covered with white dupattas and their faces pale and haggard, could be seen everywhere. A cruel and purposeless storm seemed to have blown away every red dupatta, and all the colour from the lives of the people. Condolence meetings became a common sight in every lane.

An old man who sat on the platform under the peepal of our gurudwara would say, 'The country is facing bad times—We have not seen such killing and massacre since the Partition.' Their utter helplessness was clear when he said, 'Those who are sitting in places of worship are hatching conspiracies and making plans will be vanquished only by God. One day nature will surely be kind to man. The earth and the sky stay in place because there is justice and righteousness.'

Every day, innocent people disappeared. Despite the sweltering heat of summers and power cuts, most people, particularly young men, were compelled to sleep behind locked doors. Young girls were kept hidden as if they were precious objects which could be stolen. Hands raised in their protection were often broken or severed.

Absolute anarchy!

It was being whispered that there was no difference between the one and the other. Many fair-minded people tried to foster a favourable atmosphere by trying to unite people against these murderous elements and attempting to heal the deep wounds that had been inflicted on the social fabric. They appealed for tolerance, peace, and harmony.

... Then came a time when conditions changed. The voice of the voiceless found an expression; the helpless found a refuge. Things gradually improved, and the tide turned, amicably and irrevocably, against all these merciless killings. The voice which had wanted to silence all opposition was silenced forever. The extremists were vanquished, though Shri Harmandir Sahib was desecrated.

... For the first time I happened to see the lifeless and purposeless functioning of the government agencies under the threat of fear. It was said that curfew had been imposed only once in Jalandhar during British rule; but now it was imposed in the whole state. Only the army and paramilitary forces were visible, with some stray dogs on the roads and birds in the open skies. There was desolation everywhere. The lanes and bazaars that had pulsated with life and the bright chatter of children had simply vanished! Tears had stilled the pranks of the young and taken the smiles off the faces of their elders. I often had the feeling that someone was following me. But when I spun around to look back, I saw no one! Fear and delusion stalked the land.

A burning inferno takes no heed of what comes in its way. Ultimately, it touched the highest. The capital itself was engulfed. A huge tree fell and the earth trembled. People ran amuck, wreaking vengeance, killing the innocent. Hands raised in prayer were severed. Every conceivable atrocity was committed and even corpses were spat on, urinated upon, burning tyres flung on living men. 'An eye for an eye' was the cry of the day.

Appeals for peace were made by the fair-minded and sensible elements. But many of them also met horrific ends, some died their lips still moving, trying to utter a word of peace.

During those unbelievable times, full of fear and suspicion, Bhaia advised me, 'Take off your turban and cut your hair a little more, and go to Delhi. Go and see how Bakshi and the other relatives are faring—it seems that the killings are now over ...'

Getting off the bus at the stop, as I made for Bakshi's house, I could feel the fear which hung all around. The whole atmosphere reeked of revenge. When I looked around and saw the husks of burnt houses, my thoughts went to the nest of a pair of sparrows who had made the electricity meter their home, collecting straw by straw, and which had collapsed under the onslaught of fierce winds when a storm had raged. I was so upset at what I saw in Delhi that I came back the next day. To me it seemed that there was no humanity left anywhere on the face of the earth.

And, after months, my emotions and feelings took the form of poetry

...

... 24 July 1985 was my thirtieth birthday, and it proved to be a memorable day for the country as well. The Rajiv–Longowal Agreement with its eleven points was signed on that day. People read about it in the newspapers, heard about it in the news. Chandigarh was to go to the Punjab, and the Hindi speaking regions of the Punjab to Haryana; a tribunal to decide about the waters of the Ravi and Beas; the Kanpur-Bokaro riots in November 1984 were to be investigated. The

Anandpur Sahib Resolution was referred to the Sarkaria Commission to deliberate over; rehabilitation of the army deserters, etc. ... The Rangnath Commission was already enquiring into the Delhi riots. The leaders responsible for the Agreement became the messiahs of peace overnight. The contribution made by the Leftists in this regard was not given much weight.

Voices against extremism were also heard from the moderate camp. They also supported peace and advocated brotherhood. Everyone was of the view that if the Agreement was implemented honestly, it would be a lesson for the enemies of the Punjab and country.

The exchange of Punjabi-Hindi regions was halted at Kundu Khera, and 'Kundu Khera karoo nibera' (Kundu Khera will decide the problem) became the war cry. Some elements were heard telling the government officers in Punjabi, 'Please write that Hindi is our mother tongue!'

... Eleven months elapsed in this confusion ... but the problems of the Punjab continued. Neither did the situation change, nor was peace established.

Conditions became ominous when Sant Harchand Singh Longowal fell to the bullets of the extremists, about thirty kilometres from Sangrur on 20 August 1986, in the gurudwara, as he bowed before the holy Guru Granth Sahib after delivering a speech in the village.

They were perplexing times for the common man. He was bewildered at the fast changing scenario, as also the postures adopted by the moderates and the extremist groups. Appeals for maintaining peace were being made on all sides, and also a desire to give a befitting answer to fundamentalism, was being expressed. Some owners and employees of newspapers dedicated to the cause of peace were shot down by the extremists.

It was during this dark period that I completed my probation, and having been promoted, became a gazetted officer. I went to the Party office to give them the happy news.

'Congratulations. Now that you are a part of the administration, we don't want you coming here often. Also, you have not been a card-holding member these last few years!' The district secretary of the party gave me this advice bluntly, 'This is good for you!'

I experienced a deep sense of loss.

The love of my companions, their wise guidance and comradeship seemed to be slipping away from me, and I felt bereft and crippled, the way a soldier is when he is injured and stands disabled at his post.

I was deeply affected by the prevailing social conditions. Travelling on the bus to my village, I decided to use my writing to fight all these elements which were subverting peace and the pluralist social fabric.

'I have been transferred to Delhi ...' I told Bhaia and Ma as soon as I stepped into the courtyard.

'God heeded my prayers ...' Ma exclaimed hearing only half my sentence, and bowed to Mother Earth. Her face, wreathed in smiles, was a wonderful sight for me. She touched my head and asked, 'When do you leave? I say if you have to go, leave today. ...'

After a pause, she told me what was on her mind.

'Comrade Kulwant (Comrade Kulwant, who had been the MLA twice) drops you on the periphery road daily at different places, you come home at different times. We worry about you all the time and are afraid. If you are in Delhi with your brother, at least we will not be scared all the time. ...'

'You followed the comrade whenever and wherever you see him, like an obedient dog ...! You did not listen to us ... and now look what's happened ...' Bhaia remarked. His triumphant expression was that of a victor.

'My promotion ...' But Ma interrupted me and asked, 'When do you have to pack?'

Before I could say anything further, Ma went on, 'The times are bad, and mothers all over the state are losing their sons. It is because of this, son, that I say leave as soon as you can.' Wiping her tearful eyes with the edge of her dupatta she sighed. 'This is kalyug—mothers want their sons to leave home for their safety and long life, and then yearn and cry to see them!'

Her voice became hoarse, and she could not say anything more. Her words died in her throat. I tried to give her the impression that I was a brave man, but within me I felt weak when I compared myself to my cousins Nohana, Phumman, and Maddi, who were all in the army. Whenever they prepared to return after leave, everyone, young and old, men and women, would gather around, and one would say, 'You had come on leave only a short while back and it doesn't feel as if you've been here for a month. ...'

Another would comment, 'We shall meet again ... may you live happily ... one has to work to live.'

My aunts and their daughters and daughters-in-law, would all bid them goodbye with tears in their eyes and sad silence would fill the air.

The gurgle of Bhaia's hookah broke into my thoughts.

'Gudd! We are getting old—don't forget us! They say that whosoever goes to Delhi—becomes a Delhiwalla! The whole family is yet to be married off and settled.' Bhaia's face reflected the helplessness clutching at his mind.

'Bhaia, don't you worry. I am with you ...' I assured him, aware of the responsibilities that were mine and filled with determination to fulfil them.

'You keep uttering this word "Bhai, Bhaia!" Do you understand what it means?' Pointing at his own body, he said, 'You were born from this body. So, in this way we are brothers—bhai ...' He explained with a wise look on his face, but there was a touch of reproach, lurking in his eyes.

I spent the whole night grappling with a host of troublesome thoughts. I was sad at the thought of leaving all my friends and relatives who had stood by me through all the ups and down of life and moving some four hundred odd miles away to a metropolis.

Next morning, 28 March 1987, my mother and sisters got up long before me, and began preparing for my departure.

'Bhaia, I will leave the cycle at Sharma's shop,' I said, and mounting the cycle, set off for Delhi. I groped for the bag on the carrier and looked back. I couldn't see Bhaia, but Ma and my sisters and younger brother Kuldip still stood on the road, looking at me and the fast moving cycle.

The golden crop of wheat standing in the fields, seemed to remind me that my sisters were now of marriageable age. I felt that my whole family was following me to Delhi.

# 18

## Between Life and Death

'This son of a bitch will die and also kill us! It would be best to marry him off! He would automatically become his wife's obedient servant! Then, we'll see how concerned he is about us!' Bhaia was ranting in his usual volatile manner. But Ma stood silent as if she had turned to stone. As he spoke rapidly and loudly, Bhaia's thin frame seemed to tremble slightly. His flashing eyes darted everywhere, in and out of the door. ...

'I didn't want to come this time, but did because of you ...'

'Shut up! You seed of a dog! Or else I'll hit you with my shoe!' Bhaia's voice was loud enough to bring all the neighbours crowding in.

At that moment, Gurumukh of Barias walked in, and said, 'When we heard the sound of footsteps, we wondered who was running through the sludge.'

'Yaar, do tell what happened!' Taaya Ram Singh asked impatiently, passing his hand over his beard.

'What is there to happen! He was caught by the terrorists,' Bhaia informed him.

'Really! Where?' Taaya was anxious.

'On, the other side of the Pir's khangah.'

'Hain! In broad daylight? Just outside the village! And it is not yet eight! Were you alone or was there someone else with you?' Taaya let loose a volley of questions.

'I and Dhyan were together!' I answered.

The questioning was still going on, when Dhyan arrived on the scene, followed by Sandhu of the Babas, who coughed, cleared his throat and said, 'When I saw the glint of the gun in the moonlight (it was Purnima or a couple of days after the full moon night), I stopped the pair of bullocks ...'

I noticed that Dhyan was breathing hard. Men and women were watching us sympathetically, carefully, and listening to the narration of the occurrence.

'... and I then turned them towards the fields—the harvested crop and the bundles of wheat are still standing in the wet fields and have begun sprouting. My feet were sinking in the sludgy ground,' Baba Sandhu said, and again coughed.

'Family problems are yet to be settled and we are now wholly dependent on you! I can still work on daily wages ...' Bhaia was voicing his fear of the future. His lips were quivering.

'Thakar, thank god—the boys are safe! There was danger, but it has been averted,' Taaya consoled him.

'Don't you worry ... be patient,' I tried to console and strengthen parents. I could see tears trembling in my mother's eyes, ready to roll down her cheeks.

'I thought that our turn had come ...' Dhyan tried to explain what had happened. 'They made the two of us stand side-by-side at some distance of ten-fifteen feet, and said, "Saale, you gad about smoking beedis on the road!" When this Baba turned the bullocks into the fields, their attention was diverted, and I also set off towards the fields. I could not run because my feet were sinking into the slushy ground, but still I ran! They shouted for me to stop or else they would shoot.'

'Dhyan told me to run in the opposite direction so that at least one of us might live—but there was wire fencing on my right, so where could I run to?' I added.

'Then?'

'Those bastards began cursing us: one said, "Shoot them and finish the matter off—don't talk to them anymore."'

'Really? Then?'

'I don't know what came over the man with the AK-47, that he told me, 'you are a Sikh brother, today we will let you off, but if in future, you drink or speak in English, then we will shoot you ...!'

'This means that your turban saved you this time, Gudd! ... Then, did they go away?' Taaya Ram Singh wanted to know.

'Taaya, they mounted their cycles and rode away—they had shawls wrapped around their heads ... and I ran off to Joginder Fauji's house, so that I might follow them with a gun.'

'Then?'

'He told me that the gun had been deposited with the police,' I told him.

'The police themselves are afraid of confronting the terrorists ...' Taaya chuckled.

'About five or seven of us went after them with sticks and axes, but came back from Rastgo,' I said, and they all laughed.

'You son of an owl! Sticks and axes against an AK-47!' Bhaia exclaimed in a low tone.

'Many a time traditional and common weapons are more effective. One should have courage and determination! Such people draw their courage from the weapons they have ... if you threaten them, then they may wet their pants! And then we were so many and they were only two!' I said and no one present there disagreed.

... Even in that condition, I suddenly thought of the road from where we had turned back. I had worked on that road some eight years ago under the blistering summer heat, during my holidays. I had swept it with a reed broom, swept it clear of dust, and poured boiling coal tar on to its surface along with the other workers. Lifting the basket slightly above my head, the gravel had to be thrown to the ground in an arc so that it could trickle down in a thin stream, leaving a trail of dust which would disperse in a moment. But as I had stoked the fire under the cauldron of boiling molten coal tar, some drops had fallen on my right arm, and I had cried out in pain.

'Gudd! ... You seem to be lost in thought ...' Taaya commented, shaking me by the arm.

'Hoon! They said, "Satguru has forgiven you. Now put all that you have on the ground and be gone. If you look back or tell the villagers anything, then we will shoot you! Run off, you sister ..." Then, the second one said, "Saala, low caste ... he struts about, shoot him, the mother ..."' I told them the details of what had happened.

'Taaya, at that time I was sure I would be shot the next moment. But, after a few seconds my courage revived, as it crossed my mind that they would have shot me by now if they had wanted to. Why would they go on arguing with me like this?'

'... Then Gudd, did you give them whatever you had?' Gurumukh asked, suddenly recollecting the details.

'My wallet, watch etc., I put on the ground, and started walking towards the village.'

'What would these sinners gain by killing the innocent? Those who have seen the creation of Pakistan, they can never take the name of Khalistan, even by mistake,' Taaya Ram Singh said, as he turned to leave. 'Hundred per cent right.' Some voices were heard in agreement. People were now drifting away.

We sat talking up till midnight. My sisters were silent, unable to utter even a word. It seemed that they had felt numb at the turn of events. I felt that they were silently praying for my long life.

As we sat talking we heard the sound of shots, at some distance from the village. We were all upset and our hearts beat fast.

'We know that you are lonely in Delhi. Your body may be there, but your heart is here. We and all your friends are there, but ...' Ma said, giving the matter a new turn, 'Bhatia talks about the daughter of his aunt, go and have a look at her on Wednesday.'

'... Wednesday? I have to go back to Delhi that day. I can go a day earlier,' I answered, expressing my helplessness in the face of official constraints.

'On a Tuesday?' Ma was astonished.

'I was born on a Tuesday. It is not a bad day for life or death. The sun shines every day, the earth rotates on its axis every day, and the night follows the day.' I tried to convince her of the appropriateness of the day.

'We don't understand all that you say. Go and take a look any time you feel it is convenient.' Ma answered, expressing what was in her heart. I felt that my parents were eager to see me married and settled.

We went on talking as the date changed.

Now, I was alone in my room. My mind was in a turmoil. Bhaia's lean face, lined with worry, compelled me to take some important decisions. His words still rang in my ears, 'Let this storm pass, then you can come and go as you please. The whole family has ... not yet ...'

# 19

## The Humanist Slap

'He is my dear friend ... Our friendship goes back some thirty-five years. He is an outstanding poet, and a writer of ghazals. His ghazals reflect the humanist views, and he is from our area ...' Dr Gurucharan Singh Muhay, the editor of the Punjabi edition of *Yojana* introduced me to a person with well-starched beard and red turban.

'Which department are you in?' I enquired of the poet.

'I am a free bird ... roam about and compose poetry ... it is my wife who works.'

'He spends his days on the roads, working on the ghazals that are in the process of being written, and his evenings are spent in the coffee house, and afternoons, he spends in the *chandu khana*,' Dr Muhay handed out his information about his poet friend.

'Chandu khana?'

'Yes, where musical evenings are held ... you must come with me one of these days. I'll introduce you to other writers and poets ... one should not sit in a room all day!' Dr Muhay continued eagerly, 'He is a large-hearted man. He doesn't let anyone pay in the coffee house—what payment does one get by reciting poem in *kavidarbars* (poetic assemblies)! He is enjoying himself at the expense of his wife ... she is a very good woman!'

The ghazal-writer was smiling all the while. I felt that this man was a parasite, without any work or source of income.

'You haven't told me anything about him,' the poet asked.

'He is here as an assistant editor. He is Balbir Chand, but he calls himself Balbir Madhopuri.' Muhay introduced me with some irony. To escape this daily humiliation, I had recently got my name officially changed to the present one.

The meetings were held in the afternoon outside the PTI building on Parliament Street. But no one talked about culture or literature, they were also preoccupied with backbiting, criticism, and jealousy. I avoided these meetings.

Days turned into months. Muhay and his other editorial colleagues would keep talking for hours about their religious interests and activities. They would debate over the various ways of making life better, higher, for the work one does, because one's wealth would not go with one etc., and these discussions would stretch out endlessly. They disturbed my world all the time. They called their guru 'Satguru' the true God, or 'Purna Satguru', the perfect God. They tried to persuade me to attend their religious meetings and would often make comments that it was bad to be without a guru. They called me stupid. I was tense and upset at not being able to finish my official assignments on time.

... Then, one evening I was obliged to go with them to attend a *satsang* of their guru, Ved Prakash, in a posh colony of New Delhi. Muhay's poet friend had also started attending these religious assemblies long before me. Discussions at these meetings would focus on spiritual, scientific, and technological development. I liked the atmosphere. I began attending these meetings along with Muhay.

... One day, at one such meeting, D.D. Sharma said, 'Pitaji, in Guru Ravidas's bani ...'

'Guru? He was not even a saint! The Gurubani calls him a bhakt, a devotee,' Satguru Sharma, who was addressed as Pitaji by one and all, explained what was not asked, interrupting the question. The one who had asked the question did not say anything further, perhaps because he felt that it was not appropriate to argue with the Guru.

The Satguru carried on, 'I was Yagyavalkya Rishi in my last birth, and Gargi was my wife then. She is now with me in the form of my daughter, Sheela.'

Everyone present looked at one another, wondering how the Guru had complete knowledge of the previous and future births and the whole universe.

'Pitaji, we have heard that the world is sweet. Who knows about the hereafter, for none has seen it,' I repeated what I had often heard.

'The Guru is great, no one knows the depth of the Guru's power ... whatever he does, is right; he is as pure as the lotus ... Companions of many births come along to keep an account of one another's doings,' Ved Prakash Sharma delivered many such discourses on the eternal and the unknown.

'Pitaji, you are a complete guru; help us demolish the differences and discriminations of caste—so that all can be equal,' I gave words to my deepest desire.

'Look! All this is the consequence of karma, actions of our previous births. Satguru does not interfere in these things, but teaches you to accept them—that would give you peace. You can yourself see, we wash our faces again and again, look at the mirror time and again, but how much attention do we give to our feet?'

I acquired the real knowledge of what it meant to be a shudra, by attending these assemblies of the 'Purna Satguru'. Then, I discussed it with Muhay. He said, 'It is the result of births and deeds. You keep on the straight path, you will be blessed—if a soul is full of faith and trust, then alone can it know belief, reverence, and devotion.'

After the satsang was over, a well dressed young man told a few people, 'He is my uncle, but don't be misled by him—duped by him. He drinks chicken soup and also takes liquor occasionally.'

None paid much attention to this boy.

'... Even if for a moment one accepts that there is an earlier birth, how can one accept a wife of the earlier birth as a daughter in this?' I asked Muhay.

'To criticize or to hear anyone else criticize the Guru is a sin,' Muhay answered curtly.

'But what is the harm in trying to find out the truth?'

His son Sukhbir answered his question of mine, 'If you are making allegations, then I am going to get to the bottom of this affair.'

Kicking his scooter to life, he roared off, coming back after some time, with dejection written all over his face, and said, 'I spoke to this daughter of Pitaji. She says, "She is neither married nor a virgin, all because of her father."'

After this confirmation, I thought of those shlokas of Brahmaji, which he had uttered while persuading his daughter, Padma, to yield to him—that one can have sex with mother, daughter, or sister, for the sake of progeny. It seemed to me that perhaps the Satguru may have been inspired by that mode!

Muhay noticed my dilemma, and he said, 'One has read and heard plenty of nonsense in Indian mythology, but this seems to have come true.'

All the good feelings that I had for the Guru and his satsang were wiped clean from my mind, the way corrupted files disappeared from my office computer. Despite pressing every button, the monitor showed blank. I felt redeemed.

Muhay and some of his like-minded friends now started a full-scale enquiry, like an investigating committee. 'We'll close this shop of his,' Muhay declared. Somehow the know-all guru had come to know of this determined declaration.

Earlier, Muhay and many of his friends would dismiss the charge of the Guru being a *tantrik*, but now they were themselves levelling this charge against him. The Guru could no longer amass wealth through his satsang.

In an attempt to cover up his misdeeds, the Guru told one of the satsangis who was close to him, 'All the scheduled castes have come together against me.'

The man who had declared himself the father of all, now revealed how obscurantist his views still were.

Muhay was bitterly angry, 'We have been duped. We have been humiliated. My family was connected with Radhsaomi sect for more than seventy-eight years ... I have spent nights weeping.'

'And that writer woman?' I tried to shock him.

'After fourteen years of living together, she has left me, saying that you were, and even now are, a Chamar.'

Muhay was sad and dejected—his face had shrunk and he would pass his hand over his grey beard. It seemed as if he was about to tear it out.

Dr Muhay was soon promoted as deputy secretary. He came to see me every five or seven days. As he walked in one day, he said, 'Come, let's go to the chandu khana. We will meet some friends ...'

'Gurucharan, how much longer before you retire?' His poet friend asked, after greeting Muhay.

'Six months.'

'After that you can sit here with this cobbler and his shoe-polishing kit, and I too will be coming here regularly so we that can meet.'

Dr Muhay ignored his bitter comment, and tried to steer the conversation into another direction.

'Gurucharan, what am I saying! You can get a shoe-polishing kit and sit with the cobbler here—and we will continue seeing each other ...' the poet repeated what he had said, pointing to the cobbler who was busy repairing some shoes.

'Yaar, I have a degree in homeopathy. I will help people by dispensing medicines. Then, I have plenty of experience, and can work as a journalist in English and Punjabi. I am an M.A. One shouldn't say such things to friends.'

After a few days, Dr Muhay and I visited some old friends. After enquiring about the process of retirement from government service, the poet again said, 'Gurucharan, I had advised you earlier also that you should sit here under this neem tree with a shoe-polishing kit. And it would be a way for us to keep on meeting each other ...'

Dr Muhay slapped the poet hard. I tried to ignore it by turning away. Then, as I watched them obliquely, I saw Mohan Singh Berry separating them and trying to put some sense into them.

I realized that even the mind of the other low castes had been deeply affected by the inhuman treatment meted out to them for centuries. We would like scheduled castes and backward castes to unite, but the terrible wounds inflicted on their psyche, and the deep divisions created by these wounds, will not allow them to mingle and be one. The scheduled castes had organized the movement for reservations for the backward classes after the Mandal Commission report, but the backward classes were used by the upper castes in their own interests. There was rioting and arson and lives were lost.

I was thinking of these things, when a colleague of mine, M.K. Rao from Andhra Pradesh came to Delhi. When I had discussed the details of what had happened with him, he said, 'There is no need to worry. When I was elected the president of our association, one of our senior officers, who had always projected himself as a Gandhian said, "How can we allow the scheduled castes to sit with us?" Then, when I was the general secretary of the state unit of SFI, and we had invited the communist leaders for meals during the Telengana assembly elections, the village headman refused to come to our homes. But otherwise, he is very progressive.'

It seemed to me that the curse of caste had permeated our society and there was no indication of its dying out soon. Then, it suddenly occurred to me that the Muhay formula may be the most effective method of establishing social equality—the way I had seen him deliver a sharp humanist slap on the face of casteism!

# 20

## Being a Tenant

A baraat (groom's party) of eleven reached the village of my in-laws, on the occasion of my wedding. The women of the bride's family sang welcome songs, and they also began singing *sithnis*—abusive ditties, usually sung by the women of the bride's family. These are some of verses they sang:

*You can take the money*
  *from our village,*
*And get a band to come*
  *with the groom.*
*The baraat doesn't look good,*
  *you shameless ones,*
*You should be ashamed of*
  *yourselves.*
           Or
*The baraatis could not get a band*
*They came beating their bellies.*

These women were making loud comments about us, 'They say that the groom is an officer—but they haven't even got a photographer to make a video film ... as if they have come only to take the bride ... some show of grandeur and gaiety is necessary ...'

'They say that they don't want any dowry!' This was another voice.

'Who notices or cares if they get something for free!' This came from another voice. 'If not now, they will ask for it later on—it is only said for form's sake, sister. Later, they want more.'

After the wedding ceremony of two and half hours, the worry which had been eating me for the last few months again reared its head. This was the worry of our bridal night and our married life. I was full of fears of all sorts. I was under a great deal of pressure, and felt as if a mountain had fallen on me. I had lost about ten kilos of weight in the last few months. Some of my friends had even teased me about it, 'You are losing weight even before you are married … but don't worry, you will put on a lot of weight after your marriage. It works on one like desi ghee.'

On the fifth day after our wedding, we were in Delhi. Within a month and half, I had regained my lost weight and felt happy and content. But this happiness was short-lived, and within four or five months, harsh realities had clipped the wings of my elation.

The wedding expenses of two younger sisters and my elder brother, and the house, had all created a big financial mess for me, and I was trying my best to extricate myself from it. I had been taking loans from my provident fund at frequent intervals, and my take-home salary was now less than two thousand. Out of this meagre sum, I kept a third for myself and a third I sent home to Madhopur. The rest, I gave my elder brother, for I was living with him.

Within six years we had three children. My third sister had also been married off. The loan instalments being deducted from my salary had increased. The rising cost of living and escalating expenses had added to my problems, and also to the mental tension. Then, one day, my elder brother told me rather sharply, 'Every month you say that you will move into some other accommodation, but you don't go. The eight hundred you give me—do you think that it is enough for running the household? Your friends always visit us in hordes. When you live on your own, only then will you really know how expensive everything is, and how to run a household.'

'What about the eight hundred I send home? Is that not worth anything?' I retorted. 'You keep telling me to borrow from my provident fund and that we will somehow manage.'

'You move out, we also want to live happily and on our own,' My bhabhi, clinched the argument.

To me it seemed that all my plans to help take the family forward had been demolished, the way Babri Masjid had been a few days back. There was no basis on which a compromise could be worked out. Perhaps they had not given much thought to the future of the family. Perhaps I was nothing more than a money-making machine for them!

That very morning I took a friend, who happened to be my wife's cousin, Misrdeep Bhatia, on a house-hunting trip, and succeeded in renting a room in Munirka, after a long search and various difficulties.

My office and my eldest daughter's school were only a kilometre from there. The house was new and we cooked and ate our first meal in new utensils. Our five-member family slept on one bed under one quilt. Neither did we have another bed nor was there any bed linen. I did, however, have plenty of books.

Madan, who was like a younger brother, came to see us with his wife and twin children after a couple of days. My wife and I looked askance at one another.

'Madan, lets finish this stuff first, it is not very good.' I said putting some biscuits and sugar before them. My salary had already been used to buy some essentials for the kitchen.

'This was her first visit with her babies! We didn't have even ten rupees to give them,' my wife said, almost in tears.

I was preoccupied with my own thoughts. When I returned from work, the house owner, seated in front of the house, pulling on his hookah, would often ask, 'Bhai, don't be annoyed, but which caste do you belong to?'

'We are Sikhs,' I would answer, adjusting my turban.

'Don't be angry, once I was travelling by train from Agra to Delhi and a sardar and his wife were also travelling with me. They were well dressed and the man appeared to be educated. I asked him about Punjab, and learnt many things ...'

'Really?'

'... And I asked him about his caste. Like you, he also said, that he was a Sikh. I told him, "Sikhs also have caste, Which caste do you belong to?" He hesitated at first, and that he said that he was a Ramdasia.'

'Good, your time was well spent.'

'When he told me that he was a Ramdasia, what more could I talk to him about—I turned my face the other side,' the elderly Gujjar proudly told me.

'If he had lied to you and told you that he belonged to a higher caste?'

'… Then, he would have sinned,' and with this he picked up a bottle or rum lying near him, poured some into a glass and drank it, neat!

I disliked this old man. I felt as if a new phase of humiliation had begun. Wearied of this daily interrogation, my hunt for a new house began all over again.

I went to Sector VII in R.K. Puram to a family we knew well. It was winter and the landlady was seated on the roof, knitting.

'Give me an advance of five thousand—we will give these quarters to you; these days, these class IV quarters are going for Rs 10,000. We, of course, know each other.'

We settled happily in the new house. But my daughter's school, which was in Sector III was very far away. I didn't own a cycle and there was no other mode of transport except the local bus. I had to fetch her from school in the blistering heat of the summer afternoon and drop her home, and then rush off to office. I would often think what a difference would it have made if my elder brother had let us live with him till the end of the school session? The skies would not have fallen! Time and again, I would recollect what my mother had said, 'Now, there are three houses. If only they had lived together till the marriage of the two younger children, and set up separate households after that!'

We had lived in that house for five months, when one day, a stout woman walked in, adjusting her sari, and started shouting, 'Who are you? How did you come into my quarters without my permission?'

Fresh trouble in the form of this woman added to our woes. She sat down on the bed and began talking to us in a very arrogant tone. We looked at each other. The children whispered to us, 'When will this "Tuntun" leave … she is sitting on our bed! Where will we sleep?'

'Had I been receiving rent then I would have had no objection,' she said, after she had taken some tea.

'They took five thousand advance from us, and were taking Rs 500 a month as rent. They had told us that everything had been regularized.

You can live here and needn't worry. Five hundred would be deducted from the advance,' we told her about the arrangements we had made.

'That means a thousand in rent! She herself was only giving five hundred as rent!' she retorted. We were astonished at what we had heard. She gave us some time and somehow we managed to pay her the back rent.

Actually, the family we had known was aware of the orders of the Supreme Court and that there was going to be an investigation about the subletting of these government quarters. They had taken advantage of the opportunity, and giving us the key, had made their escape. When we asked them about the fraud that they had perpetrated on us, we were thoroughly scolded, 'Any agent charges three months' rent as commission, and you go on complaining! You are insulting us by repeatedly asking about the money—don't you dare do it again!'

The Central Public Works Department people raided these government quarters every day. We came to know that neither the rent nor the electricity charges had been paid for the last ten years. The reason was that 'Tuntun' had been widowed a few years ago, and had thought of nothing except collecting rent for the quarters. Mercifully, the water and power connections of class IV quarters had not been cut off even after non-payment of charges all these years.

Dr Gurucharan Singh Muhay was sisted on my accompanying them on a visit to Kerala, on LTC. But the children had their exam during that period. I was apprehensive about my wife's reaction to this proposal for a visit to Kerala. But I did go and when I returned after ten days in the south, the people on the ground floor stopped me near the stairs and said, 'The PWD people had come to throw out your luggage—we told them to wait for your return and that you would vacate the house in two days.'

The next day, we put our luggage at a friend's, as a temporary arrangement. Within a week, we had got a room in Sector VIII of R.K. Puram, for which we paid Rs 5000 as advance. There were very strict conditions attached to the room we rented.

The owner-mistress of this government quarter was running a crèche. She would frighten the children she was looking after and force them to go to sleep. She wouldn't allow our children to go out during the day, nor let them speak. She would create problems, 'Bhai sahib, your children are very noisy, your family is also too large. You use too much water for clothes. Vacate the room in a couple of days.'

I recalled what her husband had said a few days earlier, 'Bhai sahib, you wet the whole bathroom—bathe in one corner. You are an educated man.'

My courage seemed to give way under these new developments. It was, perhaps, my fate to worry. I had just paid the children's fees in their new schools, and here I was again homeless only after three months. How much could I go on borrowing? I would think of Bhaia, his determination even in the face of adversities, the money he borrowed, and what he had earned—whatever he had earned had been spent on paying off the loans! It was his courage and grit that had enabled me to go on and I was now earning a good salary.

We both had now decided that we would not get into the vicious circle of renting government quarters. I would have fits of anger, 'The scheduled castes are all allotted government quarters quickly. But I have now been serving for fifteen years—when will I be allotted quarters? When I have only a couple of years left to serve?'

The landlady said, 'Now that you are going, and your luggage is also packed; also it is not raining heavily—it is just a drizzle, and it will go on drizzling like this ...'

Loading our things on to a tempo, we went to the Jain mohalla in Palam village. When our children saw the turds floating in the open sewers, they covered their noses. My wife had fever and she had just entered the room with the children, and had hardly sat down, when the landlady walked in. My wife seemed to be in pain, but the landlady went on talking. Finally, when she did leave my wife told me, 'The old woman was asking me, "what are you, the way people are Brahmins, etc. ..."'

'What did you tell her?' I asked.

'I told her that we were Sikhs. Let us decide what caste we are going to admit to if they ask us again. It should not happen that I tell them one thing and you another.'

We thought about it till midnight. The thought came to us that these people were only bothered about the rent, what do they have to do with our caste? The curse of caste had followed us to the city—though it is said that people living in cities are educated and open-minded!

My wife commented, 'Sesha, who was running the crèche, would question me about our caste every now and then, and I used to avoid giving her a direct answer. This old woman has not even let us unload our things and has begun asking about our caste ...' She paused and then continued, 'If only Sesha had let the children finish this school session, what difference would it have made? The meters had been disconnected and she was always watering her vegetables and lawn, and yet would always say, "You have a large family ... you have three children and I have only two."'

'Do you think she had somehow got a whiff of our caste? Did she not see the name plate outside the door, Gopal Singh Gaur?'

'What can I say about that? But she was always saying that if you are Sikhs then why don't you tie your hair into a bun?'

'The new school is at least a mile from here! Get a cycle, or arrange for a rickshaw for the children to go to school.'

Time and again I would think of what my elder brother had done. Many extended families were living together in these quarters—parents, siblings, and their children. Had we continued living together, it would have been easier to get my fourth sister married.

My wife understood what was gnawing at me mentally. She would say, 'Don't worry about it all the time. It is for children to look after their father's affairs. You should look after your health ... other things will take care of themselves. Go to sleep now.'

This gave me some strength. At least I was not alone and the two of us were together. As the saying goes, 'one and one make eleven!'

In that house of the Jains, at Palam, our policy was to endure what could not be cured. We had to pay the old electricity bill. Even when we had no power in our room, their lights would be burning. I was tired of this recurring problem and one day I said, 'There are a lot of mosquitoes. Let me connect my fan to the switch in your room so that the children might sleep!'

'No, this will mean more load on our connection,' the landlady's daughter-in-law bluntly refused, though they had themselves fixed the electric wires on to the poles, and were actually stealing power.

I had to get up for water sometimes at midnight or early in the morning. Because the pressure was very low it would often take me three hours to collect water. I could not sleep properly, and I felt that

my desire to read and write was gradually being overwhelmed by the
pressure of all these problems and I felt suffocated ... We thought about
all these problems deeply, and decided to rent a house nearer to the
school.

We now rented a house belonging to B.D. Sharma in Mahavir
Enclave in Palam village. He had moved here from Punjab, after selling
everything he had owned there, when the militancy had been at its
height. Many other businessmen from Amritsar were also living here
and carrying on their business. His daughter would often ask my wife
about our caste. My wife did not give her a clear answer, 'Perhaps,
people cannot digest their food until they are able to verify the caste of
others!' she remarked.

One of my colleagues, with whom I had been discussing the
difficulties I had been encountering in renting a house suggested, 'You
do not wear a turban now, and getting a room on a small rent is an uphill
task. Sometimes one has to pretend to be what one actually is not. Listen,
one day I was on the terrace of my house in the Jain mohalla, when I saw
a man on the adjacent roof. He had a "januo" wrapped round his ear so
that all those who saw him may be able to know that he is Brahmin, from
a distance. But when I recognized him, I was astonished and asked him,
"Purshottam yaar, you? When did you move here? And since when have
you become a Brahmin? You had yourself told me that you had been
selected on the basis of the quota." His answer was, "Softly please—
people asked a thousand questions before renting their rooms and then
they would refuse. It was then that I thought of this! I bought a length of
thread for a few annas and started wearing it! And now everyone—the
Jats and the Jains included, call me Panditji ...!"'

'I cannot indulge in this sort of fraud. We must create an awareness
against this ... But, I cannot pay a high rent!'

'Then, you should be prepared to be evicted very now and then,' he
retorted.

The next month, B.D. Sharma suddenly enhanced the rent by three
hundred rupees. He imposed another condition, 'If you don't want to
pay a higher rent, then put all your three children in my school!'

I spent two weeks looking for another house ... One Bihari told me
that I had a very large family. Another person from Himachal asked
about me and my job, and then pronounced, 'You have been living in

Delhi for so many years and are still looking for rented accommodation! Do you have any bad habits … drinking or …?'

Many house owners, after making many enquires, would quote an exorbitant rent which was beyond my means.

My wife had a childhood friend who would tell us about houses that were vacant. It was she who had brought us here to this colony. It was through her that we got a dark dingy house on the ground floor in a lane behind her house.

After a couple of days, the landlady, who was from Haryana, asked my wife, 'Are you also Jats like Baljeet (my wife's friend)? They have very large land holdings.'

At that moment, the doorbell rang and Baljeet's children rushed in calling out, 'Masi, Masi', and the landlady went away.

But her investigations did not stop.

'Balbirji, come let's have a drink.' This was the landlord, who was an ex-army man, and when I sat down on the sofa, he said, 'So your house is in the village! In the village or outside?'

'In the village.' This new trick that he had played on me shook me. I got up saying, 'I don't drink,' and came away. Who knows what other tricks he would have played on me had I stayed there.

We stayed for ten months in that house, and then told them that the children had difficulty in negotiating the roads here, and that we had bought a plot on the other side. Now we were about to build our own house.

I saw my wife smiling! Perhaps she had heard my words. We moved our luggage the very next day to the third floor of the new home we had rented.

Within four and a half years this was our sixth house and my eldest daughter's sixth change of school. Every new house meant paying money to new schools. My people in the village would send messages, *'You have taken your children and forgotten us. Whenever you think of us, send us some money—otherwise everything is fine. Goodbye.'*

I fretted and fumed, and wondered who was to blame for the predicament that I found myself in! Who was responsible for this? I was worried that these problems would drive me away from my reading and writing—I was now being recognized as a poet. I had won some awards and was now being praised. I didn't want to be distracted from my goal.

Such thoughts jostled around in my mind. I reviewed the domestic situation, and devoted myself with greater enthusiasm to translations from Hindi or English into Punjabi. For the first time I sat at a table to do my writing and reading. All along I had worked seated cross-legged on a bed. My waist, back, and legs would begin to ache.

I translated *Lajja* for Arsi Publications, and *Edwina and Nehru* for Navyug Publications. While visiting Bhapa Pritam Singh in his office near the Lal Quila, I had often seen starving kids and grown-ups hungrily hunting and licking the leftovers dumped near the street vendors hawking food. I had seen what they called home—the footpath under the open skies. I had also seen their torn, dirty clothes, and mud-spattered feet. All this had left me shaken and deeply moved.

I realized that life was a struggle and there was no escape from it. If I wanted to expand my horizons, I needed to put all the tumult within me into my writings. It hurts me to live in another's house as a tenant, which is a humiliating experience, and an insult and a curse. I wanted to extricate myself from this situation, and longing for the comfort of my own walls, began planning for my own home, which would be my castle.

# Glossary

| | |
|---|---|
| Aflatoon | Asian/Indian form of Plato |
| ahimsa | non-violence |
| Akhand Paths | continuous recitation of Guru Granth Sahib, the sacred book of the Sikhs, which is completed in seventy-two hours. |
| akhara | wrestling pit |
| Amavasya | last day of the dark forthnight of a lunar month |
| amrit | literally nectar; sweetened consecrated water, administered in the Sikh baptism. |
| angocha | a small towel |
| baazigars | acrobats or gymnasts |
| Baisakhi | the first day of the month of Baisakh (mid-April) Spring festival |
| baraat | wedding party of the groom |
| bargad | banyan tree |
| berseem | good quality fodder |
| bhabhi | brother's wife |
| bhagats | worshippers; a family name |
| bhai | a Sikh priest |
| bhaji | brother |
| bhaia | elder brother; father |
| bhaiya | term commonly used for people from Uttar Pradesh and Bihar, who are also called 'Purbias'—people from the east. |

| | |
|---|---|
| bhog | conclusion of a religious ceremony |
| Brahma | God, according to the Hindu system of belief; the divine source of the universe. |
| bibi | term of respect while addressing young girls |
| bua | father's sister |
| bumbi | tubewell |
| chaacha | father's brother |
| chaachi | father's brother's wife |
| chah | tea |
| chakra | circle, wheel |
| Chamar | member of a caste who trades in leather or weaving |
| chandu khana | a smoking den where opium etc. are smoked |
| chappar | thatch |
| chattala | low quality fodder |
| chattis | thirty-six |
| chharra | single, bachelor |
| chamarli | the place where the Chamars live |
| choora | scavenger; member of a caste usually working as a scavenger. |
| chillum | bowl of hubble bubble, into which tobacco or hemp and burning coal are put. |
| chulha | eastern hearth |
| daada | father's father |
| daadi | father's mother |
| Darbar Sahib | Guru Granth Sahib; also Shri Harmandir Sahib or the Golden temple at Amritsar. |
| dharam naal | by God, in faith |
| dhol | drum |
| doaba | the land between two rivers, particularly the one between Rivers Sutlej and Beas, called Jalandhar. |
| doli | palanquin |
| ektara | one-stringed musical instrument mostly used by itinerant mendicants or sadhus. |
| gaiwalas | those who keep and tend cows |
| gati | redemption, speed |
| gotra | Subdivision of a caste |
| granthi | priest; Sikh scripture reader |

| | |
|---|---|
| Gugga | serpent God |
| Gugga navami | Festival of Gugga, the serpent God |
| Gurus | The ten Gurus of the Sikhs |
| gurbani | the composition and sayings of the Gurus |
| Guru purab | religious festivals in commemoration of the Guru |
| hali | one who ploughs: ox used for ploughing |
| haraamzadi | an abuse; illegitimate woman |
| haveli | A large walled house; mansion |
| Heer | the heroine in the ballad of Heer and Ranjha, the legendary lovers of Punjab which is an integral part of the Punjabi folk lore. |
| hysha | a refrain an abbreviation of hy shawa-be brave |
| ichchadhari | one who can do what he wants and assume whatever form he wants. |
| janao | sacred thread |
| Jat | An agricultural class of North Western India, which owns most of the agricultural land in the Punjab and Haryana. |
| jalebis | North Indian sweet which is circular in shape. |
| jamoora | clown |
| Jatti | a woman of this caste |
| joothis | footwear |
| jhool | a blanket; a warm covering for animals |
| kabab | roasted meat delicacy |
| kachcha | underpants or underwear |
| Kafi | a type/style of song |
| kameen | low born; mean |
| kanal | a measure of land—about one eight of an acre. |
| kanjarkhap | obscene and vulgar words |
| Kavi Sammelan | a gathering of poets |
| Khangah | a Muslim shrine; habitation around a mausoleum. |
| khas chick | a curtain made of Khas grass which cools the room. |
| kharif | crop sown in summer and harvested in autumn |
| khartal | a pair of wooden bars with inset cymbals |
| khes | a hand woven cotton blanket or sheet |
| kirpan | curved sword, worn by baptized Sikhs |

| | |
|---|---|
| Kissa Puran Bhagat | Ballad of Puran, whose father ruled an area near and around Sialkot (now in Pakistan), in second century AD. Driven from his home by a lusting stepmother Luna, he underwent great suffering, attained high spiritual power and gave a new moral vision to his times. |
| khu | a well |
| Lohri | a festival celebrated on the last day of the Indian month of Paush mid-January. |
| loi | woollen sheet or wrap |
| Maghi | festival observed on 1 Magh—the eleventh month of the North-Indian calendar. |
| maama | mother's brother; a mode of address |
| maami | maama's wife |
| madari | juggler |
| mand | low-lying land along a river, subject to inundation and erosion. |
| marla | a land measure 30–35 sq yards |
| marusi | common land |
| mauli | untwisted yarn with alternate strands of red and saffron used on ceremonial occasions |
| mirasi | a humorist; a Muslim bard-cum-genealogist |
| mohalla | a ward or an area |
| moksha | salvation |
| mudda | a reed chair |
| murabba | a square of rectangular tract of 25 acres |
| Nambardar | village headman |
| Nambardarin | female nambardar or wife of a nambardar. |
| Nihang | A sect of baptized Sikhs. They were the suicide squad of the Sikh Army. Even today some Sikhs like to dress like these ancient warriors. |
| OBC | Other Backward Classes—those who are given certain protections under Article 340 of the Indian Constitution, so as to enable them to improve their social and economic condition. |
| Punj Duwanji | is a deal in which a young animal, or dry milch cattle is entrusted to someone's care, till it is fit to be sold |

|  | profitably, with an understanding of sharing the proceeds between the owner and caretaker in the ratio of 3:2. |
|---|---|
| Panchayat | A group of five elders of the village who form a council/law court. All matters of dispute pertaining to the village are settled by them . Their word is final. |
| pardesan | a female outsider; stranger, foreigner |
| pir | Muslim religious teacher or recluse |
| pita ji | father |
| Puranmasi | full moon night |
| puttar | son |
| qugi | dove |
| Rabi | crop sown in winter nd harvested in spring. |
| Ramdasia | Follower of medieval saint Ravidas; Sikhs who are converted from the chamar caste. |
| Saal | a festival observed to protect cattle from mouth and foot disease and their general welfare. |
| saala | wife's brother; a form of abuse |
| saali | wife's sister; a form of abuse |
| Sangrand/ sankranti | first day of the Indian solar month. |
| sarangi | a musical instrument |
| Sarpanch | head of the Panchayat |
| satguru | true guru or preceptor |
| satsang | religious congregation |
| sawain | vermicelli |
| seeri | agricultural worker, share cropper |
| shamshan | burning ghats/cremation grounds; babies and infants below one year are usually buried at the shamshan ghat or immersed in a river, and not cremated. |
| Suleiman | King Solomon known for his cap of wisdom. |
| SC | Scheduled Castes—the socially oppressed castes which are provided reservations for education and employment under the Indian Constitution, so as to enable them to improve their social and economic status. |

| | |
|---|---|
| ST | Scheduled Tribes—the tribes spread across the country who are protected and provided reservations in education and employment by the Indian Constitution. |
| taaya | father's elder brother |
| tagri | an ornament worn around the waist |
| tahli | a type of pine tree |
| tai | taaya's wife |
| tantrik | one who practices tantras or magic |
| tumba/tumbi | a single-stringed musical instrument mostly used by folk singers. |
| varnas | castes |
| Waheguru | Sikhs' name for the ultimate reality—God. |
| zaildar | a petty government official |
| zarda | tobacco; rice fried in saffron and yellow colour on festive occasions. |